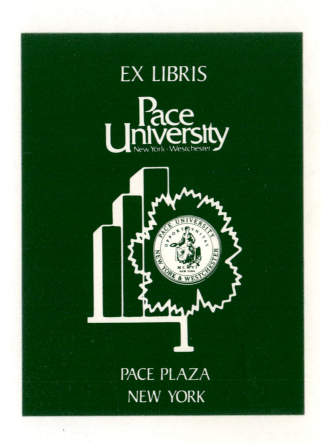

Contemporary problems in perception

Contemporary problems in perception

Edited by

A. T. Welford
L. Houssiadas

papers based on those
delivered at a NATO
Advanced Study Institute
held at the University
of Thessaloniki, Greece
22–26 July 1968

Published by

Taylor & Francis Ltd
10–14 Macklin Street
London WC2B 5NF

1975

First published 1971 by Taylor
& Francis Ltd, 10–14 Macklin
Street, London WC2B 5NF and

Reprinted 1972 and 1975.

© 1975 Taylor & Francis Ltd.

Printed by photo offset and
bound in Great Britain by
Taylor & Francis (Printers)
Ltd., Rankine Road, Basing-
stoke, Hampshire.

ISBN 0 85066 039 4

List of contributors

Cüceloglu Dogan M.
c/o Ekrem Metin
6 sok 19/6
Bahcelievler-Ankara
Turkey

Day C. M.
U.S. Air Force
Institute of Technology (AU)
Wright-Patterson Air Force Base
Ohio

Easterby R. S.
Applied Psychology Department
University of Aston in Birmingham
Gosta Green
Birmingham 4

Farne Mario
Via G. Turati, 51/3
40134 Bologna
Italy

Fatouros M.
Psychological Laboratory
University of Thessaloniki
Thessaloniki, Greece

Freeman R. B.
Department of Psychology
The Pennsylvania State University
University Park
Pennsylvania

Glick Joseph
Institute of Child Development
University of Minnesota
Minneapolis, Minnesota

Gregory R. L.
Department of Machine Intelligence
and Perception
University of Edinburgh
Forest Hill, Edinburgh

Houssiadas L.
Psychological Laboratory
University of Thessaloniki
Thessaloniki, Greece

Kabrisky M.
U.S. Air Force
Institute of Technology (AU)
Wright-Patterson Air Force Base
Ohio

Metelli F.
Istituto di Psicologie Sperimentale
Universita di Padova
Piazza Capitaniato
Padova, Italy

Radoy C. M.
U.S. Air Force
Cambridge Research & Development
Centre, Lexington, Massachusetts

Sanders A. F.
Institute for Perception RVO-TNO
Soesterberg
Kampweg 5, Postbus 23
Holland

Smith W. M.
Department of Psychology
Dartmouth College
Hanover, New Hampshire

Tallman O.
U.S. Air Force
Institute of Technology (AU)
Wright-Patterson Air Force Base
Ohio

Welford A. T.
Department of Psychology
University of Adelaide
Adelaide 5001, South Australia

Vickers D.
Department of Psychology
University of Adelaide
Adelaide 5001, South Australia

Contents

Preface

Modern theory and practice in the psychological study of human performance depends, to a much greater extent than is commonly recognized, upon the effects of co-operation between psychologists and engineers during the Second World War on problems which have since come to be known as ergonomics. The mathematical formulations of human behaviour that resulted brought a desire for precision and measurement in many areas where previous treatments had been mainly in qualitative terms. At the same time there arose a new mutual respect between those engaged in fundamental and applied research, a respect which has sometimes faltered since, but has never wholly disappeared. It has thus come to be recognized, on the one hand, that good applied research must depend on fundamental knowledge, and on the other, that applied problems can often show the way to fundamental insights. It is, therefore, with no apology that we present a series of papers on what are essentially fundamental problems of perception to the readers of *Ergonomics*.

Our aim has been to collect some of the current strands of thinking on human perception which seem likely to be important in the future on both theoretical and practical grounds. The occasion for doing so was a N.A.T.O. Advanced Study Institute which was designed to bring together students from Greece, Italy and Turkey with students and teachers from other Western European countries and North America. This not only determined the place of meeting, but also ensured a more representative set of contributions from Southern Europe than is often secured in an English-speaking symposium.

When designing the programme, it was essential to restrict the range of material covered. We therefore limited ourselves to discussions of perception in the full sense of the term, leaving aside purely sensory problems such as colour vision. The resulting papers fall into three groups. Those in the first deal with general approaches and theories. The opening paper by A. T. Welford surveys recent work on perceptual selection and integration. The paper by R. L. Gregory looks further at these problems, especially as they concern the building of conceptual frameworks. That by M. Kabrisky and his colleagues presents important suggestions, based on anatomical studies and computer analogies, regarding the mechanism by which the brain identifies patterns. Finally in this group, D. Vickers surveys the problem of giving a mathematical account of the time taken to make fine discriminations, and proposes a new model based on his own studies. The broad contents of this paper were conveyed to the meeting by Professor Welford as Dr. Vickers was not able to be present.

The second group of papers report specific studies all of which are aimed at accounting, in terms of stimuli reaching the eye, for features of perception which are often regarded as matters of inference and judgement: in other words, they attempt to specify the necessary and sufficient stimuli for certain features of perceptual integration. In this group, F. Metelli deals with the perception of transparency, and L. Houssiadas with the conditions under which one object appears to be compressed by another. The next two papers by R. B. Freeman and M. Farnè both deal with problems of three-dimensional perception, the former with the recognition of tilt and distance, and the latter with distortions due to the after effects of previous viewing. The fifth paper in this group by M. Fatouros and J. Glick examines the extent to which the apparent whiteness of objects seen in different illuminations is affected by their shape. The last paper by D. M. Cüceloglu extends discussion to the social field, showing how certain facial characteristics are associated with the perception of particular emotions, and how this ' code ' in some ways remains the same, and in some ways varies, between different cultures.

The last group of papers look at the relations between perception and action. A. F. Sanders describes some of his research on the effects of visual angle between objects on the time taken to shift attention from one to the other. W. M. Smith outlines some of his work on the effects of disturbing the spatial and temporal relations between action and the sight of its effects, and discusses the problems it raises. Finally, R. S. Easterby sketches ways in which traditional theoretical principles of perception apply to the design of signs and symbols for machine-tool and other similar displays.

It is this last group of papers which is most likely to interest an ergonomics practitioner directly, but the papers in the other groups are of fundamental concern to him, either in the design of displays, or because they bear on problems encountered in the driving of high-speed vehicles, the landing of aircraft or the comprehending of complex industrial plant, or because they illustrate one facet of the social skill that is becoming increasingly important in modern industrial society.

L. Houssiadas.
A. T. Welford.

Perceptual Selection and Integration

By A. T. Welford

University of Adelaide, South Australia

Perception involves both a selection from, and an integration of, the data conveyed to the brain from the sense organs. Selection seems to be made in terms of both simple sensory qualities and more complex semantic aspects of incoming data, and appears to result in 'unwanted' data being in a very real sense attenuated. It is achieved at some cost, as is shown by the fact that selection commonly takes a time which increases with the degree of specificity to which it is carried. Research results do not yet fully agree upon the extent to which different features of incoming data are selected simultaneously or successively.

Perceptual integration appears to achieve economy of decision in the sense that it enables a large quantity of incoming data to be handled as a limited number of 'units'. Of the various ways in which this is achieved, the extraction of rates of change and of time-sequences, the imposition of 'schemata' or 'templates' from past experience, and the building of perceptual frameworks in both space and time are considered.

Some consequences and practical implications are briefly discussed.

1. The Problem

It is well recognized that far more data are transmitted by our sense organs to the brain than we in fact perceive. It is also obvious—so obvious that its importance is commonly overlooked—that the data we do perceive are grouped and ordered. Thus as regards vision, we 'see' only a part of the data our eyes provide and we see it not as a mosaic of more and less stimulated points, but as coherent objects which have form and structure as wholes. The net result of both the selection and the integration involved is an *economy* in handling data, in the sense that fewer 'units' are dealt with and the number of items upon which decisions have to be taken is reduced. What constitute 'units' or 'items' in this context is not easy to say. The attempt to specify them has been the aim of a substantial line of research which began in continental Europe during the second and third decades of the present century, and led to several developments, notably the so-called Gestalt school's studies of the simple, closed, regular or symmetrical forms which seemed to be the ones most spontaneously and easily perceived. More recently it has continued with attempts to reformulate the problems in mathematical terms, under the dual spurs of information theory and the type of analysis involved in computer programming.

Selection and integration commonly go hand in hand: the ordering of data involved in perceiving an object as such, implies a kind of selection in that main attention is paid to some data, while the rest are relegated to a 'background' which is largely ignored and commonly cannot be reported in much detail. At the same time, deliberate selection often depends on how data are organized: for example, it is often difficult to see a simple shape embedded in a more complex design. Again, in tasks where one type of item has to be selected from among others, ease of selection depends on context, for instance if the letter *e* has to be cancelled throughout a passage of prose, it is more likely to be detected when it would normally be pronounced in the words concerned than when it would be silent (Corcoran 1966, 1967 a, Corcoran and Weening

1968).   We shall, however, for convenience, deal with selection and integration separately before looking at some general implications of both together.   Much of the main evidence has already been surveyed elsewhere (e.g. Egeth 1967, Welford 1968): here, therefore, we shall look at certain broad principles, and take note of recent trends which appear to be of both theoretical and practical interest.

2.   Selection and Identification

Recent studies of perceptual selection point to three important conclusions.

2.1. *The Basis of Selection*

Selection can be made relatively easily in terms of certain sensory qualities: classes of incoming data seem sometimes to be filtered off at a relatively early stage of the perceptual process.   The evidence comes mainly from experiments on listening in which subjects are presented with two or more messages and have to respond to one while ignoring others.   Selection is facilitated if one of the messages is in a man's voice and the other in a woman's, if one message is louder than the other, if the voices come from different sides of the subject or are made to appear to do so by stereophonic means, or if the 'wanted' message is fed into one ear and the unwanted into the other (see Broadbent 1958, Treisman 1960, 1964 b).   Evidence of this kind implies that the basis of selection can be not only simple sensory qualities, such as pitch or intensity or difference of sense organ, but also more subtle distinctions such as the differences of phase and intensity at the two ears which are the basis of auditory localization.

Selection appears also to be facilitated by semantic differences as, for example, when one message is a passage from a novel and the other from a textbook, or when messages are in different languages, or when one is sense and the other nonsense (Treisman 1964 a).   Just how far separation in these cases is truly on semantic grounds, and how far in terms of subtleties of rhythm or phonetic quality, is not certain.   Over and above all this, however, selection seems commonly to be made in terms of attitudes and hypotheses brought to a present situation from past experience—we perceive what we expect to occur or along the lines of what is familiar.   It seems clear, therefore, that selection must often be a high-grade process, concerned with data which have already been processed to a substantial extent by the mechanisms of perception.   This may well be true even when selection appears to be made in terms of simple sensory qualities.

2.2. *Results of Selection*

There is a substantial amount of evidence, again mainly from studies of selective listening, that reception of the signals from an 'unwanted' message is in some very real sense impaired.   For example, Broadbent and Gregory (1963) asked subjects to rate the confidence with which they judged a tone to be present in a burst of noise played into one ear while a string of digits was played into the other: they found that detection of the tones was poorer when the subject was told to report the digits after giving his judgment, than if he was told to ignore them.   The poorer detection could not be explained purely in terms of lower confidence, but implied that the detectability of the tones was reduced.   In terms of signal-detection theory, the effect of having to reproduce the digits was to lower d' rather than raise β, and implied that the signal-to-noise ratio was poorer in the unwanted channel. The obvious assumption is that the signal of the unwanted message is attenuated and this is supported by the fact that the electrical potentials evoked in the cortex by incoming stimuli are diminished when attention is directed away from them (Wilkinson 1967). Broadbent and Gregory found, however, that the criterion levels, as measured by β, of different degrees of confidence in whether or not the tone was present, were closer together when the digits had to be reported than when they were ignored. This bunching of criteria can be most parsimoniously interpreted as the result of increased ' noise ' in the decision process. It suggests that division of attention not only reduces signal strength, but also increases noise level.

Broadbent (1958) had originally assumed that the unwanted channel was completely blocked, but several experiments have now shown this not to be so (e.g. Moray 1959, Treisman 1960, Treisman and Geffen 1967). When a subject has two messages played, one to each ear, through headphones and has to attend to one while ignoring the other, occasional items from the ignored message will be perceived. They are especially likely to get through if they are appropriate or relevant to the unwanted message at the moment they occur, or if they are of special significance to the subject, such as his own name. Occasional ' wanted ' items played to the unattended ear can be detected better if they are readily discriminable, such as when they are spoken in a different voice (Treisman and Riley 1969), or are ' pips ' interspersed during a passage of prose (Lawson 1966). In the latter case, ' pips ' played into the unattended ear were reacted to more slowly than those played into the attended ear. Similar results have been noted for vision by Webster and Haslerud (1964) who found that attention to auditory signals, or signals in foveal vision, slowed reaction to signals shown in peripheral vision.

Looking at selectivity in more general terms, Wachtel (1967) surveyed evidence which suggests that attention can be conceived as like a beam of light which is focused more or less sharply on particular sources of incoming data. He suggested that a distinction can be drawn between the narrowness of focusing at any one time, and the extent to which the beam ranges over the field at different times. He proposed that characteristic tendencies in these two respects can be regarded as facets of personality varying from one individual, or type of individual, to another. For example, highly anxious people can be thought of as tending to have a narrow beam which roams widely over the field, so that their attention skips rapidly from item to item, but is intensely directed to any item on which it is actually resting.

2.3. *Costs of Selection*

A wide variety of experimental studies have made it clear that perceptual selection is a task which involves some mental activity or ' work ' by the observer, and that the more precise the selection has to be, the longer it takes or the more risk there is of error. The times taken may, in absolute terms, be brief, but in most cases they are appreciable and in some substantial. In this context, perceptual selection can be conceived as a special case of the identification involved in choice-reaction tasks. In the typical choice-reaction experiment any one of several signals may appear and to each the subject has to make an appropriate response. The reaction time contains the time required to observe that a signal has occurred, to identify which of the possible signals it is, to choose the required response and to initiate the responding action. Donders (1868) in his pioneer studies of reaction time attempted to measure these components separately by comparing conditions in which (*a*) there was only one signal and response for all trials, (*b*) there might be any of several signals and corresponding responses, and (*c*) any of several signals occurred but the subject was required to respond to only one, ignoring the others. Donders argued that the first and fourth components was measured by (*a*), the first two and the fourth by (*c*) and all four by (*b*), so that the difference between (*c*) and (*a*) was a measure of the time taken to identify the signal, and that between (*b*) and (*c*) of the time required to choose the response.

The argument can be criticized on the ground that in (*c*) the subject has not only to identify the signal but also to decide whether to respond or to do nothing, so that some choice of response is still included in the reaction time. Subsequent work has been based on the fact that, as the number of possible signals and responses increase, choice-reaction times rise. Most of this rise in type (*b*) experiments is due to increase in the time required to choose the response, but some of it seems to be due to longer time taken to identify the signal. Evidence is contained in several studies, notably that of Hilgendorf (1966) who required her subjects, when a signal appeared, to move as quickly as possible from a ' home ' key to make the appropriate response. As soon as they moved, the signal disappeared, so that the time taken before moving could be regarded as a measure of the time to identify the signal. She found that this time rose linearly with the logarithm of the number of possible signals at a rate of about 27 bits per sec, as opposed to about 5·5 bits per sec for the time taken to complete the response.

Research on type (*c*) reactions has been fraught with the methodological difficulty that, if the number of possible signals is increased and if all are of equal frequency and the time between successive signals is kept the same, the average interval between *responses* increases, and reaction time may be affected for this reason. However, when these complicating factors have been controlled, reaction time to the one wanted signal has still been found to increase with the number of possible signals (Brebner and Gordon 1962, 1964). Reaction times in type (*c*) tasks have also been found to rise as the number of wanted signals has been increased beyond one, even though the same response is made to them all (Nickerson and Feehrer 1964).

Two further relevant lines of evidence may be noted. One is from experiments on *scanning*, which has an obvious affinity to type (*c*) tasks: the subject scans through a list of, say, letters or words to note the presence or absence of particular items. The time taken has been found to increase with the number of different possible items from amongst which those actually shown are drawn (Oostlander and de Swart 1966, Gordon 1968), with the number of different items being sought in any one scan (Kaplan and Carvellas 1965, Kaplan *et al.* 1966, Nickerson 1966), and when the definition of a class of words or other items sought is wide rather than narrow (Foster 1962, Neisser and Beller 1965).

Secondly, several experiments have found that the time to classify objects rises with the number of criteria of classification. Thus, for example, Nickerson (1967) found it took longer to identify shapes as red *or* circular, or as red *and* circular, than either as red or as circular alone. Identifying in terms of three criteria—say red, circular and large—took longer still. Again Posner and Mitchell (1967) found it took longer to decide whether two letters were ' same ' or ' different ' according to similarity of name (e.g. Aa) than according to physical identity (e.g. AA). It took longer still to decide in terms of whether both were vowels or both consonants (e.g. Ae or BC).

The time taken for selection often seems to follow an information law, rising linearly with the logarithm of the number of equally probable alternatives, or other measure of information involved. It does not always do so, however, and in these cases the time taken seems to depend on the *discriminability* of the items to be selected from those to be rejected or ignored. Thus, for example, Neisser (1963) found that scanning for the letter Q among other rounded letters was slower than scanning for it among angular letters. It is perhaps arguable that this is the basis of the information relationship—the larger the set from which items are to be chosen, the greater the likelihood of poor discriminability. If so, both are examples of the more general principle that time taken for identification depends on how precisely the item has to be observed; in other words, how much detail has to be noted in it.

This principle cannot give a complete account of the difficulties encountered when making identifications, since it ignores many aspects of the material stored in memory with which incoming data are matched. It is, however, at least plausible in some cases. For example, Attneave (1957) required subjects to associate names with sets of irregular polygons. Each set was constructed by making minor variations in a basic design. He found that learning was better when all the variations were made to the same corner, than when any of the corners might be altered. A more subtle example is suggested in results obtained by Fitts *et al.* (1956), whose subjects had to identify particular bar

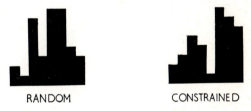

RANDOM   CONSTRAINED

Figure 1.   Examples of bar-diagrams used by Fitts *et al.* (1956).

figures of the type shown in Figure 1 from among sets of eight. The bars could be of eight different heights and, in different trials, figures were constructed with either random bar heights or with the constraint that all eight heights were represented once. It was expected that, because there were fewer possible constrained figures, they would be identified more quickly. The reverse, however, was found to be true. The authors noted that the constrained figures appeared more similar to one another than did the random. If one considers the subject's task in detail, it is easy to see how the random figures could be distinguished by means of a more cursory inspection than could the constrained. If the subject inspects bar by bar, he will be able to decide seven times out of eight on the basis of the first bar alone for either type of figure. If he needs to inspect a further bar, however, the random figure will enable him to decide again seven times out of eight for each, but the constrained only six times out of seven for the second bar, five times out of six for the third, and so on.   If instead he inspects row by row from the top down, the random figures will often have distinctive. features, such as two bars of the same height, which the constrained figures will never contain.

The full benefits of such partial inspection may, however, not be realized, because subjects seem to find it difficult to ignore parts of a display, even though they are not necessary for correct identification.   For instance, Bricker (1955) found that identification of the patterns shown in Figure 2 was quicker when the leftmost two items were omitted, than when all five were shown. Such findings raise the interesting question of why, if selection of part of the display and exclusion of the rest would have been beneficial, this was not done?   It suggests that the cost of making the selection in terms of time, effort or possibility of error may sometimes more than offset the extra ' work ' involved in attending to redundant parts of the display.

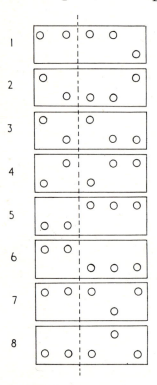

Figure 2.   Patterns used by Bricker (1955).

2.4. *The Phasing of Perceptual Analysis*

A question about which considerable uncertainty still exists is whether different features of an item, such as colour, shape and size in Nickerson's (1967) study, are identified serially or simultaneously.   If the former, adding. one feature to another should increase the time required in such a way that together they take substantially longer than either alone.   If the latter, the time taken to identify in terms of two features, say colour *or* size, should be that for whichever feature is identified faster, or in the case of colour *and* size, for whichever is identified more slowly.   Nickerson found that, on the whole, his results favoured serial identification, but the results of several studies of scanning, using very familiar or highly practised items, suggest simultaneous identification. Thus Neisser (1963) found that when subjects scanned lists of letters for both Q and Z, they took little, if any, longer than to scan for whichever was the slower of Q or Z alone. Again Neisser *et al.* (1963) found that scanning for ten or five letters took longer than scanning for one initially, but that the times became virtually identical after long practice. Similar indications came from experiments by Corcoran (1967 b).

These results have been interpreted to mean that serial processing of different features gives way in the course of practice to simultaneous. Other explanations are however possible, at least in some cases. For instance, if a subject is scanning for a large number of letters, he may have difficulty initially in remembering which he is seeking, so that there is improvement with practice due to learning. This, however, can hardly explain Neisser's results when scanning for only two letters. A second possibility is that, in the course of a series of trials each with different requirements, a subject may improve his speed of identification in general, but find it increasingly difficult to ignore irrelevant data. If so he would, when scanning for single items, inspect more thoroughly than he needed to, and a basic successiveness might be masked. A third possibility, especially with a continuous task such as scanning, is that identification of one signal comes to overlap the making of a response to a previous one—there is evidence that this occurs in some rapid serial sensory-motor tasks (see Welford 1968, p. 127). If so, scanning time may come to be set not so much by the times taken to identify signals, but by the times required to decide whether or not to respond.

There remains the possibility that, in the course of practice, the method of identification does not change from successive to simultaneous, but from analysis in terms of individual features to a process of matching the incoming data against a set of complex patterns specific to the task or long ingrained in the subject's experience. An explanation along these lines would link perceptual selection to many facts of perceptual integration, memory, habit formation and problem-solving, which seem to depend on imposing pre-formed 'templates' or 'schemata' on to incoming data. We shall consider these processes in the next section.

3. Analysis and Integration

Part of the tendency to organize incoming visual stimuli into coherent patterns can probably be attributed to the action of the retina, where stimulation of one area leads to partial inhibition of activity in surrounding areas (von Bekesy 1967). In this way, contrasts between areas of different illumination are enhanced and patterns may sometimes be distorted: for example, angles may appear less acute than they are (see Robinson 1968). Also, the rapid small eye movements, which are continually taking place, are commonly held to sweep a pattern of stimulation continually onto fresh retinal elements. Since these respond more to changes of stimulation than to steady levels, the boundaries between one area and another are enhanced. In the visual cortex, elementary analysis in terms of lines, angles and their orientations has been demonstrated (Hubel and Wiesel 1962, 1968). More subtle analyses of form by fairly elementary mechanisms also seem likely: an elegantly conceived

12   A. T. Welford

model is discussed by Kabrisky *et al.* (1970).   However, these mechanisms, at
least at their present stage of investigation, are not enough to account for the
wealth of known perceptual phenomena.   For the elucidation of this, physiological studies and theories need to be supplemented by studies of perceptual
phenomena as such, and of what may be termed ' perceptual behaviour '.

At this level two recent approaches seem especially important.   One is the
view that perceptual analysis attempts to minimize the number of items
required to account for data adequately.   For example, Hochberg and McAlister
(1953), who showed subjects designs similar to those in Figure 3, suggested
that A and B should be seen as three-dimensional more than C and D because
the number of lines and angles required to specify A and B in two dimensions
is greater than required for C and D.   Thus for specification in two dimensions,
A and B each require 16 lines and 26 angles, whereas C requires 13 lines and
20 angles and D 12 lines and 18 angles.   In three dimensions all patterns
require 12 lines and 24 angles.   The authors indeed found that the percentage
of three-dimensional responses followed expectation in being 98·7, 99·3, 51·0
and 40·0 for A, B, C and D respectively.   A, B and D were therefore most often
seen in the more economical way while C, which required about the same
number of elements in either specification, was seen about equally often in
each way.

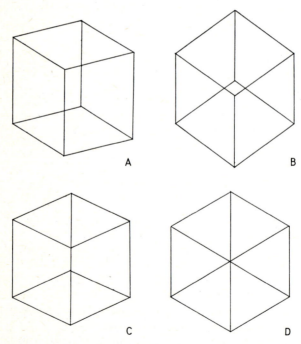

Figure 3.   Various projections of a cube.   Adapted from Hochberg and McAlister (1953).

A possible variant of this approach, although not quite so good at explaining
Hochberg and McAlister's results, would be to suggest that what the subject
minimizes is not the number of *separate* items, but the number of *different*
items.   Thus A, B and C would each contain a variety of different angles when

seen in two dimensions, but only right-angles when seen in three. On the other hand, only one angle is involved with D whether it is seen in two or three dimensions—i.e. 60° or 90° respectively.

The second type of approach assumes that ease of perception depends on the extent to which one part of a pattern can be inferred from another. It is well illustrated by a version of ' guessing game ' used for some years in class experiments at the Cambridge University Psychological Laboratory, and based on one by Attneave (1954). The experimenter has a grid in front of him containing a pattern of the type shown in Figure 4. The subject cannot see the experimenter's grid, but has his own blank grid, and is required to guess whether each square in turn will be white or black. The experimenter tells him the correct answer after each guess, and the subject records it on his grid, thus gradually building up a copy of the experimenter's grid. If the pattern is random, as in Figure 4 A, the subject cannot on average guess better than 50 per cent correct. If, however, the pattern is not random, as in Figure 4 B and C, the subject quickly detects the regularities and thereafter makes no more errors. If the pattern changes, as in Figure 4D, he makes a few errors around the point of change, but none once its nature and direction have been recognized. It is not suggested that anyone does in fact scan a pattern like this in the course of ordinary perception, but the game serves to emphasize that, once regularities have been detected, much of the rest of the pattern can be inferred—in the terminology of information-theory, it becomes redundant. Information is concentrated at the points at which regularity changes; that is at boundaries, angles and points where curved lines change their rate of curvature.

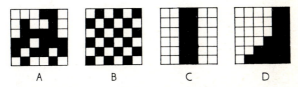

Figure 4. Designs used in ' guessing game '. The subject is required to guess, without seeing the design, whether each square is black or white, beginning at the top left corner and proceeding from left to right along each row in turn.

Both these approaches, especially the second, imply that some sort of *constants* are extracted from the data presented, and that items not included in these constants have to be noted or specified separately. Both also imply that, in so far as language reflects experience, the ease of specifying a pattern verbally—the number of words or phrases required—gives an approximate measure of the readiness with which it will be perceived.

Applications of these approaches have recently been made to classical principles of perception, such as that objects tend to be seen as grouped when they are similar in shape, or close together or continue along a line; and that simple, regular or symmetrical patterns are usually easier to perceive than those which are complex or irregular (Simon 1967, Welford 1968, Glanzer *et al.* 1968). We shall, therefore, confine discussions here to some seemingly important implications and extensions.

3.1. *Extraction of Gradients*

A considerable advance in understanding the perception of three-dimensional space was made by Gibson (1950) with a suggestion regarding the nature of perspective effects. These, he argued, can be conceived as the result of extracting a rate of change or *gradient* of size from similar objects at different distances in space. Such objects, although they subtend different visual angles, become in an important sense *invariant* once the gradient has been recognized. Perception may, in this way, be regarded as tending to maximize the invariance in the data presented. An example of a perspective gradient is shown in Figure 5. If the pattern is regarded as two-dimensional and perpendicular to the line of sight, all the black broken lines and the spaces between them are of different sizes or shapes. Once a gradient has been extracted, all become similar although at different apparent distances.

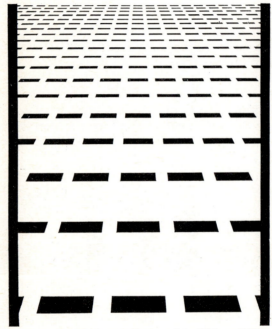

Figure 5.   Perspective gradient used by Vickers (1967).

The gradient appears to be extracted at some cost. Vickers (1967) has shown that if Figure 5 is covered by a card except for the bottom two rows of bars, these are not likely to be seen as three-dimensional. If now the card is slowly raised to expose further rows, the three-dimensional effect suddenly appears. The same is true for Figure 6, but the changeover from two to three dimensions comes later. It seems reasonable to suppose that this is so because the amount of data per row rendered invariant is greater in Figure 5 than in Figure 6. In the former length, width, shape and distances between bars all become invariant; in the latter, only distance.

We seem to have here an example of an economy principle: the gradient is extracted when the amount of data rendered invariant is enough to offset the cost of extraction. What is meant by 'cost' in this context has not yet been ascertained, although it can be defined operationally in terms of the gain in invariance required to produce it. Evidence confirming the general line of argument comes from the greater ease and accuracy with which objects are located in space as the number of surrounding objects, from which a gradient can be extracted, increases.

The gradients in Figures 5 and 6 are for flat surfaces. Gibson emphasized that these are not the only ones that can be extracted: different gradients give impressions of curved surfaces, either concave or convex, and the *rate* of change affects the apparent angle of slope relative to the observer's line of regard. Nor are such gradients confined to spatial arrangements. The fact, for example, that objects retain the same apparent whiteness when seen in different illuminations, appears to be due essentially to the same principle. It is not generally realized that perception of white and black has little to do with the absolute amounts of light reflected by objects. A few readings with a photometer, or looking at objects through a narrow tube which excludes sight of their surroundings, will reveal that a black object in good light—say near a window—may be reflecting substantially more light than a white object in shadow further into the room. The fact that the one looks black and the other white implies that the observer has extracted, albeit unconsciously, a gradient of brightness, and has thus rendered the relation between black and white invariant in the different illuminations.

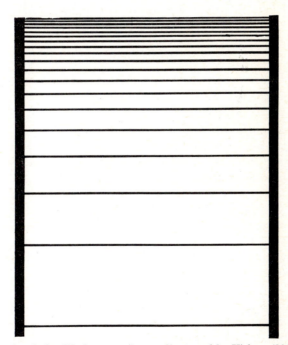

Figure 6. A simplified perspective gradient used by Vickers (1967).

Once a gradient has been extracted, all objects within its field tend to be scaled accordingly. This has been held to account for many of the geometrical illusions such as that of Figure 7 in which the lower horizontal line tends to look shorter than the upper: it is assumed that the observer automatically treats the converging lines as a perspective gradient and that the horizontal lines are scaled in terms of this (Gregory 1966).   Some have assumed that all visual illusions are to be accounted for in this way, although this seems to be an exaggeration (Fisher 1968 a, b, Robinson 1968).

Perspective gradients may not be entirely accurate in scaling objects.   It has, for example, been known since the pioneer work of Thouless (1931) that if, say, a circular disc is seen tilted and the observer is asked to assess the elliptical shape it projects at his eye, he will judge it to be fatter than it really is. Similar effects occur with other judgments: for instance, the projections of distant objects are judged too large, and horizontal distances are judged as shorter and shorter as they become more distant (Gilinsky 1951).   In sum, these distortions are as if the visual scene is foreshortened and tilted up, so as to be viewed a little more from above than it really is.   We can only speculate upon the origins of such a system: it does perhaps have a biological utility in enabling the distant scene to be examined, in a sense, more closely.

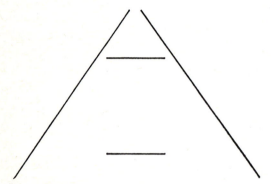

Figure 7.   A version of the Ponzo illusion.   The two horizontal lines are the same length.

3.2. *Transformations over Time*

As an observer moves, the relative positions of objects at different distances in his field of view also change, and he obtains slightly different views of the objects themselves.   Gibson was at pains to stress that these changes of position and view are to be understood as forming gradients in terms of which the *stability* of positions in space, and the shapes of solid objects, are recognized —the particular positions and shapes perceived are those which are invariant under the co-ordinated set of changes and transformations produced by the observer's movement.   By the same tokens, departure from such invariance is an indication that the objects themselves are moving or changing shape (Gibson 1968).   This is a powerful cue to movement, but probably not the only one.   Consider, for instance, the fact that when one stops after driving fast in a car, the road in front may seem to be moving away as if the car was going backwards; or after slowing down one may underestimate the present speed of the car and be unable to stop at a required point—a hazard reported from petrol stations on some main highways.   Such visual after effects seem to imply that some fairly elementary process in the perceptual mechanism tends to compensate for the movement of objects across the retinal field, and probably signals this movement to the central perceptual mechanism.

It seems possible also that the *potential* effects of change of position may influence the perception of some static objects.   For example, if minor perspective effects are neglected, all four patterns in Figure 3 are projections of a cube, but they are not all equally probable. A real outline cube would only be seen as D by an observer who viewed it with one eye from a fixed position. Viewing with one eye would also be necessary for C, and movement would be permissible only along a vertical axis. The latter condition, although not the former, would still apply to B. These limitations would not apply to A: the size of the small parallelogram in the middle would differ according to precise orientation, but the same general pattern would remain with both vertical and horizontal movement and whether viewed with one eye or two.

3.3. *Effects of Familiarity*

The effects discussed so far have had little, if anything, to do with familiarity. We have already mentioned that if objects are inspected through a narrow tube which excludes sight of their surroundings, a black object in good light may clearly be seen as brighter than, and look whiter than, a white object in shadow. Viewing them in this way does not, however, affect the perception of one as black and the other as white when they are again viewed in their context of other objects. In the same way the horizontal lines in Figure 7 look different in length even though we know they are the same. Again, it is often argued that we extract gradients from data because we are used to seeing them in this way. Clearly, however, the main reason is rather than doing so increases invariance. It is, indeed, possible to perceive something in an unfamiliar way if the invariance is thereby made greater. For example, the now famous Ames distorted rooms are often assumed to look rectangular because we are used to seeing rectangular rooms, but the reason seems rather to be that they are so scaled that their projection at the eye has maximum invariance when they are seen as rectangular. A rectangular room can be made to look distorted by suitable scaling of windows, wall-panels and floorboards so as to give maximum invariance when it is seen as other than rectangular.

On the other hand, much of the ordering of perceptual data in real-life situations is undoubtedly by the application of patterns or 'templates', or as Bartlett (1932) termed them 'schemata', built up in the course of experience. The imposition of such a schema enables complex data to be apprehended as a unitary whole, and seems to increase the discriminability of a pattern from irrelevant background 'noise' (Thierman 1968). Typically the fit does not have to be precise, but has to be within acceptable limits of approximation, and the schema itself seems constantly to be modified as the result of further experience. For example, the category 'modern car' includes a range of shapes, sizes and makes, and changes substantially during a lifetime. Bartlett noted that complex line drawings to which a match could be made in this way were regarded by his observers as 'simpler' than less objectively complex drawings that could not be readily linked to familiar objects. Consistently with this, Erdman and Neal (1968) found familiar words to be about as legible as single letters, although unfamiliar words were less so.

Bartlett was clear that the schemata actually imposed showed effects of social conventions and the observer's individual interests, which presumably affected their availability. The possibility of deliberately shaping perception by introducing bias towards particular schemata was illustrated in the classical experiment of Carmichael *et al.* (1932) who showed, for example, that the reproduction of two circles, joined by a short line and exposed briefly, differed according to whether the observer was told beforehand that he was going to see a pair of eyeglasses or a dumb-bell. This result indicates what has been repeatedly demonstrated, that when a schema is applied, detail which is apparently observed is often in fact inferred: details brought by the schema seem to be incorporated into the resulting perception. Details in the stimulus which cannot be fitted into the schema seem either to be ignored or to become what Bartlett termed ' dominant details ' which are specially noticed. Those ignored do not seem to be wholly lost, since they can in some circumstances be reported if the observer is challenged to do so (Earhard 1968).

The observer thus seems to fit the data approximately with some familiar category which, if reasonably adequate, suppresses the perception of deviant details. If, however, the lack of fit is substantial in one or two respects, the deviant features are specified separately. Attneave (1954) has argued that such a procedure could still be much more economical than no categorization. We might add that it could often be more economical to accept a *quickly found* schema and to specify deviant details, than to make an extensive search of the material stored in memory for a more precise category.

3.4. *The Building of Perceptual Frameworks*

Gibson emphasized that, when perceiving an object of substantial size, we do not see all the relevant details at a single glance: our eyes rove over it, observing first one part, then another. Our total perception is thus not the same as the observation in any one glance: rather it is a *construct* built by integrating together the data from many different glances. Such integration seems to be readily achieved when all the data are present together, so that the data in focal attention in one glance are those more peripherally observed in others. When the data are not all present at once, integration may still be achieved provided they arrive within a fairly short period of time. Experiments in which parts of patterns have been shown sequentially have indicated that the accuracy of integration falls rapidly with increasing times between the exposures of the different parts: for example, from 0 to 100 msec (Eriksen and Collins 1968) or from 125 to 800 msec (Garner and Gottwald 1968). The latter authors suggest that such integration as is achieved at longer intervals is not truly perceptual, but is rather a matter of learning to associate the different parts together.

Once integration has been achieved, it seems as if an enduring, stable framework has been built up which is immediately available as a whole. It is these visual frameworks that constitute what Gibson called our ' visual world ', in terms of which we maintain orientation. They provide a context to which fresh incoming data are either congruent and readily incorporated, or deviant, in which case attention is concentrated on them and further analysis carried out. In the same way, these frameworks lead to the challenging idea that perception can be conceived as a running hypothesis, by which events at any one moment are compared with expectations brought from the immediate past. Such a concept is consistent with the idea of perception as economical, in the sense that attention is concentrated at temporal points of change, just as we saw it was at spatial points of change in Attneave's guessing game (Figure 4).

The conditions which favour the building and maintenance of these frameworks are not fully understood, but the experiments on integration over time that we have already noted suggest that they depend to a considerable extent on some form of short-term retention. Additional evidence that this is so can perhaps be seen in the loss of orientation often shown by patients suffering from impaired short-term memory. Some further understanding might be gained from studies of the estimation of averages (Spencer 1961, 1963, Anderson 1968). These have shown, for instance, that the span of data that can be judged is limited and that highly deviant data tend to be overweighted. The task of understanding the nature of perceptual frameworks is, however, a challenging one in which several different parameters seem to be emerging. Some of the most potentially promising leads are coming from the study of complex process operations in industry. The skilled operator of these appears to build a conceptual framework or ' model ' of the plant he is using, and of its manner of functioning. The model is sometimes crude, even bizarre, but may still nevertheless be highly effective (Crossman 1960, Beishon 1967 a, b).

4. Consequences and Practical Implications

To sum up: although many details of the nature and manner of perceptual selection and integration remain in need of research, some broad principles are already clear.

(i) Perception is not to be understood as a matter of sensory data alone, but rather in terms of more or less elaborate constructs or frameworks. These enable current sensory data to be related to other sensory data present at the same time and to data drawn from the past, and thus make possible the computation of future trends. The fitting of incoming data into such a framework can be regarded as a kind of ' perceptual response ' in which the observer is active, although not always overtly so. Except with the simplest reflexes, it seems to be this perceptual response which is the stimulus for any overt motor action.

(ii) The whole process of perceptual selection and integration seems to be designed to secure economy of decision, reducing the number of ' units ' dealt with. In this process, integration operates to secure that the maximum data are treated in the minimum terms, commonly by fitting some overall schema or template and then dealing separately with discrepant details. At the same time, the mechanism of selection seems to secure that the degree of specificity of the schema and details are in line with the needs of the situation—perceptual analysis proceeds only so far as is required. For example, if we are crossing a road, it is usually sufficient to recognize the vehicle in the distance as a car, and we are often unaware of its make, model, number or other details. If, however, we were watching for a friend's car, these details become important and are noticed.

(iii) The terms in which incoming data are treated are both spatial and temporal, and both types seem commonly to operate together even in cases, such as distance perception, where reference is essentially to one type only. Both types are of several different orders of magnitude. For example, when looking at a picture, we may be aware of certain details of brushwork or the depicting of particular objects, and at the same time of broad features of overall composition and design. Similarly, when reading a book, we are concerned not only with the meanings of individual words or sentences but with the content of paragraphs and chapters, and often with broader characteristics such as the style of writing. It is, perhaps, not too far-fetched to suggest that the subject makes a kind of Fourier analysis of incoming data, treating their characteristics in terms of varying time scales or degrees of generality.* If so, the identification of characteristic time scales required or used seems to be a promising method of analysing the demands of tasks, of specifying methods of training, and of defining certain facets of individual ability and personality.

The kind of factors we have discussed have some obvious applications in industry and elsewhere. To take only one example, the building and application of templates or schemata seem to be of importance in relation to industrial inspection (Thomas 1962). Observation of inspectors at work reveals that they often do their work much faster than classical studies of the times taken for discrimination and choice would lead us to expect. Most spectacular is, perhaps, the inspection of printed sheets, which an inspector may flip rapidly through, yet readily note where some fault in the printing has occurred. Laboratory studies have shown that in many cases *identity* can be recognized relatively quickly (Sekuler and Abrams 1968). We should, therefore, expect that an inspector would benefit from building up a schema of a perfect article, which he applied to each example as it came along, rejecting deviations from it. In the most rapid inspection tasks, the succession of perfect articles might take on the character of a continuous single pattern which changed when a fault occurred. The development of a schema might, however, sometimes lead to difficulties. If it became too precise and detailed, the deviations observed would sometimes be within tolerable limits, so that satisfactory articles would be rejected. If this happened, the inspector would have to make a more complex judgment of whether an article was *similar* to a standard within a permitted range of variation. This type of judgment was shown by Sekuler and Abrams to be considerably slower than recognition of identity.

Many other examples could be quoted in which the kind of perceptual factors which have been outlined here prove to be of practical significance. Studies of perceptual factors to be taken into account in the design of instruments, control panels and other industrial displays are now classical (for summaries see Welford 1960, Murrell 1965). Again, as Easterby (1967) points out, the conventional signs used on machine tools become much easier to recognize and understand if they are designed with due regard to perceptual principles of configuration and grouping. Outside industry, similar principles have been shown to be important in, for example, the design of aircraft plotting rooms (Bartlett and Mackworth 1950), road signs (e.g. de la Mare and Walker 1962, Crawford 1963), and styles of printing (e.g. Poulton 1959); and can be applied to the layout of electrical circuit diagrams (cf. Bainbridge-Bell 1948).

Perhaps the most obvious general lesson which emerges is that, if we seek to mitigate the perceptual demands of a task, it is not sufficient to take account only of the lighting, the size of significant detail, the possibility of using

---

* This type of Fourier analysis is of a different order of magnitude from that discussed by Kabrisky *et al.* (*op. cit.*).

magnifiers or of selecting employees for eyesight. Far more important for many purposes are the form, arrangement, colour and contrasts of the visual display as a whole, the extent to which significant features can be readily identified, and their relations to the observer's expectations and knowledge. This last point emphasizes the further requirement, that not only has due consideration to be given to individual items or installations, but that wider problems of standardization have also to be tackled if flexibility in the deployment of personnel from one machine or installation to another is to be achieved.

La perception suppose, à la fois, la sélection et l'intégration, au niveau du cerveau, des données en provenance des organes sensoriels. La sélection semble s'élaborer d'emblée à partir des qualités sensorielles primaires, ainsi qu'à partir d'aspects sémantiques plus complexes liés aux données d'entrée, pour aboutir à la formation de données non pertinentes, mais effectivement atténuées. Elle ne s'effectue que moyennant un certain coût, ce dont rend bien compte le fait que le temps nécessaire au choix augmente avec le degré de spécificité requis par la sélection. Les résultats expérimentaux ne permettent pas encore de dire jusqu'à quel point les aspects des données d'entrée sont sélectionnés simultanément ou successivement.

L'intégration perceptive semble rechercher l'économie dans la décision, dans ce sens qu'elle permet à une grande quantité de données entrantes d'être traitée comme un nombre limité d'" unités ". Dans la suite, sont examinées: la façon dont s'effectue le traitement, l'extraction des taux d'altération et des séquences temporelles, l'imposition de " schémas " et de " modèles " à partir de l'expérience passée et, enfin, l'élaboration de structures perceptives spatiales et temporelles. Dans une courte discussion, on dégage quelques conséquences et implications d'ordre pratique.

Wahrnehmung umfasst beides, eine Auswahl aus, und eine Integration von Daten, die dem Gehirn durch die Sinnesorgane zugeführt werden. Die Auswahl scheint in zwei Kategorien zu erfolgen: in einfachen Sinnesqualitäten und in mehr komplexen semantischen Aspekten der eingehenden Daten, und scheint das Resultat zu haben, dass " unerwünschte " Daten im wahren Sinn des Wortes " abgehalten " werden. Das kostet einiges, wie aus der Tatsache folgt, dass diese Auswahl gemeinhin Zeit kostet, die mit dem Grad der Spezifität zumimmt, bis zu der sie durchgeführt wird. Die Forschungsergebnisse stimmen noch nicht über das Ausmaß überein, bis zu dem verschiedene Merkmale der eingehenden Daten gleichzeitig oder nacheinander ausgewählt werden.

Die Integration der Wahrnehmung scheint die Ökonomie der Entscheidung in dem Sinn zu verbessern, dass sie es ermöglicht, eine grosse Zahl eingehender Daten als begrenzte Zahl von " Einheiten " zu verarbeiten. Von den verschiedenen Wegen, auf denen das geschieht, werden folgende besprochen: die Erfassung von Frequenzen, der Einsatz von Schemata und Mustervorstellungen aus früherer Erfahrung, und der Aufbau von Rahmenvorstellungen der Wahrnehmung in Raum und Zeit. Einige Folgen und praktische Auswirkungen werden kurz diskutiert.

References

ANDERSON, N. H., 1968, Averaging of space and number stimuli with simultaneous presentation. *Journal of Experimental Psychology*, **77**, 383–392.

ATTNEAVE, F., 1954, Some informational aspects of visual perception. *Psychological Review*, **61**, 183–193.

ATTNEAVE, F., 1957, Transfer of experience with a class-schema to identification-learning of patterns and shapes. *Journal of Experimental Psychology*, **54**, 81–88.

BAINBRIDGE-BELL, L. H., 1948, Improving circuit diagrams. *Electronic Engineering*, **20**, 175–177.

BARTLETT, F. C., 1932, *Remembering* (London: CAMBRIDGE UNIVERSITY PRESS).

BARTLETT, F. C., and MACKWORTH, N. H., 1950, *Planned Seeing* (London: H.M.S.O.), Air Publication 3139B.

BEISHON, R. J., 1967 a, Problems of task description in process control. *Ergonomics*, **10**, 177–186.

BEISHON, R. J., 1967 b, An analysis and simulation of an operator's behaviour in controlling continuous baking ovens. In *Symposium O.T.A.N.: The Simulation of Human Behavior* (Paris: DUNOD) pp. 329–343.

BEKESY, G. VON, 1967, *Sensory Inhibition* (Princeton: PRINCETON UNIVERSITY PRESS).

BREBNER, J., and GORDON, I., 1962, Ensemble size and selective response times with a constant signal rate. *Quarterly Journal of Experimental Psychology*, **14**, 113–116.

BREBNER, J., and GORDON, I., 1964, The influence of signal probability and the number of non-signal categories on selective response times. *Quarterly Journal of Experimental Psychology*, **16**, 56–60.

BRICKER, P. D., 1955, The identification of redundant stimulus patterns. *Journal of Experimental Psychology*, **49**, 73–81.

BROADBENT, D. E., 1958, *Perception and Communication* (London: PERGAMON PRESS).

BROADBENT, D. E., and GREGORY, MARGARET, 1963, Division of attention and the decision theory of signal detection. *Proceedings of the Royal Society B*, **158**, 222–231.

CARMICHAEL, L., HOGAN, H. P., and WALTER, A. A., 1932, An experimental study of the effect of language on the reproduction of visually perceived form. *Journal of Experimental Psychology*, **15**, 73–86.

CORCORAN, D. W. J., 1966, An acoustic factor in letter cancellation. *Nature*, **210**, 658.

CORCORAN, D. W. J., 1967 a, Acoustic factors in proof reading. *Nature*, **214**, 851.

CORCORAN, D. W. J., 1967 b, Serial and parallel classification. *British Journal of Psychology*, **58**, 197–203.

CORCORAN, D. W. J., and WEENING, D. L., 1968, Acoustic factors in visual search. *Quarterly Journal of Experimental Psychology*, **20**, 83–85.

CRAWFORD, A., 1963, The perception of light signals: the effect of mixing flashing and steady irrelevant lights. *Ergonomics*, **6**, 287–294.

CROSSMAN, E. R. F. W., 1960, *Automation and Skill*. D.S.I.R. Problems of Progress in Industry No. 9 (London: H.M.S.O.).

DE LA MARE, GWYNNETH, and WALKER, J., 1962, The visibility of direction indicators. *Ergonomics*, **5**, 573–579.

DONDERS, F. C., 1868, Over de snelheid van psychische processen. *Onderzoekingen gedaan in het Physiologische Laboratorium der Utrechtsche Hoogeschool*, **2**, 92–120. English translation by W. G. Koster, 1969, *Acta Psychologica*, **30**, 412–431.

EARHARD, B., 1968, Perception and retention of familiar and unfamiliar material. *Journal of Experimental Psychology*, **76**, 584–595.

EASTERBY, R. S., 1967, Perceptual organization in static displays for man/machine systems. *Ergonomics*, **10**, 195–205.

EGETH, H., 1967, Selective attention. *Psychological Bulletin*, **67**, 41–57.

ERDMANN, R. L., and NEAL, A. S., 1968, Word legibility as a function of letter legibility, with word size, word familiarity and resolution as parameters. *Journal of Applied Psychology*, **52**, 403–409.

ERIKSEN, C. W., and COLLINS, J. F., 1968, Sensory traces versus the psychological moment in the temporal organization of form. *Journal of Experimental Psychology*, **77**, 376–382.

FISHER, G. H., 1968 a, Illusions and size-constancy. *American Journal of Psychology*, **81**, 2–20.

FISHER, G. H., 1968 b. An experimental comparison of rectilinear and curvilinear illusions. *British Journal of Psychology*, **59**, 23–28.

FITTS, P. M., WEINSTEIN, M., RAPPAPORT, M., ANDERSON, NANCY, and LEONARD, J. A., 1956, Stimulus correlates of visual pattern recognition: a probability approach. *Journal of Experimental Psychology*, **51**, 1–11.

FOSTER, HARRIET, 1962, The operation of set in a visual search task. *Journal of Experimental Psychology*, **63**, 74–83.

GARNER, W. R., and GOTTWALD, R. L., 1968, The perception and learning of temporal patterns. *Quarterly Journal of Experimental Psychology*, **20**, 97–109.

GIBSON, J. J., 1950, *The Perception of the Visual World* (Boston, Mass: HOUGHTON MIFFLIN).

GIBSON, J. J., 1968, What gives rise to the perception of motion? *Psychological Review*, **75**, 335–346.

GILINSKY, ALBERTA S., 1951, Perceived size and distance in visual space. *Psychological Review*, **58**, 460–482.

GLANZER, M., TAUB, THELMA, and MURPHY, R., 1968, An evaluation of three theories of figural organization. *American Journal of Psychology*, **81**, 53–66.

GORDON, I. E., 1968, Interactions between items in visual search. *Journal of Experimental Psychology*, **76**, 348–355.

GREGORY, R. L., 1966, *Eye and Brain: The Psychology of Seeing* (London: WORLD UNIVERSITY LIBRARY).

HILGENDORF, LINDEN, 1966, Information input and response time. *Ergonomics*, **9**, 31–37.

HOCHBERG, J., and McALISTER, E., 1953, A quantitative approach to figural 'goodness'. *Journal of Experimental Psychology*, **46**, 361–364.

HUBEL, D. H., and WIESEL, T. N., 1962, Receptive fields, binocular interaction and functional architecture in the cat's visual cortex. *Journal of Physiology*, **160**, 106–154.

HUBEL, D. H., and WIESEL, T. N., 1968, Receptive fields and functional architecture of monkey striate cortex. *Journal of Physiology*, **195**, 215–243.

KABRISKY, M., DAY, C. M., TALLMAN, O., and RADOY, C. M., A theory of pattern perception based on human physiology. *Ergonomics*, **13**, 129–149.

KAPLAN, IRA T., and CARVELLAS, T., 1965, Scanning for multiple targets. *Perceptual and Motor Skills*, **21**, 239–243.

KAPLAN, IRA T., CARVELLAS, T., and METLAY, W., 1966, Visual search and immediate memory. *Journal of Experimental Psychology*, **71**, 488–493.

LAWSON, EVERDINA A., 1966, Decisions concerning the rejected channel. *Quarterly Journal of Experimental Psychology*, **18**, 260–265.

MORAY, N. 1959, Attention in dichotic listening: affective cues and the influence of instructions. *Quarterly Journal of Experimental Psychology*, **11**, 56–60.

MURRELL, K. F. H., 1965, *Ergonomics* (London: CHAPMAN & HALL).

NEISSER, U., 1963, Decision-time without reaction-time: experiments in visual scanning. *American Journal of Psychology*, **76**, 376–385.

NEISSER, U., and BELLER, H. K., 1965, Searching through word lists. *British Journal of Psychology*, **56**, 349–358.

NEISSER, U., NOVICK, R., and LAZAR, R., 1963, Searching for ten targets simultaneously. *Perceptual and Motor Skills*, **17**, 955–961.

NICKERSON, R. S., 1966, Response times with a memory-dependent decision task. *Journal of Experimental Psychology*, **72**, 761–769.

NICKERSON, R. S., 1967, Categorization time with categories defined by disjunctions and conjunctions of stimulus attributes. *Journal of Experimental Psychology*, **73**, 211–219.

NICKERSON, R. S., and FEEHRER, C. E., 1964, Stimulus categorization and response time. *Perceptual and Motor Skills*, **18**, 785–793.

OOSTLANDER, A. M., and DE SWART, H., 1966, Search-discrimination time and the applicability of information theory. *Journal of Experimental Psychology*, **72**, 423–428.

POSNER, M. I., and MITCHELL, R. F., 1967, Chronometric analysis of classification. *Psychological Review*, **74**, 392–409.

POULTON, E. C., 1959, Effects of printing types and formats on the comprehension of scientific journals. *Nature*, **184**, 1824–1825.

ROBINSON, J. O., 1968, Retinal inhibition in visual distortion. *British Journal of Psychology*, **59**, 29–36.

SEKULER, R. W., and ABRAMS, M., 1968, Visual sameness: a choice time analysis of pattern recognition processes. *Journal of Experimental Psychology*, **77**, 232–238.

SIMON, H. A., 1967, An information-processing explanation of some perceptual phenomena. *British Journal of Psychology*, **58**, 1–12.

SPENCER, J., 1961, Estimating averages. *Ergonomics*, **4**, 317–328.

SPENCER, J., 1963, A further study of estimating averages. *Ergonomics*, **6**, 255–265.

THIERMAN, T., 1968, A signal detection approach to the study of set in tachistoscopic recognition. *Perceptual and Motor Skills*, **27**, 96–98.

THOMAS, L. F., 1962, Perceptual organization in industrial inspectors. *Ergonomics*, **5**, 429–434.

THOULESS, R. H., 1931, Phenomenal regression to the ' real ' object. II. *British Journal of Psychology*, **22**, 1–30.

TREISMAN, ANNE M., 1960, Contextual cues in selective listening. *Quarterly Journal of Experimental Psychology*, **12**, 242–248.

TREISMAN, ANNE M., 1964 a, Verbal cues, language and meaning in selective attention. *American Journal of Psychology*, **77**, 206–219.

TREISMAN, ANNE M., 1964 b, The effect of irrelevant material on the efficiency of selective listening. *American Journal of Psychology*, **77**, 533–546.

TREISMAN, ANNE, and GEFFEN, GINA, 1967, Selective attention: perception or response? *Quarterly Journal of Experimental Psychology*, **19**, 1–17.

TREISMAN, ANNE M., and RILEY, JENEFER G. A., 1969, Is selective attention selective perception or selective response? A further test. *Journal of Experimental Psychology*, **79**, 27–34.

VICKERS, D., 1967, Unpublished Ph.D. Thesis. University of Cambridge.

WACHTEL, P. L., 1967, Conceptions of broad and narrow attention. *Psychological Bulletin*, **68**, 417–429.

WEBSTER, R. G., and HASLERUD, G. M., 1964, Influence on extreme peripheral vision of attention to a visual or auditory task. *Journal of Experimental Psychology*, **68**, 269–272.

WELFORD, A. T., 1960, *Ergonomics of Automation*. D.S.I.R. Problems of Progress in Industry No. 8 (London: H.M.S.O.).

WELFORD, A. T., 1968, *Fundamentals of Skill* (London: METHUEN).

WILKINSON, R. T., 1967, Evoked response and reaction time. In *Attention and Performance* (Edited by A. F. SANDERS) (Amsterdam: NORTH-HOLLAND PUBLISHING CO.).

On How Little Information Controls So Much Behaviour

By R. L. GREGORY

University of Edinburgh, Scotland

Perception is discussed as a process of the selection of ' internal models ' in terms of which incoming data are used to shape behaviour. The advantages and disadvantages to the organism of using such models are outlined, and the way in which models operate is considered in the light of evidence from perceptual illusions: these can be regarded as cases where a wrong model has been selected, or errors of scaling have occurred. It is suggested that some of the bizarre imagery in dreams and certain abnormal states can also be understood in these terms. When compared with a computer, the perceptual mechanism and its models resemble an analogue rather than a digital system.

1. Types of Stored Information

Perhaps the most fundamental question in the whole field of experimental psychology is: How far is behaviour controlled by currently available sensory information and how far by information already stored in the central nervous system? Considering the origin of neurally stored information, I believe that this has only two origins: (1) ancestral disasters, changing neural structure according to the principles and processes of other phylogenetic changes occurring by natural selection; (2) previous sensory experience of the individual, stored as ' memory '. We may call these two ways of gaining stored information phylogenetic and ontogenetic learning respectively.

It is important to distinguish two quite different kinds of stored information. We learn *skills* and *events*. Some skills may be inherited, and so are examples of gaining information phylogenetically, though they may show as behaviour only after sufficient maturation: while learning or storing *particular* events is always ontogenetic. For examples of inherited skills, babies walk without special training at about fifteen months, and as Coghill (1929) showed, salamanders kept from all movement by anaesthesia will nevertheless swim normally as soon as allowed, once the neural connections of the spinal cord are complete. For examples of learned skills we may take activities such as tennis, piano playing and chess. We may be able to recall the odd particular games or concerts, but as skills it is not individual past events which are stored, but rather appropriate behaviour and strategies which give more or less complete success in later similar situations. Evidently crucial generalized features of the original situation are stored and used when appropriate. But sometimes stored features are used when inappropriate and are a handicap—for example, playing table tennis with the straight-arm movements appropriate to tennis.

It is an open question just how far individual events are stored as such, and how far they have to be ' constructed ' for recall (cf. Bartlett 1932). What is certain is that information gained phylogenetically is always of the general ' skill ' kind. We are not able to recall individual events experienced by our ancestors.

We know quite a lot about the stages by which skills are learned by individuals. I would like to suggest that this can provide clues to the nature of how behaviour is controlled by sensory information. It suggests that control is not direct, except in the special cases of reflexes, but is via internal neural models of reality. These internal models are essential for skills—including perception of the external world.

2. The Learning of Skills and the Construction of 'Internal Models'

It has been clear ever since the experiments of Blodgett (1929) that 'latent' learning occurs—that is, some information storage which does not at once show itself in behaviour nevertheless occurs during the early stages of developing a skill.   We find two features of learning curves characteristic of ontogenetic skill learning: first, in learning discriminations—which seem vital to 'map the ground' in the first stages—learning curves are positively accelerated: at first there is no progress, then later progress appears at an increasing rate.   Experiments have shown that the animal (generally a rat) is responding to other, and it turns out irrelevant, features of the situation.   Secondly, learning curves of skill show marked 'plateaux', during which no progress is observed, but each plateau is followed by a sudden jump in performance, associated with a different 'strategy'.   In learning morse code, typing or piano playing, increase in speed of performance occurrs in steps as the input is handled in larger and larger units.   Thus in typing, while each letter remains a unit, speed is limited to about two letters per second; but later, letter groups up to whole words and finally groups of words become the neural units.   Speed is then far greater than is possible with the maximum decision rate of about 0·5 sec per decision possible for the human neural system.   Lashley (1951) has described the process for piano playing: 'The finger strokes of a musician may reach sixteen per second in passages which call for a definite and changing order of successive finger movements.   The succession of movements is too quick even for visual reaction time.   In rapid sight reading it is impossible to read the individual notes of an arpeggio.   The notes must be seen in groups, and it is actually easier to read chords simultaneously and to translate them into temporal sequence than to read successive notes in an arpeggio as usually written '.

This grouping of what are at first discrete inputs is, however, done at the cost of complete flexibility.   Unusual combinations of inputs may be missed, or accepted as though they were in a more usual order, with consequent errors. Random music is very difficult to play, and random letters very difficult to type.

A system which makes use of the redundancy, in space and time, of the real world has the following advantages.

1. It can achieve high performance with a limited rate of information transmission—it is estimated that human transmission rate is only about 12 bits per second.   The gain results because the perception of objects—which are always redundant—requires identification of only certain key features of each object.   Some kind of search strategy for these features would save a great deal of processing time for object-recognition.   This is open to experimental investigation and has implications for pattern recognition, which is *not* the same as object recognition.   The latter is perhaps an artificial concept.

2. It is essentially predictive. In suitable circumstances it can cut reaction time to zero. Experimental situations for demonstrating reaction-time are somewhat artificial, seldom occurring during actual skills, such as driving, typing, piano playing, etc.

3. It can continue to function in the temporary absence of any input—as when turning the music page, blinking or sneezing while driving. Loss of input is very different from loss of output control, such as would occur if the steering wheel came off, and this difference seems important for investigating these internal selected groupings, or as Craik (1943) called them ' internal models ', of reality.

4. It can continue to function when the input changes in kind. Thus in maze learning, a rat can continue to run a maze once learned though it is denied each sensory input—vision, smell, kinaesthesis, etc.—in turn. The fact that rats can also swim a flooded maze after learning to run it dry is particularly striking, for evidently it is *not* primarily patterns of motor movements which are learned. This is important evidence for cognitive learning at the level of the rat, and we believe that it gets even more important higher up the phylogenetic scale.

5. It can extract signals from ' noise ': if the internal models are highly redundant, they can be called up with minimal sensory information. This means that the models can enormously improve the effective signal-to-noise ratio of sensory systems.

6. Provided a particular situation is similar to the situations for which a ' model ' was developed, behaviour will generally be appropriate. This, in the language of experimental psychology, is ' positive transfer of training '.

There are, however, disadvantages of systems in which behaviour is based on internal models.

1. When the current situation is sufficiently similar to past situations which have been selected and combined to give an internal model, but the current situation differs in crucial respects, then the system will *be systematically misled by its model*, producing a ' negative transfer ' effect. Since no model can be complete, and few, if any, are entirely accurate in what they represent, biological or computer systems employing internal models can always be fooled. They are fooled when characteristics which they accept for selecting a model occur in an atypical situation. It is always possible that a wildly wrong model will be selected when this happens. It will happen most often when only a few selection characteristics are demanded, or are available to the system. We know, from many learning and perceptual experiments, that there are great individual differences in what kinds of features are demanded. For instance, among rats, ' brighter ' individuals tend to demand where possible, non-visual features while the dimmer brethren are largely content with visual ones. This is curious in the case of the rat, which is generally regarded as rather a ' non-visual ' animal.

2. Internal model systems are essentially conservative—showing inertial drag to change—for internal models must reflect the past rather than the present. This implies that rapid change of environment, or social

groups is biologically dangerous, and of course it favours young members
of such groups.

A model may be selected on purely visual data, but once selected it is
generally used for non-visual predictions.   Thus in driving a car, characteristics
of the road surface such as slipperiness are ' read off ' the retinal image although
they are not properties of it.   In general, the eye's images are biologically
important only in so far as non-optical features can be read from the internal
models they select.   Images are merely patches of light—which cannot be
eaten or be dangerous—but they serve as symbols for selecting internal models,
which include the non-visual features vital to survival.   It is this reading of
object characteristics from images that *is* visual perception.

2.1. *Internal Models and Perceptual Illusions*

We have already noted that gross errors may occur when a wrong model is
selected.   Errors of scale can also occur; and these, I believe, are the familiar
perceptual distortion illusions.   These illusions are interesting because they can
tell us something of how internal models are made to fit the precise state of
affairs in the outside world (cf. Gregory 1963).

We cannot suppose that there are as many internal models as there are
perceptible objects *of all sizes, distances and positions in space*.   But it is
important for the models to represent the current sizes, distances and positions
of external objects if they are to mediate appropriate behaviour.   To solve
this problem we may suppose that the models are flexible.   They can be
adjusted to fit reality.   They are adjusted by ' size scaling, ' using visual
features, such as perspective convergence of lines, though not always
appropriately.

In the absence of any available scale-setting data, perception is determined
by average sizes and distances.   These are modified by ' scale-setting ' sensory
information when available.   When scale-setting information is inappropriate
to the prevailing reality, then perception is systematically distorted.   On this
view we can use distortion illusions as quite basic research tools.   In Muller-
Lyer, Hering or Orbison visual illusions, typical perspective depth features
are presented on a flat plane.   Features which would be distant if these
figures were truly three-dimensional are expanded in the flat illusion figures.
This expansion is normally appropriate—since it is object size and not retinal
image size which is biologically important—but here the system is misled by
the scaling information and systematic distortions occur.   By studying these
distortions, we can discover experimentally just how flexible the internal
models are; what sorts of information are used to give object scale, and also
something of how internal models are built by perceptual learning.

Biologically important features of the world must be read from available
sensory information.   To be useful, visual features must be related to the
weight, hardness and chemical properties of objects which have to be handled
or eaten.   Now it is well known that a small object of the same weight as a
larger object feels up to 50 per cent heavier.   This is the ' size-weight ' illusion.
Vision selects a model calling up appropriate muscle power for lifting the weight,
but when the internal model is inappropriate the power called up is inappropriate—and we suffer an illusion corresponding to the error. The illusion
seems to be due to the model being selected in terms of the apparent density

of the objects.   The weight setting adopted by the nervous system in the absence of information about the density of a weight corresponds to a density of one—about the average density of common objects.   If the actual density is greater, as it will be with a small, heavy object, the muscle power will be too low, and the object will appear heavier than a larger object of the same weight.

It is interesting that scale distortion illusions are similar in different individuals from the same culture, but differ somewhat in different cultures when the available characteristic features are different.   They are also very slow to change in adults.   For example, in a case of adult recovery from infant blindness, we found (Gregory and Wallace 1963) that the newly available visual inputs were only accepted when they could be directly related to previous touch experience.   In our present terms—vision was only possible after the corneal grafts when visual data could select *already available* internal models based on earlier touch experience.   Building new models was very slow, taking a year or more.   The use of vision for size-scaling occurred within a few months, the initial distortion being very great in situations where touch or other information had not previously been brought to bear—as when looking at the ground from a high window, when the ground appeared almost within touch range though actually 40 feet below.   The normal systematic distortion illusions did not occur: I suppose that there was no negative transfer of perceptual learning, where there had been no opportunity for learning to take the place of the normal size-scaling features such as perspective.

2.2. *The Operation of Models in Sensory Discrimination*

The size-weight and similar illusions can tell us something about the ' engineering ' nature of the models in the brain.   Consider the following experiment.   We have two sets of weights, such as tins filled with lead shot. Each set consists of, say, seven tins all of a certain size, while the other set has seven tins each of which is, say, twice the volume of the first set.   Each set has a tin of weight, in grams, 85, 90, 95, 100, 105, 110, 115.   The 100 gram weight in each set is the standard, and the task is to compare the other weights in the same set with this standard, and try to distinguish them as heavier or lighter.   The tins are fitted with the same sized handles for lifting to keep the touch inputs constant except for weight.   Is the discrimination the same for the set of weights which are *apparently* heavier but in fact the same? The answer is that discrimination is *worse* for weights either apparently *heavier* or *lighter* than weights having a specific gravity of about one (Gregory and Ross 1967). Why should this be so?

Suppose that sensory data are not only compared with the current internal model—as they must be to be useful—but are also *balanced against it*.   We then have systems like Wheatstone bridges, and these have useful properties. Bridge circuits are especially good (*a*) over a very large input intensity range and (*b*) with components subject to drift.   Now it is striking how large an intensity range sensory systems cover—$1 : 10^5$ or even $1 : 10^6$—and the biological components are subject to far more drift than would be tolerated by engineers confronted with similar problems.   So balanced bridge circuits seem a good engineering choice in the biological situation.

We can regard the input signals as providing one arm of our Wheatstone bridge, and the prevailing internal model·as providing the opposed arm against which the input is balanced.   Now since the internal arm is part of the model, it will be set wrongly in a scale distortion illusion: in the size-weight illusion, visual information has set the 'weight arm' wrongly.   This means that the bridge will not balance.   The illusion is the misbalance of the bridge.   Now an engineer's bridge which is not balanced suffers in its ability to discriminate changes in its input, for it is no longer a null system but relies on scale readings of the galvometer or other misbalance detector.   Thus the supposed biological system gives just what a practical engineer's bridge would give—loss of intensity discrimination associated with an error in balancing the bridge.

2.3. *Some Further Implications of Internal Models*

On the general view I have outlined, perception is not directly of sensory information but rather of the internal models selected by sensory information. Indeed, current perception *is* the prevailing set of models. Three further points may be briefly mentioned.

1. There are well known situations in which the sensory information calls up two or more incompatible internal models with equal probability.   The best known example is the spontaneously reversing Necker cube.   The available information is insufficient to decide between rival internal models, one of a cube viewed from above, and the other of a cube viewed from below, and each comes to the fore in turn.   It is interesting that in this case the addition of tactile information—provided by holding in the hand a luminous cube viewed in darkness—does not serve to abolish visual reversals, though it does reduce their rate of occurrence (Shopland and Gregory 1964).   Evidently the visual internal model system is largely autonomous, though it is partly under the control of other senses.   For example, visual size and distance can be set by other senses, especially touch.   It is also worth noting that size scaling follows not only currently available sensory information, but also changes in the internal model.   Thus, a luminous cube appears as a cube when seen correctly— though the further face is smaller at the retina—but as a truncated pyramid when depth-reversed.   Here there is no change at all in the sensory input, only in the internal model, so the scale changes *with the model*, though the sensory information remains constant.

2. Generally, as we have said, the internal model is reasonably complete and appropriate, but a wrong model may be selected and even if appropriate it may be wrongly scaled.   We know from perceptual experiments in situations where only minimal information is available, that both selection and scaling can be quite wrong.   So it is a small step to say that in the absence of any sensory information entirely wild models might be called up.   This could be the case in dreaming, and in drug or fatigue induced hallucinations.   Hallucinogenic drugs might call up internal models either by increasing neural noise in the brain or by reducing the threshold criteria for acceptance of the models stored there.

3. Abnormal conditions such as schizophrenia might be caused by inappropriate models being built in the first place, or by wrong selection criteria being employed.   Greater knowledge of the processes and conditions for perceptual learning might have implications for psychiatry.   If the models are our internal world we should find out more about them.

3. Human Perception and the Design of Robots

Devices which respond to sources of information are commonplace. There is no difficulty in arranging for a door to open itself when someone breaks a beam of light to a photocell. But such devices do not ' see ' or ' perceive ' in the sense that we do. Similarly, our reflex blink to a sudden bright light is not ' seeing ', ' perceiving ' or ' observing '.

Classical and current theories of perception lay far too much stress on sensory characteristics, giving insufficient weight to the vital point about perception: perception is geared to *objects*, for it is objects which are biologically important. Objects are useful or dangerous, food or disaster; but retinal images, and vibrations of the tympanum, are of no importance except to indicate the identity of external objects. The patterns of sensory activity are but symbols from which reality may be read. This involves far more than the recognition of patterns. Pattern recognition is only an early stage of perception, for objects are more than patterns and it is *objects* that matter. Objects have all manner of vitally important properties which are seldom sensed, so current sensory information cannot be adequate for dealing with objects.

On this theory, perception allows behaviour to be appropriate to the hidden properties of objects, when the internal models sufficiently reflect their properties. This is very like the notion of a medical syndrome—a few spots may indicate the past, present and future course of a disease such as measles, together with an appropriate strategy for dealing with it. Once recognized, the syndrome—or perceived objects—may be accepted for guiding the most complex behaviour with but little current information.

The special feature of perception is that it does not mediate behaviour directly from current sensory information; but always via internal models of reality—which themselves reflect the redundancy in space and in time of the external world. This is where perception differs from devices such as photocells actuating doors, or biological reflexes, for these give control directly from the inputs. They do not use the current information to call up appropriate models, giving information drawn from the past of the hidden features of the present situation. The past is usually a reliable guide, and our memory contains vastly more information than can be transmitted in reasonable time by the sensory channels even when the relevant information is available—which is rarely the case.

One might be tempted to think that objects, as perceived, are no more than statistical groupings of sensed events—syndromes of sensation. But to say this is to miss a vital point. Sensed events are categorized also in terms of the use made of them. A book, for example, is seen as a single object. This is because we handle the collection of pages as one object. Sensory inputs are grouped according to the repertoire of behavioural skills of the owner of the perceptual system. One man's object may be another's pattern—or be nothing but randomness.

This brings out the kind of difficulty we have in imagining the perceptual world of animals, or even people whose interests are very different from our own. It also has implications for designers of robots—machines to see and act on what they see. If they are to respond to objects via internal models—and all the biological advantages will apply to the machine—then its models must be appropriate to *its* sensory inputs and to *its* repertoire of actions. These will differ greatly from ours. But could we communicate with a robot having internal models very different from our own? We should expect the same extreme difficulty that we have in trying to communicate with other animals, or with schizophrenics. Even though we design and build our own robot, and know exactly how its circuits function, communication could be impossible when its internal models are not ours.

3.1. *The Status of Perceptual Brain Models*

We suppose that perceptual models are aggregates of data about objects, and about how objects behave and interact in various circumstances. Perceptual models bear a resemblance to hypotheses in science. We may think of sensory data suggesting, testing and sometimes modifying perceptual models in much the same way that scientific data suggest, test and modify theory and hypothesis in science. A precise comparison of perceptual processes with the logic and method of scientific inquiry could be highly rewarding. The project was actually planned by Norwood Russell Hanson with the present writer, but tragically Russ Hanson was killed in his private plane.

We are concerned here, however, with not only the logical but also the biological and the engineering status of brain models. Whatever they are— one thing is quite clear—they are not isomorphic pictures of external shapes. All sorts of information about objects must be stored, but pictures can only represent specific shapes and colours. Shape and colour have only indirect significance: what matters is whether the object is useful, a threat or food. It is non-optical properties that are important. When we look at a picture, we can read all kinds of significance beyond mere shape and colour. The picture serves to evoke our internal models, which have been developed by handling objects, so that non-optical features have become associated. Similarly the pictures in the eye, the retinal images, only have significance when related to non-optical properties of objects. Without such correlations all pictures, including retinal images, would be meaningless—mere patterns. The artist, by presenting selected visual features, plays games with our internal brain models, and may quite drastically change them by evoking new associations. It is clear that the brain models cannot be logically at all like pictures: for though pictures can evoke models their appropriateness is in terms of objects.

The computer engineer will ask: are these supposed brain models digital or analogue? It is possible to make an informed guess as to which system is adopted by the brain, in terms of speed of operation, types of errors and other characteristics typical of analogue or digital engineering systems (cf. Gregory 1953). The engineering distinction arises from the fact that in practice analogue systems work continuously, but digital systems work in precisely defined discrete steps. This difference is immensely important to the kinds of circuits or mechanical systems used. Discontinuous systems have higher reliability in the presence of ' noise ' disturbance, while analogue devices can have faster data transmission rates though their precision is limited to around $0 \cdot 1$ per cent. There is no limit in principle to the number of significant figures obtainable from a digital computer, if it has space enough and time.

Because of the clear engineering distinction between continuous and discontinuous systems, there is a temptation to define analogue in terms of continuous, and digital in terms of discontinuous. But this will not do. We can imagine click steps fitted to a slide rule; this would make it discontinuous, but it would still be an analogue device. We must seek some deeper distinction.

The point is that both 'analogue' and 'digital' systems represent things by their internal states. The essential difference between them is not in *how* they represent things but rather in *what* they represent. The distinction is between representing events *directly* by the states of the system, and representing *symbolic accounts* of real (or hypothetical) events. Real events always occur in a continuum, but symbolic systems are always discontinuous. The continuous/discontinuous computer distinction reflects this difference between representing the world of objects directly and representing symbolic systems. Even the continuous functions of differential calculus have to be handled as though they were discretely stepped.

A continuous computing device can work without going through the steps of an analytical or mathematical procedure. A digital device, on the other hand, has to work through the steps of an appropriate mathematical or logical system. This means that continuous computers functioning directly from input variables necessarily lack power of analysis, but they can work as fast as the changes in their inputs—and so are ideal for real-time computing systems provided that high accuracy is not required. The perceptual brains must work in real-time, and it does not need the accuracy or the analytical power of a digital system following the symbolic steps of a mathematical treatment of the situation. Perceptual motor performance only has an accuracy of around 1 per cent. It seems that a continuous analogue system is appropriate for perceptual data processing. This holds both for actual brains and future robots.

It is most implausible to suppose that the brain of a child contains mathematical analyses of physical situations. When a child builds a house of toy bricks, balancing them to make walls and towers, we cannot suppose that the structural problems are solved by employing analytical mathematical techniques, involving concepts such as centre of gravity, and coefficient of friction of masses. It is far better to make the lesser claim for children and animals: that they behave appropriately to objects by using analogues of sensed object-properties, without involving mathematical analyses of the properties of objects and their interactions. Perceptual learning surely cannot require the learning of mathematics. It is far more plausible to suppose that it involves the building of quite simple analogues of relevant properties of objects: relevant so far as they concern the behaviour of the animal or the child. We might say that, from the point of view of the controlling nervous system, relevant properties of objects are transfer functions between the motor output and the sensory input of the active, perceiving, organism. Behaviour is given by selecting appropriate transfer functions developed by inductive generalization from similar past situations and called up by the recognition of objects.

This and other considerations force us to question the traditional distinction between 'analogue' and 'digital'. The discontinuous–continuous distinction will not serve. It is a matter of distinguishing between computing systems which solve problems by going through the steps of a formal argument, or mathematical analysis, from systems which solve problems without 'knowing' logic or mathematics—by following the input variables and reading off solutions with a look-up system of internal functions. We need a new terminology for this distinction. This is worth making if only it helps us to think more clearly about the relation of computers to the nervous system; and what kind of man-made computer would be appropriate for a robot.

To name the first type of computer, we can go back to Charles Babbage's Analytical Engine of about 1840. Systems employing formal logical or mathematical analysis we may call *Analytical Computers*. In practice these will be discontinuous, the steps representing the steps of the analytical argument or mathematics. But this is not its defining characteristic, which is that it works by following an analysis of the prevailing problem or situation. A convenient term for computers which arrive at (rough and ready) solutions by look-up systems of internal syntheses of past data—'models' reflecting aspects of reality—is more difficult to find. We propose the term: *Synthetical Computers*.

It is reasonable to suppose that the invention of logic and mathematics has conferred much of the astonishing power humans have compared with other animals for many kinds of problem solving. We have *synthetical* brains which use, with the aid of explicit symbols, *analytical* techniques. It is interesting that even the most advanced analytical techniques are useless for some physical problems—predicting the weather, the tides, economic trends, for example—and then we have to rely on inductivity derived models and crude synthetical techniques. Almost always simplifications and corrections have to be used when analytical techniques are applied to the real world: so it is not entirely surprising that synthetical brains are so successful. Indeed we do not know how to programme an analytical computer to analyse optical information for performing tasks that would be simple for a child of three. We are on the wrong track to make the attempt—surely the child does not do it this way.

To build a seeing machine, we must provide more than an 'eye' and a computer. It must have limbs, or the equivalent, to discover non-optical properties of objects for its eyes' images to take on significance in terms of objects and not merely patterns. The computer must work in real time. It need not work according to analytical descriptions of the physical world: all it requires are quite crude synthetical analogues of input–output functions, selected by distinguishing features of objects. These collections of transfer functions give appropriate behaviour through predictions, made possible by the redundancy of the world of objects. Ultimately, the perceptual brain reflects the redundancy of the external world: when it does so correctly, we see aspects of reality without illusion.

La perception est considérée, dans cet article, comme un processus de sélection par des "modèles internes", de l'information d'entrée destinée à modeler le comportement. Les avantages et les inconvénients que représente pour l'organisme le recours à de tels modèles sont soulignés. Les modalités de fonctionnement de ces modèles sont étudiées à la lumière de données en provenance des recherches sur les illusions perceptives: celles-ci peuvent être considérées comme des cas où un modèle erroné a été choisi ou qu'une erreur d'échelle a été commise. Ce sont probablement aussi ces arguments qui permettrai ent d'expliquer certaines imageries bizarres survenant dans le rêve et dans certains états anormaux. Comparés à un ordinateur, les mécanismes perceptifs et leurs modèles fonctionnent davantage comme un système analogique que comme un système digital.

Wahrnehmung wird als ein Prozess der Auswahl " innerer Modelle " diskutiert, nach deren Struktur Daten verwendet werden, um das Verhalten zu formen. Vorteile und Nachteile für den Organismus bei der Benutzung dieser Modelle werden umrissen, und die Wege, auf denen diese Modelle wirken, im Lichte deutlicher Wahrnehmungs- Illusionen betrachtet: diese können als Fälle angesehen werden, in denen ein falsches Modell gewählt wurde, oder Bewertungsfehler gemacht wurden. Es wird vermutet, dass bizarre Bilder in Träumen und einige abnormen Zust ände auch in dieser Weise verstanden werden können. Mit einem Computer verglichen, ähnelt der Wahrnehmungs- Mechanismus mit seinen Modellen eher einem analogen als einem digitalen System.

References

BARTLETT, F. C., 1932, *Remembering* (London: CAMBRIDGE UNIVERSITY PRESS).

BLODGETT, H. C., 1929, The effect of the introduction of reward on the maze performance of rats. *University of California Publications in Psychology*, **4**, 113–134.

COGHILL, G. E., 1929, *Anatomy and the Problem of Behaviour* (London: CAMBRIDGE UNIVERSITY PRESS).

CRAIK, K. J. W., 1943, *The Nature of Explanation* (London: CAMBRIDGE UNIVERSITY PRESS).

GREGORY, R. L., 1953, Physical explanations in psychology. *British Journal of Philosophica Science*, **4**, 192–197.

GREGORY, R. L., 1963, Distortion of visual space as inappropriate constancy scaling. *Nature*, **199**, 678–680.

GREGORY, R. L., and WALLACE, JEAN G., 1963, *Recovery from Early Blindness*: 1 *Case Study* (Cambridge: HEFFERS).

GREGORY, R. L., and ROSS, HELEN E., 1967, Arm weight, adaptation, and weight discrimination. *Perceptual and Motor Skills*, **24**, 1127–1130.

LASHLEY, K. S., 1951, The problem of serial order in behaviour. In *Cerebral Mechanisms in Behaviour* (Edited by L. A. JEFFRESS) (New York: WILEY).

SHOPLAND, C., and GREGORY, R. L., 1964, The effect of touch on a visually ambiguous three-dimensional figure. *Quarterly Journal of Psychology*, **26**, 66–70.

Evidence for an Accumulator Model of Psychophysical Discrimination

By D. VICKERS

University of Adelaide, South Australia

Recent theoretical approaches to the problem of psychophysical discrimination have produced what may be classified as 'statistical decision' or 'data accumulation' models. While the former have received much attention their application to judgment and choice meets with some difficulties. Among the latter, the two types which have received most attention are a 'runs' and a 'recruitment' model, but neither seems able to account for all of the relevant data. It is suggested instead that an 'accumulator' model, in which sampled events may vary in magnitude as well as probability, can be developed to give a good account of much of the available data on psychophysical discrimination. Two experiments are reported, in which the subject presses one of two keys as soon as he has decided whether the longer of two simultaneously presented lines is on the left or right. Results are found to be inconsistent with a runs or recruitment process, but to accord well with predictions from the accumulator model. Other evidence consistent with such a mechanism is briefly reviewed.

1. Introduction

The many attempts which have been made during the last 100 years to understand the process of sensory discrimination have generally been concerned to devise a model which can predict the observed relationships between, on the one hand, the detectability of the difference between two quantities and a subject's degree of caution in making a judgment, and on the other, the observed latency of a response and the probability of its being correct. Some attempts, such as the 'information' and 'confusion' models of Crossman (1955), have been restricted to relating signal difference to latency, and may be criticized as inaccurate or incomplete (Vickers 1967). Those which have considered all four variables fall into two broad classes, the so-called statistical decision models and what may be termed data-accumulation models. Both types assume that, owing to momentary fluctuations in the observer arising from randomness in his neural activity, two signals of physical magnitudes A and B may be thought of as represented in the brain by two overlapping normal distributions of perceived signal magnitudes. If an unknown signal equal to A or B is presented, the subject is assumed to take a series of samples of perceived magnitudes of the signal until sufficient data have been accumulated to decide, within acceptable limits of error, to which of the two distributions the presented signal belongs.

1.1. Statistical Decision Models of Choice Behaviour

With different authors the statistical procedures proposed vary, but Welford (1968, p. 50) points out that, if errors are held constant, they all imply that the mean latency ($\bar{L}$) should be given by

$$\bar{L} = k/d'^2,$$ (1)

where k is some constant determined by the length of time needed to take a sample, and the percentage of errors made by the subject, while d' is the conventional measure of detectability, determined by the ratio of the difference between the means to the square root of the sum of the variances of the two distributions of perceived signals, i.e. the signal-to-noise ratio. So far the models have dealt only with the case where two signals are presented together by assuming that the subject consistently adopts one or other of the signals as a standard, or that he deals with differences between signal magnitudes rather than the magnitudes themselves.

1.2. *Difficulties with Statistical Decision Models*

While statistical decision models of the above kind have recently enjoyed a considerable vogue, their application to judgment and choice has also met with some difficulties.

(i) In an experiment where tones were discriminated from background noise Green *et al.* (1957) found that, when the duration of the signal exceeded some minimum, which varied for different subjects between 108 and 276 msec, Equation 1 held fairly well. However, the most economical description of the overall pattern of results plotted by Green *et al.* (1952, Figure 5) is that it shows a sigmoidal relation between d' and signal duration. In a later experiment, where subjects made repeated observations of signals in noise, Swets *et al.* (1959) claimed that d' is a direct, approximately linear, function of the square root of the number of observations. The data they plot, however, cannot be accepted as clear confirmation of a square root relation. Some data might equally well be taken as evidence of a sigmoidal relation, and others clearly suggest it. Again, attempts by Welford (1960) and Vickers (*op. cit.*) to test Equation 1 found that it did not provide a good description of the results of other experiments using signals relatively free from external noise (e.g. Crossman 1955; Birren and Botwinick 1955; Vickers *op. cit.*). Finally, Taylor *et al.* (1967) claimed that data by Schouten and Bekker (1967) illustrate a linear relationship between L and d'^2. The data they plot, however, do not seem to justify that conclusion; if anything, their analysis clearly demonstrates a sigmoidal relationship between the two.

(ii) Statistical decision models in which the number of samples is fixed (e.g. Crossman *op. cit.*) or variable (e.g. Stone 1960) account for increased L with decreased d' by supposing that the subject adjusts the size (or number) of samples to maintain an approximately constant error rate. Vickers (*op. cit.*), however, analysed results from a series of his own experiments, as well as those by Shallice and Vickers (1964), and found that in all cases the proportion of errors was a monotonic decreasing function of d'. Again, a very plausible interpretation of a subject's reported confidence is that it represents his subjective estimate of the probability of making an error (Cartwright and Festinger 1943) and hence, if he were trying to maintain a constant error rate, his reported confidence should also remain roughly constant with changes in d'^2 and L. However, reported confidence appears to be a monotonic increasing function of d' (Johnson 1939; Festinger 1943 a; Garrett 1922; Volkmann 1934; Johnson 1945). This seems difficult to reconcile with the notion of sampling to a fixed level of error (Crossman *op. cit.*) or with that of an ' acceptable outgoing quality level ' (AOQL), which is used by quality control statistics (Grant 1952), and which underlies the variable sample models of the kind proposed by Stone (*op. cit.*).

(iii) In addition to the general difficulties mentioned above, the variable sample model developed by Stone (*op. cit.*) and Laming (1962) suffers from several practical disadvantages:

    (*a*) as Audley and Jonckheere (1956) pointed out, it may be inappropriate to use group data because the latency equation includes a term (log $\sqrt{(\alpha\beta)}$), in which α is the proportion of errors made on one signal and β the proportion made on the other. The value of this term varies with each subject's proportion of errors, and, because of the logarithm, cannot be averaged over a group;

    (*b*) when no errors are made log $\sqrt{(\alpha\beta)} = \infty$ which can make the model unworkable for very easy discriminations; and

    (*c*) when the two signals are identical, so that $\bar{A} = \bar{B}$, the equation given by Laming (1968, p. 32, Equations 3·7 and 3·8) assumes an indeterminate value, so that no direct prediction can be made concerning the decision latencies for discriminating between them. The effect of the last two restrictions is to make theoretical predictions for two limiting conditions uncertain, so that the model cannot deal with a considerable amount of existing data (e.g. Kellogg 1931; Johnson 1939; Cartwright 1941 a; Festinger 1943).

1.3. *Data Accumulation Models of Choice*

One feature which fixed and variable sample statistical decision models have in common is that both postulate some kind of bidirectional counter, registering either the mean of a sampling distribution or a (log) likelihood ratio that the mean of this distribution is greater (or less) than zero (i.e. for signals which are equiprobable, the logarithm of the ratio of the probability that the series of observations would arise given that one signal were presented to the probability that the series would arise given the alternative signal). The value stored in this counter can be increased or decreased by additional stimulus information, successive values taking, in the variable sample case, the form of a random walk. This feature distinguishes them from another class of decision models, which may be termed data accumulation models, in which different counters are postulated for each possible kind of information and the value in each counter can only be increased—never decreased—by new stimulus information. The properties of these ' undirectional ' counters and their application to reaction time experiments have been discussed by many writers, including La Berge (1962), McGill (1963), Laming (1968) and Smith (1968). It is generally assumed that sampled events fall into distinct classes (e.g. $A > B$ or $B > A$), and that samples are accumulated until particular criteria are met. Audley and Pike (1965) distinguished two main types:

    (i) a ' runs ' model in which the criterion for making a response is the accumulation of K successive events of the same class (e.g. Audley 1960; Estes 1960; Bower 1959, Model B);

    (ii) a ' recruitment ' model in which the criterion is the accumulation of K events in any class (e.g. La Berge *op. cit.*).

1.4. *Difficulties with the ' Runs ' Model*

Although the ' runs ' model is intuitively plausible in so far as it is reminiscent of neurophysiological conditions for the firing of a nerve fibre, as well as providing a first approximation to some of the data (Audley *op cit*.), results from several experiments (e.g. Cross and Lane 1962; Pike 1968 b; Pickett 1967, 1968), when analysed in the form of latency–probability functions (Audley and Pike *op. cit*.), are clearly inconsistent with a runs process (Pike 1968 a). Despite this, data from some individual Ss (e.g. Pike 1968 b; Wollen 1963) are consistent with a runs process. The discrepancy cannot be explained by a change in criterion, i.e. the length of run required for a decision. For slow responders, who would presumably have a high criterion, the empirical latency–probability function is least symmetrical, while the theoretical function for a runs process becomes increasingly symmetrical as the criterion is made stricter. Rather than make the very complex supposition of a ' change in strategy ' to explain these differences in performance, it would seem preferable to turn attention to models in which the shape of the latency–probability function is appropriately sensitive to changes in criterion.

1.5. *Difficulties with the ' Recruitment ' Model*

Although there seems to be a fair amount of evidence in the shape of latency–probability functions suggesting that a recruitment process operates in tasks involving psychophysical judgment (La Berge *op. cit*.; Pike, 1968 a) as well as in more complex ' perceptual ' processes (Pickett 1967, 1968), the recruitment model, as it has been developed so far, is not entirely free from difficulties when more direct confrontations with data are attempted. The first of these is the difficulty of estimating the variances in the signals (σ) upon which depends the amount of overlap between signals, and hence the proportion of events falling into one category rather than another. Without such an estimate it does not seem possible to go further and estimate K. If an attempt is made to estimate K according to the assumptions presented below (2.1) a further difficulty arises. The proportion of errors made by subjects generally indicates a value of $K \geqslant 7$. At such low values of K, however, the expected number of events that have to be sampled before reaching a decision has a range of less than 4, although p, the probability of a sampled event falling into one particular category, may vary over the whole ' effective ' range from 0·50 to 1·0. Since response latencies are supposed to be linearly related to the number of events sampled, and since the range of latencies is often large, the time taken to accumulate each sample must usually be assumed to be also rather large (> 100 msec). When this is multiplied by the minimum number of events required for a decision, however, the predicted latencies may considerably exceed those observed.

Again, Pickett (1967) conducted a texture discrimination task in which the probability of two horizontally adjacent cells being both black or white was varied, and response latencies recorded from subjects who were required to sort the textures into ' coarse ' (high transition probability) and ' even ' (low transition probability). The form of the latency–probability functions is approximately consistent with those predicted by a recruitment model if subjects are assumed to sample pairs of horizontally adjacent cells, adding 1 to one counter for each pair of similar cells and 1 to a different counter for each pair of dissimilar cells, responding ' coarse ' or ' even ' according to which counter first reaches the criterion. However, more detailed matching with a recruitment model is difficult; accuracy increases with larger matrices, which means that the criterion must be assumed to be stricter. But this would lead us to expect longer latencies, whereas the latencies for larger patterns are shorter than those for smaller.

It might be that subjects take more than the probability of sampled events into account. For example, the distribution of run lengths, if the patterns are scanned in a horizontal direction, will be different from that obtained by vertical scanning, provided the horizontal transition probability does not equal 0·5. Moreover, distributions will change as a function of the size of the pattern since longer runs become more probable with larger patterns. If, as seems likely, the distributions will become more distinct with increased pattern size, and if subjects take both the probability and magnitude of sampled runs into account, then we should expect to find that larger patterns make for increased accuracy and shorter latencies. At any rate there seems to be some intuitive implausibility in supposing that the nervous system, in which stimulus information is coded in analogue form as pulse repetition rate, should operate in tasks involving magnitude estimation in such a manner that the effective variable is merely the probability of an event, irrespective of any magnitude which might be assigned to it.

At this juncture, therefore, it seems worth while to explore two further possibilities. The first is that subjects may accumulate information representing not only the occurrence of an event but also its magnitude. The second, which is pointed out by Pike (1968 a) and is partly dealt with by McCarthy (1947), is that the quantity which has to be accumulated may fluctuate from trial to trial, or even during a trial. While this last hypothesis seems to be neurophysiologically plausible (Oswald 1962; Haider 1967), it involves the addition of another theoretical parameter as well as presupposing the nature of the 'quantity' to be accumulated. The object of the present paper, therefore, is to explore the first possibility, and to suggest that an 'accumulator' model, in which the sampled events may vary in magnitude as well as probability (making the criterion for a response 'an amount C in any class'), can be developed to give a good account, obviating some of the above difficulties, of much of the available data on sensory discrimination.

2. Outline of an 'Accumulator' Model of Discrimination

2.1. *Stimulus Representation*

Although the present approach is quite general, a description of the stimulus display for which the model was worked out may clarify its application. This is shown in Figure 1 and consists of two black vertical lines against a rectangular white background. The lines in different presentations were always equidistant from each other, and had their upper ends always terminating at the upper horizontal boundary of the background.

In this context a 'signal' refers to the physical magnitude of a line of variable length. The perceived signal is supposed to undergo some random disturbance of its value, due either to momentary fluctuations in the physical magnitude of the signal or in the sensitivity of the observer, i.e. to external or internal 'noise' respectively. Where two signals A and B, such as those in Figure 1 are presented simultaneously, we assume that the distributions of their perceived intensities remain stationary over time, and that they may thus be represented by two normal curves of equal and constant variance, as shown in Figure 2 (*a*).

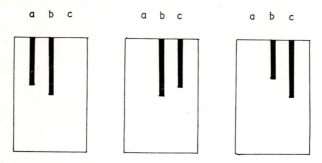

Figure 1. Sample signals used in Experiment I. Both the absolute position (i.e. *ab* or *bc*) of each pair and the relative position (i.e. left or right) of the greater signal were varied randomly from trial to trial.

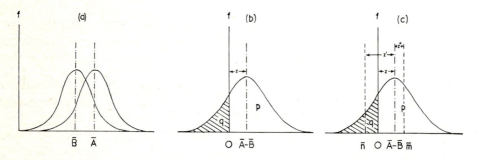

magnitude of perceived signal   magnitude of perceived difference   magnitude of perceived difference

Figure 2.   Diagrammatic representation of the supposed distributions of perceived signal magnitudes and differences. (*a*) Hypothetical representation of a perceived display. Perceived values of A and B are supposed to be randmoly disturbed by noise, and may be characterized by two normal distributions with means $\bar{A}$ and $\bar{B}$ and $\sigma_a = \sigma_b$. (*b*) Representation of sampling distribution of perceived signal differences, with mean $(\bar{A} - \bar{B}) = \bar{A} - \bar{B}$ and $\sigma_{(a-b)} = \sqrt{(\sigma_a{}^2 + \sigma_b{}^2)}$. The probability of a positive $(A - B)$ difference is p, while that of a negative is q. The proportion p is given by $z = (\bar{A} - \bar{B})/\sqrt{(\sigma_a{}^2 + \sigma_b{}^2)}$. (*c*) Representation of the sampling distribution in (*b*), with the mean value of the distribution of positive differences $(\bar{m})$ given by $z + z''$, and the mean $(\bar{n})$ of the negative differences given by $z' - z$.

If we assume that the subject makes a series of comparisons between values of A and simultaneous values of B, then, if the perturbations in A and B are independent, and if $\bar{A} \geqslant \bar{B}$, we may represent the sampling distribution of $(A - B)$ differences by a normal curve with mean $(\bar{A} - \bar{B}) = \bar{A} - \bar{B}$ and $\sigma_{(a-b)} = \sqrt{(\sigma_a{}^2 + \sigma_b{}^2)}$, as shown in Figure 2 (*b*). The mean $(\bar{A} - \bar{B})$ can be expressed as a standard score

$$z = 0 - (\bar{A} - \bar{B})/\sqrt{(\sigma_a{}^2 + \sigma_b{}^2)}],$$

and the value of p (the probability of a positive value of $(A - B)$), and hence of $q = 1 - p$ can be found using cumulative normal probability tables.

If we know the value of $(\bar{A} - \bar{B})$ and of $\sigma_{(a-b)}$ we can assign probability distributions to the positive and negative sections, respectively, of the distribution of $(A - B)$ differences shown in Figure 2 (c). We can also calculate mean values $\bar{m}$ and $\bar{n}$ for the positive and negative distributions (Hartley and Pearson 1950, pp. 2–3).

2.2. *Stimulus Sampling*

Since perturbations in perceived A and B have been assumed to be independent, we may regard the results of this series of comparison as a succession of Bernouilli trials, where the probability of a 'success' corresponds to the probability (p) that the result of a comparison will be $A > B$ and the probability of a 'failure' ($A < B$) is q, with $p + q = 1$. Since $\bar{m}$ and $\bar{n}$ are calculable we can also attach average magnitudes to the successes and failures.

The essence of the 'accumulator' model consists in supposing that the subject continuously samples the outcomes of these trials, and makes two running totals T_a and T_b of the *amounts* of success and failure respectively. We suppose in addition that the subject continuously samples the outcome of this succession of trials until T_a or T_b reaches some criterion value C_a or C_b. When either of these totals is reached, he stops sampling, and makes response R_a ('*A* is greater than *B*') or R_b ('*B* is greater than *A*'), respectively.

The values C_a and C_b are assumed to be linearly related to the variability of the perceived signals, i.e. $C_a = c\sigma_a$ and $C_b = c\sigma_b$, where c is simply a coefficient assumed to be constant for any one subject under any one set of experimental conditions, but whose value may vary as a result of changes in motivation, incentive, arousal, etc. The values C_a and C_b are supposed to be predetermined by the subject and capable of adjustment by him.

2.3. *Relations between d′, c, P(R), and L*

Although the model is conceptually simple its mathematical description seems to be very difficult. One possible approach is to view the model as a kind of recruitment process. According to this approach, if the $(A - B)$ differences are sampled by the subject until $T_a \geqslant C_a$ or $T_b \geqslant C_b$, then the number of events that must be sampled in order that $T_a \geqslant C_a$ will be given by a random variable C_a/m (where m is the magnitude of a success) with a distribution given by

$$C_a \Big/ \int_0^\infty \frac{1}{\sqrt{(2\pi)}} \exp\left(-d'^2\right)/2.$$

Similarly the number of events that must be sampled before $T_b \geqslant C_b$ will be given by a random variable C_b/n (where n is the magnitude of a failure) with a distribution given by

$$C_b \Big/ \int_{-\infty}^0 \frac{1}{\sqrt{(2\pi)}} \exp\left(-d'^2\right)/2.$$

If the $(A - B)$ differences are sampled at a steady rate, each sample taking a constant time (λ), then, in accordance with the above assumptions, the mean number ($\bar{N}$) required to make any response (either R_a or R_b) is shown by McCarthy (*op. cit.*, Equations 3.8 and 4.17) to be given by:

$$\bar{N} = \left\{ \frac{r_a}{p} I_p(r_a + 1, r_b) + \frac{r_b}{q} I_q(r_b + 1, r_a) \right\}, \tag{2}$$

where p is the proportion of successes ($A > B$ outcomes) sampled by the subject, $q = 1 - p$, $r_a = C_a/\bar{m}$, $r_b = C_b/\bar{n}$, and $I_p(r_a, r_b)$ is the incomplete beta-function, values of which are tabulated by Pearson (1932). Values of $\bar{N}$ can also be obtained from the graphs prepared by McCarthy (*op. cit.*, pp. 373–380). Comparison of theoretical sample numbers with observed latencies then depends on the relation

$$\bar{L} = \lambda \bar{N} + t_0, \tag{3}$$

where $\bar{L}$ is the mean overall latency and t_0 is a time constant inserted to allow for delays in apparatus and response systems.

It is tempting to proceed further and to develop the accumulator model, using $C_a/\bar{m}$ and $C_b/\bar{n}$ for r_a and r_b in the expressions derived by La Berge (*op. cit.*) for the recruitment model, to evaluate the probability of making a particular response and to predict the latencies of correct and incorrect responses considered separately. So far, however, no way of justifying this procedure has been found.

Because of the uncertainties involved in an approximate approach, together with the complexities involved in taking into account the precise distributions of C_a/m and C_b/n, it was decided to side-step the theoretical difficulties for the moment by using a computer simulation of the process to obtain the derived predictions. For two signals A and B, where $A > B$, with a constant 'noise' level given by $\sigma_a = \sigma_b$ and differing by amounts of 0 to 25 per cent, the programme calculated the probabilities of error, mean expected latencies for correct, incorrect and all responses, and second, third and fourth moments of the various latency distributions at each of several criterion levels from $C = 0 \cdot 5 \sigma$ up to $C = 5\sigma$. For a noise level given by ($\sigma_a/\bar{A} \times 100$) varying from 2 to 3 per cent the probabilities of an error at different criterion levels are given in Tables 1 and 2 (Appendix A).

More striking than the patterns of predicted errors are the forms of the latency–probability functions for $\sigma = 2$ per cent and c varying from 0·5 to 5, shown in Figure 3. Several features of the plotted data deserve mention.

(1) The recruitment, runs, and random walk models each predict different types of latency–probability functions, and much of the controversy about which model should be preferred has centred upon these. The present model seems able to reconcile this conflict. For high values of c (e.g. $c = 5 \cdot 0$) its latency–probability function resembles that predicted by a recruitment process, for intermediate values (e.g. $c = 1 \cdot 5$ or $2 \cdot 0$) the function resembles that for a runs model with a strict criterion, and for low values (e.g. $c = 0 \cdot 5$) the function resembles that predicted by the random walk model, with latencies for errors closely approaching those for correct responses.

(2) The fluctuations in latency for improbable errors particularly at high criterion levels are not due simply to increased variance arising from a smaller sample of observations but are a stable feature of the functions, and remain even with a greatly increased number of observations.

(3) With increase in σ the general height of each curve remains constant, but the data points, which are based on probabilities of making an incorrect response, move towards the centre, and their associated latencies also change, so that the detailed pattern may change completely.

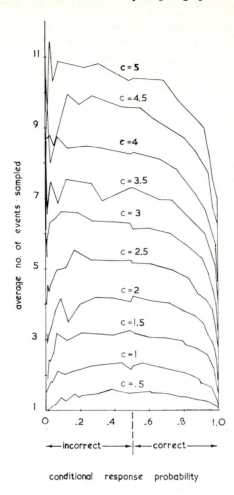

Figure 3. Latency–probability functions for a simulation of the proposed accumulator model operating on 20 different ratios with 10 different criteria. Curves are based on 500 responses to each ratio. For all ratios $\bar{A} \geqslant \bar{B}$, and $\sigma = 0{\cdot}03A$. The functions represent the average of (i) the time taken to respond '$\bar{A} > \bar{B}$', plotted against the probability of making that response as the probability of a positive difference (p) is varied from 0 to 1; and (ii) the corresponding time to respond '$B > A$' against the probability of making that response as $q = 1 - p$ is varied from 1 to 0. The two conditional probabilities have been averaged, as have the two corresponding latencies. Responses with a 'conditional probability' $> 0{\cdot}5$, therefore, have that probability of being correct, while those with a conditional probability $< 0{\cdot}5$ would have been classified as incorrect with the corresponding probability.

2.4. *Estimation of Parameter Values*

Estimation of the parameters λ, t_0, and C depends upon considering the accumulator process as it operates on very easy discriminations, where the probability of sampling a positive difference approaches unity, as analogous to the periodic latency mechanism proposed by McGill (1962), in which excitations arriving at regular intervals (λ) evoke a response after a delay which is random. If the analogy holds, then, according to McGill (1962, Equations (2) and (3)), the observed latencies should approach the sharply peaked Laplace distribution in which λ may be estimated as the difference between the minimum and the modal latencies.

Since we have supposed that excitations follow the period λ, rather than precede it as McGill envisages, then the modal response for a very easy discrimination should coincide with the attainment of the second excitation (i.e. sampled difference). This means that in order to estimate t_0 we should subtract twice the estimated value of σ from the observed modal latency.

If data are plotted in the form of latency–probability curves and scaled so that an increase of λ in the observed latency corresponds to an increase of 1 in the number of events sampled as shown in Figure 3, then the value of the criterion c can be estimated by aligning the response latency corresponding to $t_0 + \lambda$ with $N = 1$ in Figure 3, and directly comparing the obtained with the theoretical curves.

Lastly, where no independent estimate of σ is possible, the tables in Appendix A can be used in conjunction with the observed probabilities of error to provide an estimate of σ. Where, as in Experiment II σ is independently known, the tables may be used to provide an estimate of it which should then correspond closely with its known value.

3.   Experiment I.   Comparison of latencies for correct and incorrect responses

Discriminanda in this experiment were pairs of black, vertical lines, a constant 4 mm apart, on a white background. The lines were a uniform 1 mm in width, with their upper ends terminating at a common horizontal base-line as shown in Figure 1. In order to discourage the subject from making successive comparisons each pair could occur in one of two randomly varied positions (a, b or b, c in Figure 1). The longer line was always 20 mm in height while the shorter took values of 19·7, 19·5, 19·0, 18·5 and 17·5 mm. Stimuli were originally drawn in Indian ink on Bristol board to ten times these dimensions, and photographed on to alternate frames of a high-contrast cine-film. The stimuli were back-projected on to a ground glass screen 2·5 m from the subject. A manual signal from the experimenter brought on the first stimulus and triggered a Venner Digital Counter Type TSA 6634 measuring reaction times to the nearest 0·001 sec. The subject responded by pressing one of two micro-switched morse keys. Depression of either key (a) stopped the reaction timer; (b) removed the signal frame, leaving a blank white background; (c) lit a lamp on the experimenter's console which indicated whether the response was correct or incorrect; (d) disengaged both keys; and (e) triggered a delay timer, preset to issue a pulse after 3·5 sec (± 3 msec). This pulse in turn simultaneously (a) switched off the response lamp on the console; (b) re-engaged the response keys; (c) projected the next stimulus frame on to the screen; and (d) reset and restarted the reaction timer. The task was thus a self-paced cycle, and in this respect similar to earlier experiments in discrimination using card-sorting (e.g. Crossman *op. cit.*; Shallice and Vickers *op. cit.*).

For each subject the experiment was conducted in five exactly similar sessions on five closely consecutive days at the same hour and with the same background illumination. Each sesssion consisted of one practice run of 30 discriminations, followed by five test runs each with 100 discriminations. The occurrence of each ratio, the relative position of the longer line, and the absolute position of each pair were determined by a random number programme with no special restriction, except that each ratio should occur an equal number of times. Five subjects performed the five sessions in the same order.

Five female volunteers, aged 22–27, all with normal or corrected vision served as subjects. They were instructed to press the key on the side of the longer line as quickly as possible, *trying* not to make mistakes (the emphasis on *trying* being intended to convey to subjects that they should not be unduly perturbed by occasional errors). In addition, subjects were told at the beginning of each session that they should try to tackle the task in ' the same way ' as on previous sessions. After each run there was a pause of about 2 min. The whole experiment lasted 40–50 min.

3.1. *Results*

Because of the great volume of results and because of the variation within any one subject's results from session to session, as well as the variation between subjects, only the main findings can be presented here. Figure 4 (*a*) shows the distribution of latencies from all five sessions for the correct responses of one subject (*M*), to the easiest ratio (20/17·5). The distribution clearly shows the expected approach to the Laplace distribution: for high probabilities it is roughly symmetrical but the long upper tail gives it a highly significant positive skew, ($\gamma_1 = 3\cdot724$, $N = 493$), and it is also strongly leptokurtic ($\gamma_2 = 19\cdot003$, $N = 493$). The distributions for all five sessions for the remaining four subjects also show these characteristics, in each case to a highly significant extent, so that a sign test allows us to generalize the finding ($p = 0\cdot031$, $N = 5$, one tail). A computer simulation of the accumulator process operating on discriminanda in the ratio 20/17·5, and with several levels of noise from $\sigma = 0\cdot02\,\bar{A}$ up to $0\cdot20\,\bar{A}$ was carried out. The distribution of the number of sampled events produced by the simulation resembled the empirical latency distribution in being positively skewed and leptokurtic to a significant extent for values of $c \geqslant 0\cdot5$ up to $c \leqslant 2$, though for higher values of c occasional departures from this pattern did occur. In contrast, a similar simulation carried out for a

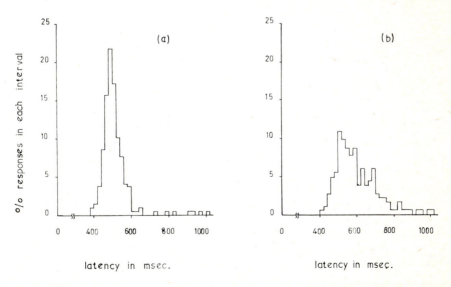

Figure 4 (*a*) Distribution of latencies for 493 responses from subject (H) to the easiest ratio (20/17·5); (*b*) distribution of latencies for 436 responses from subject (H) to a difficult ratio (20/19·5).

recruitment model for the same range of σ and with criterion values ranging from 2 to 7 produced theoretical distributions which were generally platykurtic and which had only a slight tendency to be positively skewed for very easy discriminations at low criterion values; for high criterion values (>3) distributions for correct, incorrect, and all responses were generally negatively skewed.

As the discrimination becomes slightly more difficult, changes in the shapes of the latency distributions are complex. Visually the modal ' column ' in the distribution of latencies becomes fatter, with the peak tending to shift slightly to the right. With increased difficulty this build-up suddenly collapses and the distribution breaks up into a family of two or more component distributions of decreasing proportion with each component appearing to have a slight negative skew. Generally, numerical measures of skewness tend to decrease, though even for the most difficult discriminations the positive skewness in the latency distributions for correct responses remains highly significant for each subject. Figure 4 (*b*) shows a typical distribution for correct responses to the ratio 20/19·5 and illustrates the above points.

For each subject in each session the distance between the lower limit of the interval containing the shortest latency and the value at the first peak (which coincided with the mode of the whole distribution in all but two instances) was taken as a measure of λ. Then for each subject the values of this estimate were averaged over the five sessions. The mean of these averages turned out to be 100 msec, which as well as being a convenient number, well within the range 50–200 msec suggested by Stroud (1955) for the length of the perceptual ' moment ', offers a strong enticement to connect it with some rhythmic physiological activity such as the alpha rhythm (Murphree 1954). Because of the possibility of ' empty ' sample periods, it seems likely that a truer estimate would be slightly less than 100 msec.

For each subject, for each session, values of t_0 and c were then calculated in the manner suggested above. With four out of the five subjects the latency–probability functions change shape markedly from session to session, and run the gamut of curves predicted by a recruitment, a runs, and a random walk model. Figures 5, 6 and 7 show the latency–probability functions for the slowest and fastest sessions from the most and the least accurate subjects. For all subjects λ has been approximated by 100 msec since this allows data from different sessions and different subjects to be directly compared, and in any case differs very little from the individual estimates. Values of t_0 and c have been estimated from the data in the way suggested above.

It is clear from Figures 5, 6 and 7 that the accumulator process is capable of giving a good account of the main features of these results. For the high criterion values used by subject Y (session B) the shape of both theoretical and empirical curves approaches that predicted by a recruitment process, but with a dip in latencies for incorrect responses with a low probability of occurring. In contrast the theoretical and empirical curves for low criteria (e.g. subject M, sessions C and D) more closely resemble those predicted by a runs model, or (in other cases) a random walk. Again the successive ' escarpments ' in the patterns of latencies for errors which are observable in these results (e.g. subject K, session A), and which are more clearly evident in the scatterplots, are also a stable feature of the simulated data, as are the slight discontinuities (subject K, sessions A and C) in that section of the curve showing correct

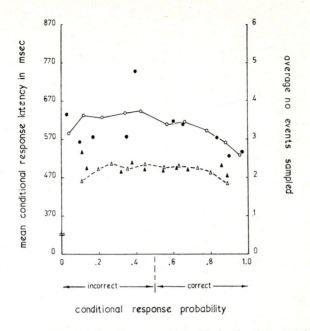

Figure 5. Latency-probability functions for one subject (M) for the slowest (●) and fastest (▲) sessions in Experiment I. The lines joining the empty circles and triangles are for a computer simulation of the accumulator process, with parameters estimated as explained in the text. For the slowest session $c = 1.7$, and for the fastest $c = 1.0$, while $\sigma = 0.011\bar{A}$ in both cases.

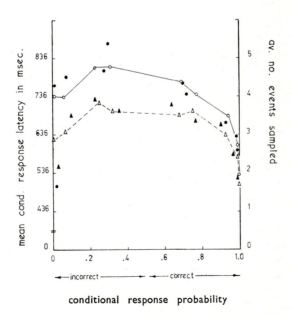

Figure 6. Latency–probability functions for one subject (K) for the slowest (●) and fastest (▲) sessions in Experiment I. The lines joining the empty circles and triangles are for a computer simulation of the accumulator process, with parameters estimated as explained in the text. For the slowest session $c = 2.2$, and for the fastest $c = 1.7$, while $\dot{\sigma} = 0.05\bar{A}$ in both cases.

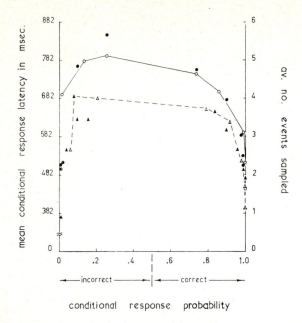

Figure 7. Latency–probability functions for one subject (Y) for the slowest (●) and fastest (▲) sessions in Experiment I. The lines joining the empty circles and triangles are for a computer simulation of the accumulator process with parameters estimated as explained in the text. For the slowest session $c = 2 \cdot 5$, and for the fastest $c = 1 \cdot 7$, while $\sigma = 0 \cdot 04 \, \bar{A}$ and $0 \cdot 03 \bar{A}$ respectively.

latencies only. Finally, although criteria in some cases (e.g. subject Y) may vary considerably between the two sessions, the latencies for highly probably correct responses remain quite close, i.e. the curves tend to emanate from a common source rather than form a regular series, each with a distinct origin.

As McGill (1962) points out, it should be possible to estimate the ' noise ' in the underlying distribution of signal differences from the variance in the distribution of latencies, but it is not yet clear exactly how it should be done in this case.

4. Experiment II

In an attempt to determine the value of σ in an empirical way, an experiment is being conducted, using a computer generated display in which the lengths of two vertical lines similar to those in Experiment I are subject to simultaneous random fluctuation. The distributions of line lengths are normal and of equal variance, and the fluctuation rate is constant, so that some empirical estimate of both λ and σ is possible. So far only a few results from one subject (Y in the previous experiment) have been obtained, but these seem sufficiently clear to be worth inclusion.

Figure 8 shows a latency–probability function based on 300 responses from subject Y to each of five different ratios. The value of λ has been estimated as 100 msec. This accords with the fluctuation rate of 10/sec predetermined for the display and with the value of 97 msec estimated from this subject's data in Experiment I. As in Experiment I the value of t_0 has been estimated as 282, making $c = 3 \cdot 0$. The best estimate of σ was the very high one of $\sigma \simeq 0 \cdot 21 \bar{A}$, which accords well with the predetermined value of $\sigma = 0.20\bar{A}$. Figure 8 shows the reasonably close matching of the empirical data by a computer simulation carried out for these ratios and with the appropriate values of σ and c.

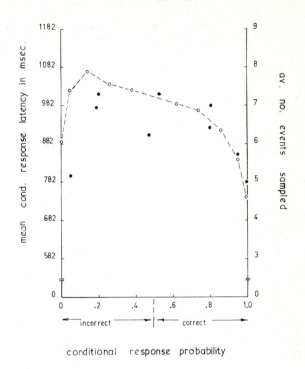

Figure 8.　Latency–probability function for 300 responses from one subject (Y) in Experiment II. The simulation is for $c = 3.5$, $\sigma = 0.10\bar{A}$.

5.　Discussion

5.1.　*Response Probability*

It is not possible, within the scope of this report, to attempt to test the present model quantitatively against all of the relevant data, since this would involve a too lengthy justification of the values chosen for the parameters c and σ. However, the probability of making a response changes as a roughly sigmoidal function of the percentage difference between two signals, and the slope of this function becomes steeper with increase in c. Since d' will be a linear function of percentage difference we may roughly characterize the predicted relationship between d' and $P(R)$ as that of a sigmoid curve which becomes less steep for 'noisy' signals (i.e. signals showing less rapid increases in d' for a given increase in the difference $\bar{A} - \bar{B}$), and more steep with increases in c. This sigmoidal relationship between $P(R)$ and d' corresponds to the classical psychometric function obtained in 'untimed' differential magnitude judgments (Duncan and Sheppard 1963; Corso 1967). A similar relationship is also the general finding in 'timed discrimination experiments' (e.g. Johnson 1939; Festinger 1943 and Pickett 1967), although the data are sometimes presented in a way which obscures this.

An increase in c in an accumulator model resembles an increase in r in a recruitment model in that it is interpreted as a change towards greater rigour in

52   *D. Vickers*

the subject's criterion. Some evidence that the psychometric function in 'timed' discrimination experiments becomes steeper with greater emphasis on accuracy is given by Festinger (1943, pp. 413–418) who found that, as instructions were varied from 'speed' through 'usual' to 'accuracy', the curve relating frequency of a particular response to confidence became steeper. Since confidence is a monotonic increasing function of detectability (Johnson 1939; Festinger 1943 a and b) this finding confirms the expected qualitative changes in the relation between $P(R)$ and d' as c is varied.

5.2. *Response Latency*

A detailed assessment of the capacity of the accumulator model to account for the results of previous experiments is made difficult by the incompleteness of most of the relevant experimental results: many experiments have taken too few observations for the data from individual results to be analysed; usually mean latencies alone are reported, and their distributions are not indicated; only in a few cases are error frequencies reported, and any comparison between the latencies for correct and incorrect responses is usually impossible. As a result, the evaluation of the various parameters cannot be guided by any strict empirical constraints and the 'adequacy' of the model depends on the degree of diligence and ingenuity exercised in selecting parameter values. Figure 15, for example, shows data from experiments by Vickers (*op. cit.*), Birren and Botwinick (1955) and Shallice and Vickers (*op. cit.*), which have been fairly well fitted by supposing $\lambda = 100$ msec for all three, t_0 equal to 740, 640 and 390 msec, and $c = 3$, 4 and 3, respectively. The linearity is fairly good but can be questioned because of the freedom in estimating c and σ.

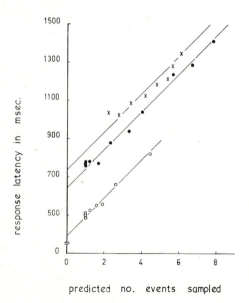

Figure 9. Latencies obtained in experiments by Vickers (1967, expt. IX), Birren and Botwinick (1955, old subjects), and Shallice and Vickers (1964, expt. III), plotted against the required number of sampled events predicted by the accumulator model with parameter values as given in the text. The straight lines have been drawn with a slope of 100, making $\lambda = 100$ msec for all three sets of data. Data from Vickers are represented by crosses, those from Birren and Botwinick by filled circles, and those from Shallice and Vickers by empty circles.

5.3. *The Relation between Latencies for Correct and Incorrect Responses*

In general, statistical decision models agree in predicting that the distribution of errors for correct responses should be the same as that for incorrect responses, while the recruitment model of La Berge predicts an inverse relationship between response probability and latency (cf. Audley and Pike 1965, Figure 1). Although this prediction seems clear-cut, there are, however, some conflicting interpretations of the relevant experimental evidence. For example, Laming (1968, p. 44) states that Schouten and Bekker (*op. cit.*) 'have found errors faster than correct responses in a two choice experiment', which seems to conflict with Pickett's (1967) finding, in a texture discrimination task, that the latency for incorrect responses was markedly higher than that for correct responses. However, Schouten and Bekker's main finding, that the proportion of errors increased as subjects were forced to respond faster, is quite different from Pickett's results. The apparent conflict can be resolved if we suppose that Pickett varied d', while holding c constant, and Schouten and Bekker varied c, while holding d' constant.

Again, in the case of Pickett's experiment, Laming (1968, p. 29) suggests that subjects ' appear to have striven for maximum accuracy without consideration of the time taken ', pointing out that it is not clear if they knew their latencies were being recorded, and concluding that the significance of the response latencies is uncertain. It is not clear, however, what grounds there are for the first contention, since the error rate rises as high as 20 per cent in the ' Small ' condition, while the lowest maximum and minimum latencies are recorded in the ' Extra Large ' condition, which also produced the lowest error rate. Enquiry from the author further revealed that it was made ' abundantly clear to subjects that response latencies were being recorded ', the instructions being to respond ' as quickly and as accurately as possible ', and in any case within 10 sec after presentation of the stimulus. This being the case, it is clear that Pickett's results accord well with the latency–probability relationship predicted by the present accumulator model, if we suppose subjects to be operating with a high criterion. In view of the magnitude of response latencies recorded, this last supposition seems very plausible. Pickett also found that for 30 of the 88 subjects the conditional response latency curves appeared to ' tip back down ' where the incorrect responses on which they are based were very infrequent, which agrees well with the pattern of results predicted by an accumulator process.

Finally, Pike (1968) has shown in a recent review that while data from several experiments appear to suggest a recruitment process, data from the fast responders of Wollen (*op. cit.*) and some of his own data from individual subjects were more consistent with a runs process. This apparent conflict can be resolved by supposing an accumulator process with a high criterion to be operating in the case of ' slow ' responders, while those results that suggest a runs model would be due to a lowering of the amount to be accumulated.

5.4. *Discriminating Signals with Equal Mean Values*

As $\bar{B} \to \bar{A}$ so that for $p \to 0{\cdot}5$, $\bar{L}$ on the present accumulator, as on the recruitment model, approaches a finite maximum value. This contrasts with the sequential sampling model where, in principle, as $\bar{B} \to \bar{A}$, it is possible to have exceedingly long random walks or sampling times. This difficulty can be avoided (cf. Laming 1958, p. 85) by postulating a time-dependent stopping rule, but only at the expense of thereby including an additional parameter and further complicating the model.

Evidence that when $\bar{A} = \bar{B}$, subjects still come to a decision in a relatively short finite time is provided by the data of Johnson (1939), Festinger (1943 a, p. 302; 1943 b, pp. 413–418), Kellogg (*op. cit.*) and Cartwright (*op. cit.*). This prediction is similar to one made by Cartwright and Festinger (*op. cit.*, p. 606, Derivation 1), and is in direct contrast to the exponential rise in $\bar{L}$ predicted by a fixed sample statistical model (e.g. Hammerton 1959).

5.5. *Is C Variable or Constant?*

A number of writers, including Hebb (1955) and Duffy (1957), have suggested that most of the effects of drugs or hormones, physical exertion, incentives, and other 'stress' factors on skin conductance, muscle tension, EEG, pulse rate, respiration and some other measures can be ascribed to changes in a continuum of arousal or activation. Although some difficulties with this hypothesis have been pointed out by Broadbent (1963), a great deal of evidence can be ordered by it (Duffy *op. cit.*; Malmo 1957), and the following discussion is based on this general concept of arousal.

On the present model, instead of supposing (i) that a subject's criterion C varies (for which it is difficult to find a neurophysiological interpretation) and (ii) that it varies in a way which correlates with certain physiological measures of arousal (which leaves the connection unexplained), we may suppose that apparent variations in C with changes in factors influencing arousal occur as the result of a number of random signals arriving in the neuronal accumulator (say T_a or T_b as above) from other heightened cortical activity. This would partially fill the accumulator, thereby diminishing the effective threshold (C). On this view we should expect that in vigilance experiments, during which arousal presumably declines (Lindsley 1952; Oswald 1962), and in the course of which cortical activity diminishes (Coleman *et al.* 1959) the effective value of C should increase, i.e. we should expect that mean response latency should increase as a direct function of time spent on watch. Evidence from several experiments reviewed by Buck (1966) does indeed show that mean reaction time increases during a vigilance task, while Aseyev (1960) found, among workers employed on monotonous conveyor-belt work, that both mean and standard deviation of reaction time increased directly with time spent on the job.

On the present view, the reductions in C shown by the data of Johnson (1939) and Cartwright and Festinger (*op. cit.*), as instructions are changed from 'accuracy' through 'normal' to 'speed', are seen as resulting directly from a heightening of the subject's state of arousal. Provided only the effective level of C were varied by the general level of activation, precisely similar effects on performance would be expected following the administration of stimulants such as benzedrine. Some complications might result, however, if heightened physiological activity could also result in a shorter sampling time (λ). Where this was the main effect, subjects would be expected to produce both faster and more accurate reaction times. If data were analysed in the same way as those of Experiment I, it should be possible, however, to distinguish between these two possibilities.

5.6. *Other Evidence of Similar Mechanisms*

From the discussion it is clear that the model presented is a kind of variable (or sequential) sampling decision model which has the distinguishing characteristic of postulating two unidirectional counters for the storage of incoming stimulus information, as opposed to one bidirectional counter. Credit for suggesting the application of this kind of model must be shared between Stone (*op. cit.*), La Berge (*op. cit.*), and McGill (1963). McGill (1963), La Berge (*op. cit.*) and more recently Grice (1968) have shown that the notion of a neural counter which accumulates an impulse count over time can be used to account for latencies under different conditions of incentive in simple reaction time tasks. Similarly, Sekuler (1965), Bindra *et al.* (1965) and Nickerson (1968) have shown that unidirectional counter models can be used to account for the observed differences in the latencies of judgments of ' same ' and ' different '.

Recently some interest has arisen among neurophysiologists about the evidence for what is termed ' rein control ' or ' unidirectional rate sensitivity ' in biological systems. This interest is manifested, for example, by a recent conference on the topic (Clynes 1967), and is concentrated on two main kinds of finding; the first concerns the specificity of neuronal units sensitive to certain types of signal (e.g. units sensitive to one direction of change of pitch (Whitfield 1967)); the second concerns the frequent assymetries in the responses of certain physiological systems (e.g. responding faster to increases in blood pressure than to decreases (Katona *et al.* 1967)). It has been argued, particularly by Clynes (1961, 1967) that these response characteristics are consistent with the notion of unidirectional, rate-sensitive neuronal units of the kind presupposed by data accumulation models, of which the accumulator process proposed here is one example.

I should like to thank Professor A. T. Welford for his advice and encouragement, and Mr. R. Willson for his invaluable computing assistance. Part of the work for this paper was carried out at the Psychological Laboratory, Cambridge, and was financed by a studentship from the Science Research Council. The remainder was carried out in the Psychology Department, University of Adelaide, and was supported by the Australian Research Grants Council.

Appendix A

Tables giving probabilities of error for various ratios, noise levels and values of c

Table 1.. $\sigma = 0.02\bar{A}$

% difference between signals	Values of the criterion c									
	0·5	1·0	1·5	2·0	2·5	3·0	3·5	4·0	4·5	5·0
0·5	0·370	0·410	0·344	0·364	0·350	0·314	0·312	0·288	0·252	0·284
1·0	0·312	0·258	0·244	0·180	0·204	0·180	0·130	0·126	0·110	0·112
1·5	0·212	0·176	0·138	0·110	0·066	0·082	0·046	0·042	0·032	0·028
2·0	0·172	0·088	0·078	0·060	0·038	0·032	0·018	0·020	0·000	0·004
2·5	0·120	0·064	0·044	0·048	0·016	0·004	0·004	0·000		0·006
3·0	0·080	0·046	0·020	0·016	0·002	0·000	0·000			0·000
3·5	0·080	0·030	0·010	0·000	0·004					
4·0	0·042	0·012	0·000		0·000					
4·5	0·024	0·004								
5·0	0·022	0·000								
7·5	0·000									
10·0										

Table 2. $\sigma = 0.03\bar{A}$

% difference between signals	Values of the criterion c									
	0·5	1·0	1·5	2·0	2·5	3·0	3·5	4·0	4·5	5·0
0·5	0·396	0·438	0·398	0·422	0·414	0·388	0·334	0·336	0·372	0·310
1·0	0·380	0·330	0·296	0·272	0·242	0·300	0·264	0·240	0·196	0·224
1·5	0·302	0·274	0·206	0·194	0·190	0·168	0·120	0·124	0·132	0·076
2·0	0·254	0·194	0·202	0·140	0·114	0·088	0·074	0·070	0·052	0·044
2·5	0·212	0·158	0·120	0·102	0·068	0·058	0·034	0·030	0·030	0·026
3·0	0·192	0·114	0·052	0·046	0·030	0·024	0·014	0·006	0·002	0·004
3·5	0·166	0·092	0·042	0·032	0·022	0·016	0·008	0·004	0·002	0·006
4·0	0·118	0·072	0·028	0·014	0·008	0·002	0·004	0·000	0·006	0·002
4·5	0·088	0·036	0·026	0·010	0·004	0·004	0·000		0·000	0·000
5·0	0·064	0·034	0·018	0·006	0·000	0·000				
7·5	0·010	0·002	0·000	0·000						
10·0	0·000	0·000								

Les études récentes consacrées au problème de la discrimination en psychophysique ont abouti à l'élaboration de deux types de modèles: le modèle de la " décision statistique " et celui de " l'accumulation des données ". Le premier a beaucoup retenu l'attention des chercheurs, mais quelques difficultés sont apparues lorsqu'on voulait l'appliquer au problème du choix et du jugement. Quant au deuxième, dont les types " sequentiels " et " à recruitment " ont été les plus étudiés, il s'est avéré qu'il ne rendait pas suffisamment compte de toutes les données pertinentes. Cependant, il semble qu'un modèle " d'accumulation " dans lequel les évènements échantillonnés peuvent varier en grandeur et en probabilité, puisse être élaboré pour rendre compte de la presque totalité de l'information disponible pour la discrimination psychophysique.

Deux expériences sont décrites dans lesquelles le sujet disposant de deux clés de réponse, devait appuyer sur l'une ou sur l'autre dès qu'il avait déterminé que la plus longue de deux barres présentées simultanément se trouvait à droite oujà gauche. Les résultats obtenus ne peuvent pas s'expliquer par un processus séquentiel ou de recrutement, mais le modele " d'accumulation " les décrit de manière satisfaisante. D'autres faits relatifs aux mécanismes mis en jeu sont décrits brièvement.

Neue theoretische Bearbeitungen des Problems psychophysiologischer Unterscheidung haben zu Modellen geführt, die als " statistische Entscheidung " oder " Daten-Akkumulation " klassifiziert werden können. Während die erstgenannten viel beachtet wurden, stösst ihre Anwendung aud Urteil und Auswahl auf einige Schwierigkeiten. Unter den letztgenannten haben zwei Typen das grösste Interesse fegunden, ein " runs " und ein " recruitment " Modell, aber keines scheint in der Lage zu sein, alle relevanten Daten zu decken. Stattdessen wird angenommen, dass ein "Akkumulator-Modell ", in dem gesammelte Ereignisse sowohl nach Grösse, als auch nach Wahrscheinlichkeit variieren können, entwickelt werden kann, das viele der verfügbaren Daten psychophysischer Unterscheidung gut zu deuten vermag. Zwei Experimente werden wiedergegeben, in welchen eine Person einen von zwei Knöpfen drückt, sobald sie entschieden hat, ob die längere von zwei dargebotenen Linien auf dei linken oder rechten Seite liegt. Die Resultate stimmen nicht mit einem " runs " oder " recruitment " Prozess überein, aber passen gut zu den Vorhersagen des "Akkumulator-Modells ". Andere Beweise für einen solchen Mechanismus werden kurz erörtert.

References

ASEYEV, V. G., 1960, The effect of monotonous work on simple motor reaction time and the lability of the excitation process in the visual analyser. *Doklady Akademiya Pedagogichespikj Nauk RSFSR*, **3**, 121–124.

AUDLEY, R. J., 1960, A stochastic model for individual choice behaviour. *Psychological Review*, **67**, 1–15.

AUDLEY, R. J., and JONCKHEERE, A. R., 1956, The statistical analysis of the learning process. *British Journal of Statistical Psychology*, **9**, 87–94.

AUDLEY, R. J., and PIKE, A. R., 1965, Some alternative stochastic models of choice. *British Journal of Mathematical and Statistical Psychology*, **18**, 207–225.

BINDRA, D., WILLIAMS, J. A., and WISE, J. S., 1965, Judgments of sameness and difference; experiments on decision time. *Science*, **150**, 1625–1628.

BIRREN, J. E., and BOTWINICK, J., 1955, Speed of response as a function of perceptual difficulty and age. *Journal of Gerontology*, **10**, 433–436.

BOTWINICK, J., BRINDLEY, J. F., and ROBBIN, J. S., 1958, The interaction effects of perceptual difficulty and stimulus exposure time on age differences in speed and accuracy of response *Gerontologia*, **2,** 1–10.

BOWER, G. H., 1959, Choice-point behaviour. In *Studies in Mathematical Learning Theory* (Edited by R. R. BUSH and W. K. ESTES.) (Stanford: UNIVERSITY PRESS).

BROADBENT, D. E., 1963, Possibilities and difficulties in the concept of arousal. In *Vigilance: A Symposium* (Edited by D. N. BUCKNER and J. J. MCGRATH) (New York: MCGRAW-HILL),

BUCK, L., 1966, Reaction time as a measure of perceptual vigilance. *Psychological Bulletin.* 291–304.

CARTWRIGHT, D., 1941 a, Decision-time in relation to the differentiation of the phenomenal field. *Psychological Review*, **48,** 425–442.

CARTWRIGHT, D., 1941 b, Relation of decision-time to the categories of response. *American Journal of Psychology*, **54,** 174–196.

CARTWRIGHT, D., and FESTINGER, L., 1953, A quantitative theory of decision. *Psychological Review*, **50,** 595–621.

CLYNES, M., 1961, Unidirectional rate sensitivity: a biocybernetic law of the reflex and humoral systems as physiologic channels of control and communication. *Annals of the New York Academy of Science*, **92,** 946.

CLYNES, M. E., 1967, Implications of rein control in perceptual and conceptual organization. *Proceedings of the New York Academy of Science.*

COLEMAN, P. D., GRAY, F. E., and WATANABE, K., 1959, EEG amplitude and reaction time during sleep. *Journal of Applied Physiology*, **14,** 397–400.

CORSO, J. F., 1967, *The Experimental Psychology of Sensory Behaviour* (New York: HOLT, RINEHART, WINSTON).

CROSS, D. V., and LANE, H. L., 1962, On the discriminative control of concurrent responses. *Journal of Experimental Analysis of Behaviour*, **5,** 487–496.

CROSSMAN, E. R. F. W., 1955, The measurement of discriminability. *Quarterly Journal of Experimental Psychology*, **7,** 176–195.

DUFFY, E., 1957, The psychological significance of the concept of 'arousal' or 'activation'. *Psychological Review*, **64,** 265–275.

DUNCAN, C. J., and SHEPPARD, P. M., 1963, Continuous and quantal theories of sensory discrimination. *Proceedings of the Royal Society of London*, Ser. B, **158,** 343–363.

ESTES, W. K., 1960, A random walk model for choice behaviour. In *Mathematical Methods in the Social Sciences* (Edited by K. J. ARROW, S. KARLIN and P. SUPPES) (Stanford: UNIVERSITY PRESS).

FESTINGER, L., 1943, Studies in decision: II. An empirical test of a quantitative theory of decision. *Journal of Experimental Psychology*, **32,** 411–423.

GARRETT, H. E., 1922, A study of the relation of accuracy to speed. *Arch. Psychol.*, 56.

GRANT, E. L., 1952, *Statistical Quality Control* (New York: MCGRAW-HILL).

GREEN, D. M., BIRDSALL, T. G., and TANNER, W. P., 1957, Signal detection as a function of signal intensity and duration. *Journal of the Acoustical Society of America*, **29,** 523–531.

GRICE, G. R., 1968, Stimulus intensity and response evocation. *Psychological Review*, **75,** 359–373.

HAIDER, M., 1967, Vigilance, attention, expectation and cortical evoked potentials. In *Attention and Performance* (Edited by A. F. SANDERS) (Amsterdam: NORTH HOLLAND).

HEBB, D. O., 1955, Drives and the C.N.S. (conceptual nervous system). *Psychological Review*, **62,** 243–254.

JOHNSON, D. M., 1945, A systematic treatment of judgment. *Psychological Bulletin*, **42,** 192–224.

JOHNSON, D. M., 1939, Confidence and speed in the two-category judgment. *Archives of Psychology,* **34,** 1–52.

KATONA, P., BARNETT, G. P., and LEVISON, W. H., 1967, Directional sensitivity of the carotid sinus reflex. *Proceedings of the New York Academy of Sciences.*

KELLOGG, W. N., 1931, Time of judgment in psychometric measures. *American Journal of Psychology*, **43,** 65–86.

LA BERGE, D., 1962, A recruitment theory of simple behaviour. *Psychometrika*, **27,** 375–396.

LAMING, D. R. J., 1962, A statistical test of a prediction from Information Theory in a card sorting situation. *Quarterly Journal of Experimental Psychology*, **14,** 38–48.

LAMING, D. R. J., 1968, *Information-Theory of Choice-Reaction Times* (New York: ACADEMIC PRESS).

LINDSLEY, D. B., 1952, Psychological phenomena and the electroencephalogram. *Electroencephalography and Clinical Neurophysiology*, **4,** 443–456.

MCCARTHY, P. I., 1947, Approximate solutions for means and variances in a certain class of box problems. *Annals of Mathematical Statistics*, **18,** 349–383.

MCGILL, W. J., 1962, Random fluctuations of response rate. *Psychometrika*, **27,** 3–17.

MCGILL, W. J., 1963, Stochastic latency mechanisms. In *Handbook of Mathematical Psychology,* Vol. 1 (Edited by R. R. BUSH and E. GALANTER) (New York: JOHN WILEY & SONS).

MALMO, R. B., 1957, Anxiety and behavioural arousal. *Psychological Review*, **64**, 276–287.

MURPHREE, O. D., 1954, Maximum rates of form perception and the alpha rhythm: an investigation and test of current nerve net theory. *Journal of Experimental Psychology*, **48**, 57–61.

NICKERSON, R. S., 1968, ' Same '–' Different ' response times: a model and a preliminary test. *Bolt Beraneck, & Newman Inc. Report No.* 1729.

OSWALD, I., 1962, *Sleeping and Waking* (Amsterdam: ELSEVIER).

PEARSON, E. S., and HARTLEY, H. O., 1966, (ed.) *Biometrika Tables for Statisticians*, Vol. I, 3rd Edition (London: CAMBRIDGE UNIVERSITY PRESS).

PEARSON, K., 1932, *Tables of the Incomplete Beta-function* (London: CAMBRIDGE UNIVERSITY PRESS).

PICKETT, R. M., 1962, Response latency in a pattern perception situation. In *Attention and Performance* (Edited by A. F. SANDERS) (Amsterdam: NORTH HOLLAND), 160–169.

PICKETT, R. M., 1968, The visual perception of random line segment texture. *Paper read at Ninth Meeting of the Psychonomic Society*.

PIKE, A. R., 1968 a, Latency and relative frequency of response in psychophysical discrimination. *British Journal of Mathematical and Statistical Psychology*, **21**, 161–182.

PIKE, A. R., 1968 b, Latency and response probability in simple discrimination. *In preparation*.

SCHOUTEN, J. F., and BEKKER, J. A. M., 1967, Reaction time and accuracy. In *Attention and Performance* (Edited by A. F. SANDERS) (Amsterdam: NORTH-HOLLAND), 143–153.

SEKULER, R. W., 1965, Signal detection, choice response times and visual backward masking. *Canadian Journal of Psychology*, **19**, 118–132.

SHALLICE, T., and VICKERS, D., 1964, Theories and experiments on discrimination times. *Ergonomics*, **7**, 37–49.

SMITH, E. E., 1968, Choice reaction time: an analysis of the major theoretical positions. *Psychological Bulletin*, **69**, 77–110.

STONE, M., 1960, Models for reaction time. *Psychometrika*, **25**, 251–260.

STROUD, J. M., 1955, The fine structure of psychological time. In *Information Theory in Psychology* (Edited by M. QUASTLER) (Glencoe, Ill.: FREE PRESS).

SWETS, J. A., SHIPLEY, E. F., McKEY, M. J., and GREEN, D. M., 1959, Multiple observations of signals in noise. *Journal of the Acoustical Society of America*, **31**, 514–521.

TAYLOR, M. M., LINDSAY, P. H., and FORBES, S. M., 1967, Quantification of shared capacity processing in auditory and visual discrimination. In *Attention and Performance* (Edited by A. F. SANDERS) (Amsterdam: NORTH HOLLAND), 223–229.

VICKERS, D., 1967, Theories and experiments on visual discrimination and the perception of visual depth. *Unpublished thesis (Ph.D.) Cambridge University*.

VOLKMANN, J., 1934, The relation of time of judgment to certainty of judgment. *Psychological Bulletin*, **31**, 672–673.

WELFORD, A. T., 1969, The measurement of sensori-motor performance. *Ergonomics*, **3**, 189–229.

WELFORD, A. T., 1968, *Fundamentals of Skill* (London: METHUEN).

WHITFIELD, I. E., 1967, The response of the auditory nervous system to simple time-dependent acoustic stimuli. *Proceedings of the New York Academy of Science*.

WOLLEN, K. A., 1963, Relationship between choice time and frequency during discrimination training and generalization tests. *Journal of Experimental Psychology*, **66**, 474–484.

An Algebraic Development of the Theory of Perceptual Transparency

By F. METELLI

University of Padova, Italy

By expressing in algebraic terms the chromatic aspects of the perceptual phenomenon of transparency and solving the resulting system of 2 equations, it has been possible to deduce from the solutions some necessary conditions of the phenomenon, which were confirmed by results of qualitative experiments.

1. A Coefficient of Transparency

The perceptual problem of transparency is epitomized in the fact that if we put a sheet of transparent plastic or glass on a homogeneous background we do not perceive it as transparent, while in arrangements such as that of Figure 1, transparency is perceived although it is not physically present. Admittedly the impression of transparency in Figure 1 may be imperfect, but it is possible to produce figures containing only different shades of grey paper which are indistinguishable from those incorporating true transparencies. One obvious suggestion is that in the first case the change of colour of a surface seen through a transparent film is not observed, because the surface covered by the film is homogeneous, whereas in Figure 1 differently coloured parts of the figure are seen through a covering film. Yet with irregular patterns it is by no means clear why in Figure 2 we perceive two surfaces one seen through the other, whereas in Figure 3 we perceive only several juxtaposed blots.

Figure 1. Transparency obtained by juxtaposing eight pieces of opaque material.

The conditions under which transparency is seen were discussed by Helmholtz (1867) and by Hering (1888), and further research was done by Fuchs (1923 a, b), Tudor-Hart (1928), Heider (1933), Koffka (1935), Metzger (1953), Kanizsa

(1955) and Metelli (1967). Figures 2 3 and 6 show that the perception of transparency depends upon both figural relationships and colour-relationships in a pattern. It is with the latter that we shall here be concerned.

Figure 2.   Transparency with irregular patterns.

Let us start with Figure 4 which is generally perceived as a transparent disc (T) upon a square (AB) which is half white and half black. We distinguish four different regions A, P, Q, and B with reflectances a, p, q and b respectively (Figure 4 (i)). What will be the relationships between these reflectances and that of the disc (t)? The question can be more clearly understood if it is asked in relation to the 'episcotizer' apparatus Which is a convenient means of studying many problems of transparency. With this apparatus a rapidly

Figure 3.   Lack of transparency, although colours and their orders are the same as in Figure 2.

rotating disc is seen in front of the background AB. A variable sized sector of the rotating disc can be removed, and when this is done the areas P and Q are partially visible behind the rotating disc as if covered by a translucent film. The reflectances p and q are thus mixtures of the background reflectances a and b and of that of the disc t in a proportion depending on the size of the absent sector.

The answer to the question can be seen in Talbot's law of colour mixture which states that

$$\alpha x + (1 - \alpha)y = z,$$

where x and y are two achromatic colours measured by their reflectances, z is the reflectance of the resulting mixture and α and $(1 - \alpha)$ are the proportions in which the colours are mixed. The same equation should imply that in Figure 4

$$p = \alpha a + (1 - \alpha)t,$$

with α representing the portion of the episcotizer disc T which has been removed. If it is assumed (as it would be in the case of the episcotizer) that t is the same for regions P and Q, then

$$q = \alpha b + (1 - \alpha)t$$

and

$$\alpha = \frac{p - q}{a - b}$$

and

$$t = \frac{aq - pb}{(a + q) - (p + b)}.$$

It can be seen that when $\alpha = 0$ both p and q are equal to t—in other words T is completely opaque. When $\alpha = 1$, $p = a$ and $q = b$—in other words T is completely transparent and wholly invisible. α can thus under these conditions be taken as a coefficient of transparency.

2. Tests of this Formulation

A series of predictions was made from these equations.

1. For transparency to be seen $(a - b)$ must be greater than $(p - q)$. In Figure 5 where $(a - b)$ is less than $(p - q)$ we seem to see a black and white square through a hole in a transparent screen.

2. The brightness differences between a and b and between p and q must always be in the same direction. The truth of this can be seen from Figure 6 (i) and (ii). In the former the condition is met, in the latter it is not.

3. When $(a - b)$ is much greater than $(p - q)$ transparency is low as in Figure 7 (i). When $(a - b)$ is only slightly greater than $(p - q)$ transparency is high, as in Figure 7 (ii).

4. If a is greater than p (i.e. A is brighter than P) and b than q (i.e. B is brighter than Q), then the reflectance of the transparent layer t will be less than either a or b and the layer will thus appear dark, as in Figure 8.

5. If a is greater than p, p than q and q than b, then the transparent layer will appear darker than a and p but brighter than q and b, as in Figure 6 (i).

6. If p is greater than a and q than b then the transparent layer will appear light as in Figure 9.

F. Metelli

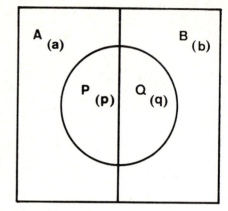

Figure 4. (i) A standard model for perceptual   Figure 4.   (ii) Symbols of regions (capital
transparency: four regions (A, P, Q, B)   letters) and colours (small letters).
of different achromatic colours.

Figure 5.   Transparency depends on colour relations.   Lack of transparency in the central field,
because $|a - |b < |p - q|$, namely the difference in brightness between the outer regions
A and B is less than the difference in brightness between the inner regions P and Q.

Figure 6.   (i) By analogy with Figure 4 we can identify regions in the upper row from left to right thus: A = white, P = light grey, Q = dark grey, B = black.   The same transition can be seen in the lower row, from right to left.

Figure 6.   (ii) Lack of transparency due to modified colour relations.   Here the transitions are A (white), P (*dark* grey), Q (*light* grey), B (black).

F. Metelli

Figure 7.   (i) When the difference in brightness between the outer regions A and B is slightly greater than the difference between the inner regions P and Q, transparency is high.

Figure 7.   (ii) When the difference in brightness between the outer regions A and B is much greater than the difference between the inner regions P and Q, transparency is low.

Figure 8.　When the region A is brighter than the region P, and the region B is brighter than the region Q, the transparent layer is dark.

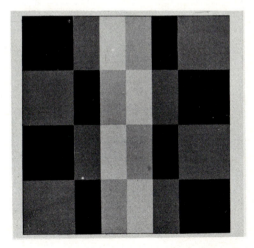

Figure 9.　When P is brighter than A, and Q is brighter than B, the transparent layer is bright.

Par l'expression en termes algébriques des aspects chromatiques du phénomène perceptif de la rantsparence et par la résolution du système de deux équations auquel on aboutit, il a été possible de déduire, à partir des solutions, quelques conditions nécessaires à la production du phénomène.   Ces conditions ont été confirmées par l'expérimentation qualitative.

Wenn man die chromatischen Aspekte des Wahrnehmungs-Phänomens der Transparenz in algebraischen Werten ausdrückt und das sich ergebende System von zwei Gleichungen lösst, wird es möglich, aus der Lösung einige notwendige Voraussetzungen dieses Phänomens abzuleiten, die sich durch Resultate qualitativer Experimente bestätigen lassen.

References

FUCHS, W., 1923 a, Untersuchungen über das simultane Hintereinandersehen auf derselben Sehrichtung. *Zeitschr. f. Psychol.*, **91**, 195–235.

FUCHS, W., 1923 b, Experimentelle Untersuchungen über die Aenderung von Farben unter dem Einfluss von Gestalten. *Zeitsch. f. Psychol.*, **92**, 299–325.

HEIDER, G., 1933, New studies in transparency, form and colour. *Psych. Forsch.*, **17**, 13–55.

HELMHOLTZ, H., 1867, *Handbuch der Physiologischen Optik* (Leipzig: L. Voss).

HERING, E., 1888, Ueber die Theorie des simultanen Kontrastes von Helmholtz, 4.   Mitteilung, *Pflügers Archiv*, **43**, 1–21.

KANIZSA, G., 1955, Condizioni ed effetti della trasparenza fenomenica. *Rivista di Psicologia*, **49**, 3–19.

KOFFKA, K., 1935, *Principles of Gestalt Psychology* (New York: HARCOURT).

METELLI, F., 1967, Zur Analyse der phänomenalen Durchsichtigkeitserscheinungen· *Gestalt und Wirklichkeit, Festgabe für Ferdinand Weinhand* (Berlin: DUNCKER & HUMBOLDT).

METZGER, W., 1953, *Gesetze des Sehens* (Frankfurt am Main: W. KRAMER).

TUDOR-HART, B., 1928, Studies in transparency, form and colour. *Psych. Forsch.*, **10**, 255–298.

Perception of Changes of Form Associated with Phenomenal Compression

By L. HOUSSIADAS

University of Thessaloniki, Greece

This paper is concerned with the description of some visual stimuli which are associated with the perception of 'pressure' or 'compression'. It is suggested that (a) such experiences are mediated by specific changes of form of a stimulus in connection with the simultaneous movement of another stimulus; (b) subjective factors are either ineffective or, at most, play a limited role.

The experiments to be reported briefly may be regarded as a contribution towards an understanding of the conditions which determine our perception of causal relations. In this sense, the present study is an extension of Michotte's work on the perception of causality. More specifically, this extension consists (a) in describing a stimulus structure associated with experiences of 'compression' which Michotte regarded as impossible to produce experimentally; (b) in showing that prior movement by the 'agent' is not always essential for the perception of causal relations.

1.   The Problem

In the world that surrounds us we often see various events as causally related. For instance, when the wind blows, we see the trees bending in a certain direction; when the weather is rainy, people use umbrellas for protection; when I push a table it is displaced.

The problem is whether such relations are learned during the lifetime of the individual or whether events involving causal relations, or at least certain types of causal relations, are structured in such a way that they give rise to an immediate impression that they are causally related. In other words, do we learn to *associate separate events* because they seem to occur together or in succession in our daily life, and attribute to them a relation of cause and effect for this reason, or are the conditions under which certain categories of events present themselves such that the visual system and the brain perceive them *immediately* as causally related without mediation of learning?

The perception of causality has been extensively investigated from a psychological standpoint by the late Professor Michotte of Louvain. A number of other investigators have extended his work in a variety of directions (for a bibliography see Thinès 1962, Crabbé 1967). Briefly, Michotte argued that causal relations are perceived under specific conditions which are of two basic types:

1. '*Lancement*'—'launching effect' or 'pushing with impact'.
2. '*Entraînement*'—'entraining effect' or 'pushing with contact'.

In the former an object A appears moving towards a stationary object B and comes into contact with it; following contact B moves away from A which remains stationary. Under these conditions, observers report that B is 'launched away' or 'pushed away' by A.

In the 'entraining' or 'pushing with contact' effect, object A appears moving towards a stationary object B and comes into contact with it; after contact, A and B move together. Under these conditions of stimulation, observers report that B is ' carried away ' or ' pushed away ' by A.

Experimental conditions required to produce these effects are highly specific —movements of A and B before and after contact must have certain speeds, duration of contact must not exceed certain time limits, etc. Given such conditions, however, observers regularly experience a relationship of cause and effect. This seems also to apply to conditions in everyday life: within the limits of certain conditions of timing, causal relations are experienced ' immediately '. Outside these conditions we may experience causal relations, but such experiences are the outcome of learning and are not immediate.

In both ' launching ' and ' entraining ' effects, there is a ' pre-existing ' movement of the object A which, in Michotte's terminology, ' extends ' to object B. A, therefore, is ' active ' while B is ' passive ', its activity being caused by the activity of A. According to Michotte, these relationships are the essential conditions which give rise to experiences of causality.

The study described here is an extension of this work to the perception of *compression*.

2.   Experimental Method

The apparatus was similar in principle to that used by Michotte (1954), and has been described in detail by Houssiadas (1964). Subjects viewed with both eyes at a distance of 1·7 m a screen in which there was a narrow horizontal slot at the level of the subject's head. The moving objects were rectangular patches which moved along this slot. Subjects were told to ' Look at this slot and describe carefully in your own words what you see happening '. The experimental session lasted approximately half an hour.

The aim of the experiments was not revealed to the subjects. All they knew was that they were participating in experiments in which ' perception of movement ' was investigated. The subjects were university students.

3.   The 'Basic' Experiment

The sequence of events was as follows: a red object (B) 25 mm long and 5 mm wide appeared stationary in the middle of the slot. At a given moment a black object (A) appeared 70 mm from B at the right of the slot and moved in the direction of B at a speed of 28 mm/sec or 50 mm/sec. When A came into contact with B, B diminished in length as if ' compressed ' by A. Then A changed direction, moving back at the same speed as that of its initial movement, while B regained its original length. The side of B which was not in contact with A remained stationary throughout. The contact between A and B was in fact only apparent because a small gap 1·5 mm wide was preserved between A and B.

Three points about the results of this experiment deserve to be noted.

(*a*) Although the experimental stimuli were in no sense ' real ', yet they did give rise to experiences normally associated with real objects. Subjects reported that object A was ' pushing in ' or ' compressing ' object B. Of course three-dimensional responses to two-dimensional stimuli are not unusual. They form the basis for understanding photographs or watching pictures in the cinema, and indeed, form the basis for all visual perception.

(b) The stimuli were giving rise to a single unified experience, that of ' pressure ' or ' compression '.   Only a few of the subjects described their experiences in ' objective ' terms, i.e. that object A was performing a movement coordinated with the deformation of B.   Most subjects gave such ' analytical ' or ' objective ' reports only when they were asked questions inviting analytical or objective descriptions.

(c) Contact between objects was not essential for reports of ' pressure ' or ' compression '.   It would be common sense to say that things deform each other when they actually come into some kind of contact with each other.   Most subjects noticed the small gap that remained between A and B when they were ' in contact ', yet this did not prevent them from *seeing* one stimulus compressing the other.   This finding, together with similar paradoxical findings by Michotte (*op. cit.*, pp. 80–81) and Yela (1952), suggests that our experiences are not always a reflection of what we know about things in terms of past experience.   Such paradoxical experiences are, however, induced much more easily in the laboratory than in daily life (Crabbé *op. cit.*, p. 136).

4.   Contact and Proximity

We will now describe briefly the conditions and results of ten experimental situations in which this last point was investigated further by varying the distance between A and B at the time of apparent contact.   In each case A travelled a distance of about 70 mm before it contacted B which was motionless; its speeds were those of the basic experiment (i.e. 28 mm/sec and 50 mm/sec).   The size of A was 4×5 mm and of B 5×16 mm.   Ten distances were used: 0, 1·5, 5, 10, 15, 20, 25, 30, 50 and 90 mm.

Table 1.   Percentages of different types of response in experiment on closeness of contact in relation to the perception of compression.   Each subject made two observations with A moving at 28 mm/sec and two more with A moving at 50 mm/sec

EFFECTS REPORTED

Distance between A and B (in mm) when B begins to change	Number of subjects	Compression	Instrumental compression	Screen effect	Erasing effect	Traction effect	Simple deformation
0	11	91	—	9	—	—	—
1·5	16	88	—	6	6	—	—
5	13	100	—	—	—	—	—
10	12	100	—	—	—	—	—
15	10	60	10	—	—	—	30
20	10	55	10	—	—	—	35
25	8	50	13	—	—	—	38
30	10	30	20	—	—	—	50
50	12	25	25	—	—	8	42
90	10	20	30	—	—	—	50

The results are shown in Table 1 from which it can be seen that certain other effects than apparent compression were associated with the longer and the shortest distances between A and B.   These were as follows.

(i) ' Screen effect ': subjects report that A is ' passing over ' B; that A becomes a ' screen ' behind which part of B is ' hidden ' (Sampaio 1943; Knops 1947; Michotte *et. al.* 1967).

    (ii) 'Erasing effect': part of *B* is seen as 'wiped out' when it comes in contact with *A*.

   (iii) 'Traction effect': *B* is seen as attracting stimulus *A* (Kanizsa and Metelli 1956; Tognazzo 1959, 1961; Kanizsa and Metelli 1961).

   (iv) 'Instrumental compression': the gap between *A* and *B* becomes a 'solid body', 'colourless' or 'invisible', through which *B* is seen as 'compressed' by *A*.

   (v) 'Simple deformation' denotes a mere coordination in space and time of the movements of *A* and *B*. In their descriptions subjects used expressions like *A* 'influences' *B* 'somehow'; *B* 'changes its form' because 'it fears' *A*; or, *A* and *B* 'perform certain movements together' or 'at the same time'.

Several subjects commented, during or after the experimental sessions, that what they were seeing 'did not make sense', yet this did not stop them from seeing *A* 'compressing' *B*. Reports of compression were given at all the distances used, although the most favourable distances were 5 mm and 10 mm. Some subjects were instructed to try to impose a different 'interpretation' on the stimuli—for example to try to see two independent movements performed by stimuli *A* and *B*—but frequently failed to do so. This was particularly true with distances of 5 mm and 10 mm, and became less so with longer distances—that is, at the distances at which spontaneous reports varied from one subject to another.

It is interesting that complete absence of gap between *A* and *B* or a gap of only 1·5 mm led to some cases in which 'compression' was not seen. It seems reasonable to suppose that for the appearance of phenomenal compression the contours of *A* and *B* should be clearly defined and that the gap enhanced this definition.

In cases of 'instrumental compression' the empty space between A and *B* assumes a definite quality; it becomes a 'colourless substance' or an 'invisible solid'. Phenomenally, this substance possesses the same qualities as *A* and *B*: it is pushing or pushed, just as they are. Perhaps we are dealing here with what Brunswik (1955) has named a 'ratiomorphic' perceptual structure. It seems possible that practice may have produced a 'set' in some subjects to organize the events into a 'meaningful' experience, and it was this tendency that led to these reports of 'compression at a distance' or 'compression through a solid body'.

Only one subject reported 'traction' effects, yet experiences of 'traction' are not infrequent in everyday life, and the stimuli used in the experimental sessions seemed on the face of it to provide many opportunities for the subjects to report 'pulling', 'dragging', etc. Other research has shown, however, that 'traction' reports are associated with fairly specific patterns of stimuli (Kanizsa and Metelli 1956, 1961; Tognazzo 1959, 1961), and we may suppose that those used here were not very favourable.

5. Size of Stimuli

We have seen that, within limits, closeness of contact is not very important for experiences of compression. However, no attempt was made to control the size of the stimuli. We therefore conducted experiments in which we varied the size of A (7×5 mm, 2×5 mm, 5×16 mm) while the size of B was kept constant (5×16 mm).

The subjects were instructed to compare the three stimulus situations with one from the experimental series already reported, and to say whether they noticed any differences in the 'strength' of compression. All 32 subjects used were in agreement that the changes in size of A did not have any effect on their impressions. Results obtained by Michotte regarding the 'pushing with impact' effect (Michotte *op. cit.*, p. 78) seem to support the view that size does not determine or influence reports of this effect either.

6.   Effects of Movement

In the experiments so far reported A covered a distance of about 70 mm before and after it came into contact with B. It is reasonable to ask whether these movements of 'approaching' and 'moving away' affect the experience of compression. This question becomes important in view of the fact that in Michotte's experiments prior movement of A was necessary for seeing causal relations. We therefore carried out a series of experiments in which we gradually eliminated the movements of A before and after contact with B, and the exposure of B when not in contact with A: distance between A and B at the point of contact in this series of experiments was 1 mm.

Experiment 1. B appeared first motionless in the middle of the slot. A moved in and made its usual contact. A disappeared suddenly before it detached itself from B on its way back.

Experiment 2. B appeared first, as in Experiment 1. A appeared suddenly by the side of B which then started changing its form. A moved away after it had been in contact with B.

These two patterns of stimulation were shown in the same session and the subjects were asked to make two observations for each pattern at a speed of 28 mm/sec and two more at 50 mm/sec. Seven subjects took part in the experiments. All reported compression for both patterns and for both speeds.

Experiment 3. B appeared first, motionless, and A appeared suddenly by its side as in Experiment 2. B changed form, then A disappeared suddenly.

Sixteen subjects participated in this experiment and made four observations each. Fourteen of them reported that A was pressing B, one reported the 'screen effect' while the other reported the 'erasing effect'.

Experiment 4. A and B emerged suddenly side by side. B changed its form, but before A 'moved back' they both disappeared.

Of the twelve subjects used in this experiment only one did not report compression.

The results of these experiments indicate clearly that, unlike Michotte's effects of 'pushing with impact' and 'pushing with contact' the experience of compression does not depend on prior or subsequent movements of A or on the pre-existence of B. In this they seem to be in line with some other findings by the present writer (Houssiadas 1964, pt. III) and others (Tognazzo 1959, 1961; Kanizsa and Metelli 1961), who have shown that one object may appear, under certain conditions, to push another even though the movement of both starts at the same time.

Cet article décrit certains phénomènes visuels tels que la perception de la " pression " ou " compression ". Il apparaît que:

(*a*) cette forme de perception est due aux variations spécifiques dans la forme du stimulus en liaison avec le mouvement simultané d'un autre stimulus;

(*b*) les facteurs subjectifs n'ont aucun effet ou, tout au plus, jouent un rôle minime.

Les expériences décrites brièvement dans cet article constituent une contribution à l'étude de la perception des liaisons causales. Ce travail se situe dans le prolongement des techerches de Michotte sur la perception de la causalité. Il en constitue une extension dans ce sens:

(*a*) qu'il y est décrit une structure de stimulus liée à une expérience de la " compression " et que Michotte avait considérée comme étant impossible à reproduire expérimentalement;

(*b*) qu'un mouvement préalable d'un " agent " n'est pas toujours essentiel pour percevirt les relations causales.

Die Arbeit befasst sich mit der Beschreibung einiger visueller Reize, die mit der Wahrnehmung von " Druck " und " Kompression " verbunden sind. Es wird angenommen, dass (*a*) solche Wahrnehmungen durch spezi—fische Formänderungen eines Reizes bei gleichzeitiger Bewegung eines anderen Reizes vermittelt werden: (*b*) subjektive Faktoren sind entweder wirkungslos oder spielen höchstens eine begrenzte Rolle.

Die beschriebenen Versuche sollen zum Verständnis der Bedingungen beitragen, welche unsere Wahrnehmung kausaler Zusammenhänge bestimmen. In diesem Sinn ist die gegenwärtige Untersuchung eine Erweiterung der Arbeit von Michotte über die Wahrnehmung der Kausalität. Genauer gesagt, diese Erweiterung besteht (*a*) in der Beschreibung einer Reizstruktur, verbunden mit der Erfahrung von Kompression, deren experimentelle Erzeugung Michotte für unmöglich hielt: (*b*) im Nachweis, dass vorhergegangene Bewegung des wirkenden Reizes nicht immer für die Wahrnehmung einer kausalen Beziehung notwendig ist.

References

BRUNSWIK, E., 1955, ' Ratiomorphic ' models of perception and thinking. *Proc. 14th International Congress of Psychology, Montreal*, 1954, pp. 108–109.

CRABBÉ, G., 1967, Les conditions d'une perception de la causalité. *Monogr. Franc. Psychol.*

HOUSSIADAS, L., 1964, An exploratory study of the perception of causality. *British Journal of Psychology Monograph Supplements*, No. 36.

KANIZSA, G., and METELLI, F., 1956, Connessioni di tipo causale fra eventi percettivi: l'effetto attrazione e l'effetto lancio inverso. *Proc. XI Congresso degli Psicologi Italiani, Milano,* 1956.

KANIZSA, G., and METELLI, F., 1961, Recherches expérimentales sur la perception visuelle d'attraction. *J. Psychol. norm. pathol.*, **58**, 385–420.

KNOPS, L., 1947, Contribution à l'étude de la ' naissance ' et de la ' permanence ' phénoménales dans le champ visuel. *Miscellanea Psychologica Albert Michotte* (Louvain: INSTITUTE SUPERIEUR DE PHILOSOPHIE), pp. 298–322.

MICHOTTE, A., 1954, *La Perception de la Causalité* (2nd edition) (Louvain: PUBLICATIONS UNIVERSITAIRES). Trans., 1963, as *The Perception of Causality* (T. R. and E. MILES) (London: METHUEN).

MICHOTTE, A., THINÈS, G., and CRABBÉ, G., 1967, *Les Compléments Amodaux des Structures Perceptives* (2nd edition) (Louvain: PUBLICATIONS UNIVERSITAIRES).

SAMPAIO, A. C., 1943, *La Translation des objets comme Facteur de leur Permanence Phénoménale* (Louvain: WARNY).

THINÈS, G., 1962, *Contribution à la Theorie de la Causalité Perceptive: Nouvelles Recherches sur l'Effet Entraînement* (Louvain: PUBLICATIONS UNIVERSITAIRES, and Paris: EDITIONS NAUWELAERTS).

TOGNAZZO, D. P., 1959, Contributo all' analisi degli effetti causali ' entraînement ' e ' traction '. *Mem. Accad. Patavina di SS.LL.AA: Classe di Scienze Matematiche e Naturali*, **71.**

TOGNAZZO, D. P., 1961, Ulteriori contributi all' analisi degli effetti causali ' entraînement ' e ' traction '. *Mem. Accad. Patavina di SS.LL.AA: Classe di Scienze Matematiche e Naturali,* **73.**

YELA, M., 1952, Phenomenal causation at a distance. *Quarterly Journal of Experimental Psychology,* **4,** 139–154.

A Psychophysical Metric for Visual Space Perception

By R. B. Freeman, Jr.

Department of Psychology, Pennsylvania State University, U.S.A.

A new psychophysical metric is proposed for the measurement of visual cues in space perception. Its application to the discrimination of distance by means of binocular disparity, monocular movement parallax and linear perspective is discussed. Experiments are described in which the validity of the proposed psychophysical metric is tested in relation to judgments of visual slant and shape.

1. Introduction

The purpose of this paper is to present a method for specifying the stimuli for visual space perception, together with some data showing its application to the perception of the slant and shape of rectangular stimuli. The paper is divided into three parts. The first part reviews some of the history of the concept of cues. In the second part the metrics of visual cues are described, using several cue-dimensions as examples. Finally, the broad outlines of two experiments are described in which the predictions of cue-theory are tested.

1.1. *Visual Cues*

It is a surprising fact that much of what we know about visual space perception is due not to the investigation of visual scientists but rather to the writings and paintings of the Renaissance artists. By the time of Leonardo da Vinci, whose death 450 years ago we celebrate this year, all the principles of perspective drawing had been thoroughly worked out. It was then a short step from the understanding of the laws of perspective in paintings to the understanding of the laws of perspective in the retinal image, based as they were on geometrical optics of a form equally well understood by the 16th century. Therefore, when Descartes demonstrated experimentally the existence of an optical image on the back of the eye of a bull, one might have expected that Kepler's notion that a retinal image was the initiating event in the process of vision would become thoroughly entrenched in subsequent scientific investigations. But such was not to be the case. For beginning with George Berkeley's *New Theory of Vision*, published in 1709, the notion of visual perceptions as dependent upon retinal images was to be supplanted by a dominant interest among British philosophers in the experiential basis of visual perception. For Berkeley, the strange shapes of retinal images were a code whose secrets were decipherable only as a consequence of learning the nature of corporeal objects whose forms retinal images represented.

Thus it is understandable that Helmholtz, when constrained to account for visual perceptions, should resort to unconscious inference as an explanatory concept. For Helmholtz, ' such objects are always imagined as being present in the field of vision as would have to be there in order to produce the same impression on the nervous mechanism, the eyes being used under ordinary normal conditions ' (Helmholtz, 1962, Vol. III, p. 2). Furthermore, according to Helmholtz, such inferential processes are involved in the visual interpretation of several stimulus dimensions, such as the variation of apparent size with distance, the occlusion of the images of farther objects by nearer ones (interposition), and the aerial perspective that makes distant mountains blue on hazy days.

However, there were, according to Helmholtz, other 'factors', as he called them, involved in the judgment of size and distance that were not dependent upon antecedent experience but were, instead, of the form of 'definite sensations' (Helmholtz *op. cit.*, Vol. III, p. 294). They included the changes of parallax that result from motions of the head, and from binocular vision, which contribute to the judgment of relative distance, and binocular convergence which provides somewhat unreliable information regarding the absolute distance of objects from the observer.

Helmholtz's classification has been perpetuated into modern times. The 'primary criteria' are the sensations (or at least stimulation) that arise from accommodation, convergence, and binocular parallax; the 'secondary criteria' are linear perspective, aerial perspective, the distribution of light and shade, apparent (or retinal) size, and interposition (Titchener 1911; Boring 1963). Motion parallax is called a secondary criterion by Titchener, and this usage was accepted by Boring (1942). Carr (1935) used the term 'signs', 'cues' and 'factors' interchangeably for both primary and secondary criteria.

The effectiveness of many, if not all, of the cues to distance have been demonstrated at least in laboratory experiments (cf. Carr for an extensive survey of the literature), and some cues (e.g. retinal disparity) have been investigated extensively (Ogle 1964). But the predominant interest in the nature and origin of cues has diverted the attention of investigators from the necessity of finding a psychophysical metric for their measurement. It is the purpose of this report to suggest an approach to the measurement of such cues, using linear perspective as a principal example.

1.2. *Requirements for a Psychophysical Metric*

For the purpose of psychophysical measurement, then, a cue may be defined as some geometrical property of the retinal images of the two eyes where the properties that are chosen for specification and measurement depend, like light itself, upon both geometrical and psychological requirements. To take an example, the retinal size of an object varies with its distance from the observer's eye. As Carr pointed out 35 years ago, it is reasonable to assume that, because of this variation, we may expect that retinal size will be a 'cue' to perceived distance, in the sense that variation in retinal size, whether or not caused by variation in physical distance of an observed object, will be accompanied by variation in *perceived* distance. The quantitative measurement of the variation of retinal size with variation in physical distance is determinable by the laws of geometrical optics. The quantitative measurement of the variation of perceived size with variation of retinal size is a matter for determination by psychophysical experiment. It is obvious that perceived size is not *necessarily* a linear function of retinal-image size, and therefore not necessarily linearly related to physical distance.

A 'cue-theory' of visual space perception therefore requires two sets of postulates, which may or may not be related to each other. One set consists of statements relating the positions of objects to the configurations of the

retinal image. In this set the statements are derived from the laws of geometrical optics and are not necessarily dependent upon knowledge of the
sensitivities of the visual system, although the choice of variables may be
influenced by them. The second set contains statements regarding the response
of the eye to stimulus dimensions, defined as variations in the geometrical
properties of the retinal images. Such postulates may be independent of
known physical relationships of objects in space. It is on the basis of such
statements, for example, that we are able to understand why the artist is able
to paint pictures which will be seen by observers as representing three-
dimensional space.

A complete understanding of the perception of objects in physical space,
therefore, requires both geometrical and psychophysical analysis of cues to
visual space perception. A useful treatment of the present knowledge of the
several cues, such as monocular movement parallax, interposition, accommodation, convergence and binocular disparity, is given by Graham (1965).
The present paper will present a similar analysis of linear perspective as a
visual cue.

2. A Psychophysical Metric for Visual Cues

Because of the difficulty inherent in measuring the linear dimensions of the
retinal image, the angle subtended by an object at the eye—the visual angle—
is generally accepted as a convenient substitute for the direct measurement of
the retinal image (Graham *op. cit.*). Like the retinal image itself, the visual
angle subtended by an object will increase with increasing physical size and
nearness. It is commonly held that we respond to the physical size and
distance, shape and slant of objects in space (e.g. Gilinsky 1951). The question
is how far those variables can be specified solely in terms of the visual-angle
subtense of objects together with visual-angle specifications of other cues in
the visual field. The theory put forward here is that they can, and that *the
eye responds solely to visual-angle differences projected by the contours of objects
at different distances*.

However, the variation in visual-angle dimensions of objects at different
distances, as noted above, depends solely on geometrical considerations, and
does not take into account the sensitivity of the eye to such visual-angle values.
It is necessary therefore to consider the sensitivity of the eye, as well as the
geometry of visual optics. Two measures of sensitivity are relevant: the
absolute threshold and the differential threshold. The former is of importance
in the scaling of visual distance and slant, while the latter is of significance in
the scaling of visual size and shape.

Let us assume that the psychophysical magnitude or value of a cue is
proportional to the threshold for the cue when measured under comparable
conditions of observation. This relationship can be expressed in general terms
as follows

$$V = \frac{\kappa}{\kappa_0}, \tag{1}$$

where V = the psychophysical value of the cue, κ = a measure of the cue in
question in visual-angle units, and κ_0 = the threshold visual-angle subtense of
that cue, defined as that subtense which is just detectable by the eye, or more

precisely the subtense which is at the change-over point from detectability to non-detectability.   An example will show how κ and κ_0 may operate in the perception of distance.   If a man is standing 100 m away and another of equal height is standing 110 m away the retinal angle subtended by the second is 10 per cent less than that subtended by the first.   If, however, the men are at 1000 and 1010 m, the difference of retinal angle is only 1 per cent and κ is thus only 1/10 as great.   Suppose, however, also that the second man is standing 10 m to the side of the first as well as further away, then at 1000 m the visual angle separation between the two men will also be reduced to 1/10 of that at 100 m.   There is evidence that, with the decrease in the visual-angle separation of contours whose relative distance is to be discriminated, the threshold value κ_0 decreases in an approximately linear manner.   This has been shown to be the case for stereoscopic acuity by Matsubayashi (1937) and by Graham *et al.* (1949).   It was also true, in at least one experimental condition used by Zegers (1948), for the absolute threshold for relative monocular movement parallax.   It has further been shown to hold for the threshold for retinal perspective in the discrimination of slant, as described later in this paper (see also Freeman 1969).   Although we cannot know, until the appropriate experiment is done, by what amount the eye's sensitivity to small differences in visual-angle size is increased by reducing the visual-angle separation of the targets whose relative distance is to be judged, there is obviously here the possibility that a mechanism is built into the visual system which tends to compensate for the loss in geometric magnitude of spatial cues as distances from the eye increase.

The manner of determining κ depends, of necessity, upon the nature of the cue to be measured.   For cues of absolute distance, such as accommodation, convergence and monocular movement parallax for single objects, κ may take the form, respectively, of wave-front curvature, convergence angle and angular displacement of an object in the visual field per unit motion of the head.   In the case of cues such as monocular movement parallax, retinal disparity and linear perspective that are effective only in the discrimination of differences in distance, or depth, to use LeGrand's terminology (LeGrand 1967), κ may be an angular *difference* (Graham *op. cit.*, Freeman 1966 a, b).   In either case, κ_0 will be the threshold for discrimination of the cue under the same conditions of viewing as those for the measurement of κ.

The usefulness of the psychophysical specification of cues depends, of course, on the knowledge of the threshold values of cues under a wide variety of conditions of observation.   Graham *et al.* (1948) obtained threshold values of monocular motion parallax under varying conditions of stimulus size, illumination intensity, rate of object motion and axis of movement.   The effects of illumination on stereoscopic acuity have been studied by Mueller and Lloyd (1948), Berry *et al.* (1950), and by others.   There are, however, surprisingly few studies of cue thresholds.

3.   The Discrimination of Shape and Slant

I should like now to turn to a consideration of two experiments on the discrimination of visual slant and shape whose purpose was to test the validity of the psychophysical analysis of visual space perception described above. In these experiments subjects viewed rectangles slanted in such a way that the top and bottom edges were horizontal, and the one farther away than the other. The only discriminable cue for slant was the linear perspective due to this difference of distance.

3.1. *Definition of Retinal Perspective*

The value used for specifying the linear perspective was $\delta = \beta_N - \beta_F$, where β_N and β_F are one-half the visual-angle subtense of the nearer and farther edges, respectively. δ increases approximately as a sine-function of slant. At the same time, the height (α) in terms of the visual-angle subtended by the projected image of the rectangle decreases as a cosine-function of slant. The relation of rate of change of δ and α with variation in slant is thus complex. It was nevertheless expected that threshold slant would be a function of both threshold perspective (δ_0) and visual-angle height (α_0) (i.e. angular separation) of the rectangle at threshold slant. Nomograms relating δ to α with variation in slant for the stimuli used in Experiment I are shown in Figure 1.

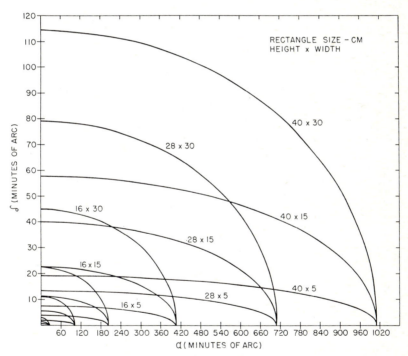

Figure 1.   Nomograms showing the relationship between retinal perspective (δ) and the visual-angle height (α) of slanted rectangles as slant increases from lower right to upper left, with stimulus dimensions as parameter.   Height and width for the first three sets of curves, from top to bottom and left to right are, respectively, 1×30, 1×15, 1×5, 4×30, 4×15, 4×5, 8×30, 8×15, 8×5 cm.   Viewing distance throughout is 135 cm.

3.2. *Slant Threshold*

The purposes of Experiment I were, first, to determine δ_0, and second, to determine how, if at all, δ_0 varies with α_0.   This was accomplished by obtaining slant thresholds for 18 different textureless rectangles, whose linear heights were 1, 4, 8, 16, 28 and 40 cm, and whose widths were 5, 15 and 30 cm.   All were viewed monocularly from a distance of 135 cm through a hole (artificial pupil) whose diameter was smaller than the diameter of the natural pupil so as to eliminate other cues, such as binocular parallax, motion parallax, accommodation and convergence, from the visual display.

Slant thresholds were obtained from 72 observers, 4 for each of the 18 rectangles, using conventional psychophysical techniques. The threshold for slant is defined as the smallest slant that is discriminable from the frontal-parallel (wall) plane position. From the slant thresholds, values of δ_0 and α_0 were computed for each observer and plotted in Figure 2. The best-fitting curve for each of the three stimulus widths is also plotted, according to the equations shown in the insert. All three of the functions are nearly linear, of positive slope, and of different levels. They show that, for constant physical (and visual-angle) width, threshold perspective increases as an approximately linear function of visual-angle height of the threshold stimulus. This finding is a direct analogue of the results obtained by Matsubayashi (*op. cit.*) and by Graham *et al.* (*op. cit.*) in their experiments on the effects of visual-angle separation on threshold retinal disparity.

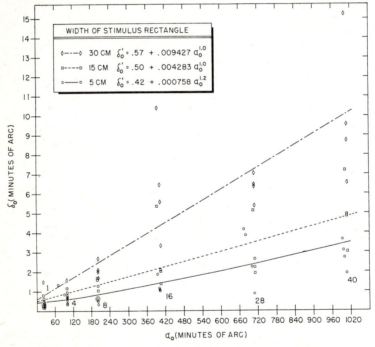

Figure 2.   Threshold retinal perspective (δ_0) as a function of threshold visual-angle height (α_0) (Experiment I). The heights of the stimulus rectangles (in cm) are shown just above the lower edge of the graph. The symbols corresponding to the different widths are shown in the insert.

3.3. *Discrimination of Shape: Experiment II*

So far, we have been concerned solely with the psychophysical scaling of visual distance and slant, and we have seen the validity of using threshold retinal perspective as a measure of discriminability of visual slant. Now I shall describe an experiment, the purpose of which was to test the notion that just-discriminable increases in visual perspective result in just-discriminable changes of visual shape in slanted rectangular targets.

In this experiment it was assumed that, when the visual-angle height of a slanted rectangle is held constant, the *perceived* height of the rectangle would increase as a linear function of retinal perspective. It was further assumed that just-discriminable changes in the dimensions of rectangles will be proportional to their visual-angle size—in other words Weber's Law holds for visual-angle.

The rationale of Experiment II was therefore as follows. If an observer is required to adjust the height of a rectangle to match its width, he will approximately match the vertical and horizontal visual-angle subtense of the image when the linear perspective is zero (i.e. when the rectangle is not slanted). As perspective increases with either forward or backward slant, the observer will *decrease* the visual-angle height of the image by an amount proportional to the amount of discriminable perspective (δ/δ_0). Furthermore, for any given increase in perspective measured in terms of Equation 1, there will be a just-discriminable decrease in visual-angle height—the decrease being proportional to the visual-angle width of the stimulus in conformity with Weber's Law. Therefore, for any slant (and hence any perspective), predicted height (α) should be

$$\alpha = \beta - \Delta\beta\left(\frac{\delta}{\delta_0}\right) - \frac{I}{\delta_0}, \qquad (2)$$

where α = visual-angle height to which the rectangle is adjusted by the subject, β = visual-angle width, $\Delta\beta$ = just-discriminable change in visual-angle height, I = judgmental error in the frontal plane (corresponding to the well-known horizontal-vertical illusion), and the other terms are as previously defined.

In the first part of Experiment II, slant thresholds were obtained from two female observers (JL and TN) for rectangles at each of a large number of slants, both forward and backward. These thresholds were then used to obtain thresholds for retinal perspective (δ_0) which in turn were used as predictive constants in Equation 2. In the second part of Experiment II, each subject made height–width matches of the same slanted rectangles by adjusting the height until the resulting stimulus appeared to be as tall as it was wide—i.e. square. Observations were, as before, through an artificial pupil from a distance of 135 cm.

The results are shown in Figure 3, in which the visual-angle height α is plotted as a function of threshold units of perspective (δ/δ_0). Negative values of perspective are for ' forward ' slants (top nearer the observer) and positive values for ' backward '. The straight lines passing through the data points were obtained by the method of least-squares, in each direction of slant separately.

The slopes of the fitted regression lines represent $\Delta\beta$ in Equation 2. It was then an easy matter to divide $\Delta\beta$ by β for each of the visual-angle widths to determine the Weber fractions for each width of stimulus rectangle and direction of slant. The Weber fractions all fell within the range 0·005 to 0·022, and there was little consistent variation with change of β, supporting the assumption that visual size of the rectangles was a linear function of retinal size. Finally, the mean Weber ratio was within 0·1 per cent of the value obtained by Veniar (1948) for the discrimination of deviation from squareness in frontal-plane shape judgments.

The alternative *a priori* possibilities to the results obtained in Experiment II are either that the visual-angle height α would have, in all cases, been equal to the visual-angle width β, in which case the data in Figure 3 would have fallen on horizontal straight lines, or that the observer would have always adjusted the physical height of the rectangle to equal the physical width.   If responses had followed this pattern they would have fallen on the bell-shaped curves shown in Figure 3, and would have accorded with the law of ' shape-constancy ' —i.e. the judged shape of the stimulus would have remained constant irrespective of the slant of the stimulus.   Clearly under the conditions of Experiment II the observer's responses fell far short of shape constancy.

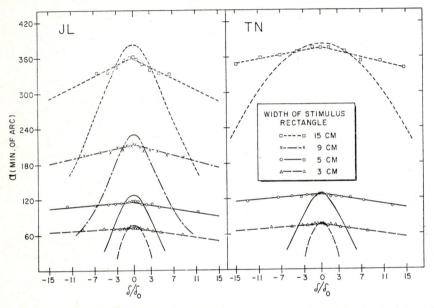

Figure 3.   Visual-angle height (α) of apparently square rectangles ranging in slant from 0 to ± 75 deg, as a function of effective retinal perspective (δ/δ_0) (Experiment II, Part 2).

Why is it, therefore, that under more normal conditions of binocular viewing, observations seem commonly to approximate to the shape-constancy pattern? There are no theories available to explain this tendency.   However, the psychophysical metric suggested in this paper, if extended to include visual cues to slant other than linear perspective, might well account for it.   If the observer had available to him the cues of retinal parallax, movement parallax, and perhaps some others, the functions of Figure 3 might more nearly conform to the bell-shaped curves predicted by shape constancy, although this is not necessarily so, for we do not know how such cues combine.   Do their effects summate?   Or are the effects of some cues contingent upon the effects of others? Are they mutually exclusive in some way?   One might find that, with such additional cues, the data points more nearly approximated the constancy curves than they do in Figure 3, but still fell on a best-fitting curve which had a shape different in some way from the constancy curve.

    The research described in this paper was supported by Grants MH–08856 and MH–10,691 from the National Institute of Mental Health, United States Public Health Service.

Une nouvelle métrique psychophysique est proposée pour évaluer les indices visuels intervenant dans la perception spatiale.   On argumente son applicabilité à la discrimination des distances fournie par la disparité binoculaire, la parallaxe du mouvement monoculaire et la perspective linéaire.   Quelques expériences sont citées dans lesquelles la validité de la métrique psychophysique proposée est éprouvée en relation avec le jugement visuel de la forme et de l'obliquité.

Ein neues psychophysische metrisches System wird zur Messung visueller Merkmale bei der räumlichen Wahrnehmung vorgeschlagen.   Seine Anwendung bei der Erkennung der Entfernung durch binokulare Unglciehheit, monokulare Bewegungs-Parallaxe und lineare Perspektive wird diskutiert.   Es werden Experimente beschrieben, in denen die Gültigkeit des vorgeschlagenen psychophysischen metrischen Systems in Realtion zur Beurteilung visueller Schrägheit und Form getestet wird.

References

BERRY, R. N., RIGGS, L. A., and DUNCAN, C. P., 1950, The relation of vernier and depth discrimination to field brightness. *Journal of Experimental Psychology*, **40**, 349–354.

BORING, E. G., 1942, *Sensation and Perception in the History of Experimental Psychology* (New York: APPLETON-CENTURY-CROFTS).

BORING, E. G., 1963, *The Physical Dimensions of Consciousness* (New York: DOVER).

CARR, H. A., 1935, *An Introduction to Space Perception* (New York: LONGMANS, GREEN).

FREEMAN, R. B., JR., 1966 a, Function of cues in the perceptual learning of visual slant: An experimental and theoretical analysis.   *Psychological Monographs* 80, No. 2 (Whole No. 610).

FREEMAN, R. B., JR., 1966 b, Optical texture versus retinal perspective: A reply to Flock. *Psychological Review*, **73**, 365–371.

FREEMAN, R. B. JR., 1969, A perspective metric for visual slant and shape.   *Psychologische Forschung* **32**, 296–323.

GILINSKY, A. S., 1951, Perceived size and distance in visual space.   *Psychological Review*, **58**, 460–482.

GRAHAM, C. H., 1965, Visual space perception.   In *Vision and Visual Perception* (Edited by C. H. GRAHAM) (New York: WILEY), pp. 504–547.

GRAHAM, C. H., BAKER, K. E., HECHT, M., and LLOYD, V. V., 1948, Factors influencing thresholds for monocular movement parallax.   *Journal of Experimental Psychology*, **38**, 205–223.

GRAHAM, C. H., RIGGS, L. A., MUELLER, C. G., and SOLOMON, R. L., 1949, Precision of stereoscopic settings as influenced by distance of target from a fiducial line.   *Journal of Psychology*, **27**, 203–207.

HELMHOLTZ, H. L. F. VON, 1962, *Treatise on Physiological Optics* (trans. J. P. C. SOUTHALL) (New York: DOVER), Vol. 111.

LEGRAND, Y., 1967, *Form and Space Vision* (Bloomington, Indiana: INDIANA UNIVERSITY PRESS).

MATSUBAYASHI, A., 1937, Forschung über die Tiefenwahrnehmung.   II.   *Acta. Soc. Ophthal. Jap.*, **41**, 2055–2074.

MUELLER, C. G., and LLOYD, V. V., 1948, Stereoscopic acuity for various levels of illumination. *Proceedings of the National Academy of Sciences*, **34**, 223–227.

OGLE, K. N., 1964, *Researches in Binocular Vision* (New York: HAFNER).

TITCHENER, E. B., 1911, *A Text-Book of Psychology* (New York: MACMILLAN).

VENIAR, F. A., 1948, Difference thresholds for shape distortion of geometrical squares.   *Journal of Psychology*, **26**, 461–476.

ZEGERS, R. T., 1948, Monocular movement parallax thresholds as functions of field size, filed position, and speed of stimulus movement.   *Journal of Psychology*, **26**, 477–498.

Visual After-Effects in the Third Dimension: the Importance of Margins

By M. Farnè

University of Bologna, Italy

Visual after-effects in the third dimension were studied under four different conditions. In each case subjects viewed a surface slanted from the frontal plane at 67 degrees. In the first condition this surface had a regular, horizontal texture and was seen through a square window that hid its edges. In the second condition the same surface was seen between margins which, of course, appeared to converge with distance due to perspective effects. In the third condition the texture was oriented vertically, and seen through the window. In the last condition the surface from the third condition was seen with margins as in the second condition. After having inspected this surface for 5 sec, subjects had to judge the distances of two vertical, parallel lines, shown for 250 msec. The results show that the line falling in the place that corresponded to the more distant part of the surface was seen as nearer than the other. This illusory displacement was stronger when the texture of the surface was vertical, and when it was displayed between margins. The third condition presents a clear example of visual after-effects in the third dimension that cannot be explained in terms of after-effects which occur in the frontal plane.

1. Introduction

It is now well known that looking steadily at an object or pattern can often distort the perception of an object seen immediately after, for example looking at a curved line may make a straight line seen subsequently look curved in the opposite direction. The pioneer work on these 'figural' or 'visual after-effects' by Köhler and Wallach (1944) has been continued by a large number of subsequent investigators. Visual after-effects in three-dimensional perception were demonstrated by Köhler and Emery (1947). All the conditions they used, however, could be reduced to those that generate after-effects on the frontal plane (Ancona 1950, Osgood and Heyer 1952, Farnè 1965 b). For example, in one of the conditions used by Köhler and Emery (*op. cit.*, pp. 176–184) subjects looked at a square (the 'inspection' or I-stimulus) which was then replaced by another square (the 'test' or T-stimulus (identical to the previous one. If this new stimulus was placed nearer to the subject than the first, it appeared even nearer than it was; the contrary happened if T was put farther away than I. Since I and T were objectively of the same size, the retinal image of the second was larger when it was placed nearer to the subject. This means that the contours of I fell entirely within those of T. This condition, if reproduced in the frontal plane with I smaller than T but at the same distance, produces a similar after-effect, as described by Köhler and Wallach (*op cit.*): T appears to be increased in size, which may also be interpreted as being decreased in distance. Köhler and Emery (*op cit.*) assert that after-effects in the third dimension are concentrated about contours.

More recently, Bergman and Gibson (1959) have suggested that it is possible to obtain after-effects in the third dimension not reducible to those in the frontal plane, and not depending on the perception of contours or edges, *if the surface has a visible texture.* They presented, as I, a coarsely textured burlap slanted at either 15, 30 or 45 degrees which subjects viewed through a window that concealed its edges.   The impression of depth, in this case, was given by the gradient of texture density (Gibson 1950), while the contour of the stimulus, given by the edge of the window, remained constant in the visual field despite changes in the slant of the surface.   After an inspection period of 4 min a slanted *T*-surface appeared noticeably less slanted, a less slanted *T*-surface appeared frontal, and a frontal *T*-surface appeared slanted in the opposite direction.   Bergman and Gibson found that the degree of slant of the *I*-surface did not affect the amount of after-effect.   Farnè and Gianninoni (1968), however, using a wider range of slants (0–67 degrees) obtained a significant increase of the effect with degree of slant.

Bergman and Gibson argue in their discussion, ' the stimulation in this experiment was an optical texture, not an optical contour or figure. . . . Important as contour and closed contour may be for visual perception, it is not the only, or necessarily the most fundamental, kind of stimulus in the array of light to an eye ' (p. 373).   The problem now arises: to what extent is the presence of the margin important for the perception of slant and, in our case, for obtaining after-effects?   In other words, is there any difference in the after-effect if the *I*-surface is presented with and without its margins?   And how large is this difference, if any?

The following experiment aimed at answering these questions.

2.   Experimental Method

The experiment was carried out in a dark room.   Figure 1 shows a sketch of the apparatus as seen from above.   The *I*-surface (*IS*) was a sheet of glass on which were applied stripes of black plastic overlay forming a pattern like that of Figure 2 (*a*).   It had an inclination of 67 degrees and transmitted the light coming from a panel placed at the back (P).   The two *T*-lines (*T*$_1$ and *T*$_2$) were luminous areas of 5×0.2 cm with a distance between them of 8.5 cm, each of them set on a track so that they could be moved towards or away from a partly reflecting mirror (M) set at 45 degrees.   The subject could observe these lines reflected in the mirror, where they appeared vertical as in Figure 2 (*b*).

The subject looked monocularly with his dominant eye through an 8 cm wide square window (W) from a distance of 25 cm.   His head was kept steady by a chinrest and headrest.

Four experimental conditions were used.

   (i) The *I*-surface contained seven stripes of the type shown in Figure 2 (*a*) but oriented horizontally, and seen through the square window, which hid its edges.

   (ii) The *I*-surface was the same but with two parallel black bands, one at the top and one at the bottom.   The surface was thus seen with horizontal margins which, owing to perspective effects, appeared to converge towards the right.   The resulting trapezoidal projection at the subject's eye subtended a visual angle of 18.33 degrees at the left and 10.31 degrees at the right.

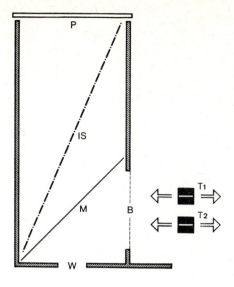

Figure 1. Experimental apparatus.

Figure 2. Experimental presentation.

(iii) The lines of the *I*-surface were oriented vertically and seen through the window. The surface contained 28 black stripes of the type shown in Figure 2 (*a*).

(iv) The same as the third condition but with the horizontal margins as in Condition (ii).

Forty experimentally naïve medical students acted as subjects—10 for each condition. Each subject was given two blocks of 20 presentations in which the *I*-surface was shown for 5 sec followed by the *T*-lines for 250 msec. One of the *T*-lines was always at a fixed distance of 10 cm from the border *B* in Figure 1, the other at a different distance which varied randomly. The subject was instructed to judge the distance of the variable line according to a scale which took the distance of the fixed line as ' 50 ', so that if the variable line looked twice as far it would be judged ' 100 ' (Stevens and Galanter 1957, Stevens 1958). Twenty presentations of the T-lines alone were given before the first block, between the first and second and after the second. With half the subjects in each group the line at fixed distance was on the left, and with half on the right.

3. Results and Discussion

The results are shown in Table 1. For most subjects, following presentation of the I-surface the right-hand T-line appeared nearer than it should have done. Sometimes when the lines were at the same distance, subjects had the immediate impression that the right-hand line was ' larger ' or ' longer ' than

Table 1.   Distance in mm between right-hand and left-hand lines required to make them appear to be equidistant from the viewer. Figures are for individual subjects: each is based on 40 readings

	No margins		Margins	
I-lines:	Horizontal	Vertical	Horizontal	Vertical
Individual subject means	24·1	38·9	35·6	38·0
	22·2	32·0	32·4	37·6
	22·1	27·3	25·0	35·9
	9·9	25·8	27·9	33·8
	5·9	19·1*	13·1	33·6
	5·8	19·0	9·6	32·5
	−3·6	16·3	7·3	30·2
	−8·3	−1·7	7·1	29·3
	−9·1	−2·6	1·6	28·9
	−22·1	−3·0	−19·6	19·0
Group mean	4·69	17·11	14·00	31·88
Group mean for readings when no I-lines shown before T-lines	−1·81	0·24	3·22	−2·10

An analysis of variance showed that the overall difference between readings with and without margins was significant ($p < 0.01$) as also was the overall difference between horizontal and vertical stripes on the I-surface ($p < 0.005$). The interaction between these variables was not significant ($p > 0.05$).

the other, followed by the impression that it was also nearer. One subject (marked * in Table 1) at times observed that the right-hand line seemed nearer than the other, but also smaller and thinner.

The vertical I-lines were more effective than the horizontal in generating an after-effect. Osgood and Heyer (*op. cit.*, p. 111) reported that in Köhler and Emery's (*op. cit.*) research also the depth effect was more striking with vertical lines than with horizontal.

The fact that the margins were not essential for obtaining an after-effect in the third dimension is in line with the results of several previous experiments (Bergman and Gibson *op. cit.*, Farnè 1965 b, Farnè and Gianninoni *op. cit.*). The effect was, however, very much stronger when margins were present. The significance of such margins has been demonstrated by many experimenters (Hochberg 1969). Slant generally tends to be underestimated when texture is the only cue (Clark *et al.* 1956, Gruber and Clark 1956, Flock 1964), whereas judgment is rather good when slanting, textureless rectangles are presented (Clark *et al.* 1955, Freeman 1966, 1968). Farnè (1969), using a surface presented under the same four conditions as those of the present experiment, obtained better evaluations of the slant with margins and with a vertical texture. It is difficult to interpret such experiments, however, because Gibson (*op. cit.*) did not specify the threshold for detecting a gradient of texture-density, so that we cannot tell whether the gradients involved in these studies were adequate and comparable to the perspective cues inherent in the outline of a slanted rectangle. This difficulty is apparent in the work of Flock (1965) who makes attempts to overcome it.

Three additional conclusions can be drawn from the results. In the first place, there is confirmation that we can obtain after-effects in the third dimension which cannot be reduced to those on the frontal plane. Our second condition (horizontal lines and margins) could remind us of the Ponzo illusion (see p. 16 of this Symposium) which produces very clear after-effects in two dimensions (Köhler and Wallach *op. cit.*, Figure 28, p. 288), but our third condition in which there were no margins and the texture had vertical lines, could produce an impression of depth only by means of the gradient within the surface. As far as the writer knows, this is the only condition under which an after-effect not reducible to two dimensions can be obtained.

A second conclusion is that after-effects in the third dimension can be obtained with very short exposure times, as has also been found for effects in the frontal plane (Farnè 1965 a). In the present experiment, an *I*-time of 5 sec and a *T*-time of 250 msec were used, and in pilot experiments displacement of the *T*-lines was also evident with *I*- and *T*-times of 100 msec each.

The third conclusion is that, for after-effects in the third dimension, the presence of a steady fixation point is not necessary (Bergman and Gibson *op. cit.*, Farnè 1965 b), but the subject can move his eye over the *I*-surface.

Two further observations made as a result of pilot studies seem worth noting. Firstly, during the inspection of the *I*-surface, the window (W) sometimes appeared to have trapezoidal contours, the right side corresponding to the farther part of the *I*-surface seeming longer than the left side. The phenomenon was more evident (*a*) when the window, instead of being a square, was a rectangle with the length longer than the height, and (*b*) when the texture had horizontal lines. In other words, there was a variation of the Ponzo illusion with the pattern producing the illusion included in the pattern which suffered the illusion instead of vice versa as in the normal Ponzo figure. Secondly, the illusion of seeing the right-hand line nearer than the left when they were objectively at the same distance was stronger when the two stimuli were presented successively than simultaneously.

L'effet consécutif visuel tridimensionnel a été étudié sous quatre conditions différentes. Dans chaque cas, les sujets observaient une surface faisant un angle de 67° avec le plan horizontal. Dans la première condition, la surface présentait une texture régulière horizontale et était vue à travers une fenêtre carrée qui masquait ses bords. Dans la seconde condition, la même surface était vue entre des marges qui, reproduisant l'effet de la perspective, paraissaient converger en fonction de la distance. Dans la troisième condition, la texture était verticale et vue à travers la fenêtre. Dans la dernière condition, on présentait la texture précédente, mais vue entre les marges, comme dans la seconde condition. Après avoir examiné les surfaces pendant 5 secondes, les sujets devaient estimer les distances de deux lignes verticales parallèles qui leur étaient présentées pendant 250 ms.   Les résultats montrent que la ligne correspondant à la région périphérique de la surface était jugée comme étant plus rapprochée que l'autre.   Cet affet était plus net encore pour la texture verticale de la surface vue entre les marges.   La troisième condition montre clairement qu'il n'est pas possible d'expliquer les effets consécutifs visuels tridimensionnels en se référant aux effets consécutifs qui intéressent le plan frontal.

Visuelle Nachwirkungen in der dritten Dimension wurden unter vier verschsiedenen Bedingungen studiert.   In jedem Fall sahen die Versuchpersonen eine Oberfläche, die—um eine vertikale Achse—um 67 Grad gegen die Frontalebene gedreht war.   Bei der ersten Bedingung hatte die Oberfläche regelmässige, horizontale Streifen und wurde durch ein quadratisches Fenster gesehen, das ihre Ränder verdeckte.   Bei der zweiten Bedingung wurde die gleiche Fläche zwischen Rändern gesehen, welche—natürliche—mit der Entfernung perspektivisch convergierten.   Bei der dritten Bedingung war die Streifung der Oberfläche vertikal und wurde wieder durch das Fenster gesehen.   Bei der letzten Bedingung wurde die Oberfläche der dritten Bedingung wie bei der zweiten Bedingung zwischen zwei Rändern gesehen.   Nach Betrachtung dieser Oberfläche für 5 sek. haben die Personen den Abstand zweier paralleler vertikaler Linien zu schätzen, die 250 msek. gezeigt werden.   Die Resultate zeigen, dass die Linie, welche auf die entferntere Hälfte der schrägen Oberfläche fällt, näher als die andere gesehen wird.   Die illusorische Versetzung war stärker, wenn die Streifen der Oberfläche vertikal lagen, und wenn sie zwischen Rändern gezeigt wurden.   Die dritte Bedingung gibt ein klares Beispiel visueller Nachwirkungen in der dritten Dimension, die nicht als Nachwirkungen erklärt werden können, die in der Frontalebene stattfinden.

References

ANCONA, L., Gli after-effects nella terza dimensione dello spazio e la teoria della ' saziazione cerebrale, *Contributi del Laboratorio di Psicologia*, **14**, 55–79.

BERGMAN, R., and GIBSON, J. J., 1959, The negative after-effect of the perception of a surface slanted in the third dimension. *American Journal of Psychology*, **72**, 364–374.

CLARK, W. C., SMITH, A. H., and RABE, A., 1955, Retinal gradient of outline as a stimulus for slant. *Canadian Journal of Psychology*, **9**, 247–253.

CLARK, W. C., SMITH, A. H., and RABE, A., 1956, The interaction of surface texture, outline gradient and ground in the perception of slant.   *Canadian Journal of Psychology*, **10**, 1–8.

FARNÈ, M., 1965 a, Figural after-effects with short exposure time.   *Psychol. Forsch.*, **28**, 519–534.

FARNÈ, M., 1965 b, Un nuovo caso di effetto postumo figurale nella terza dimensione.   *Boll. Soc. Ital. Biol. Sper.*, **41**, 1510–1513.

FARNÈ, M., 1969, Influenza dei margini sulla valutazione dell'inclinazione di una superficie. *Rivista di Psicologia*, **63**, 814–817.

FARNÈ, M., and GIANNINONI, T., 1968, Alcune ricerche sugli effetti postumi nella terza dimensione dello spazio visivo.   *Rivista di Psicologia*, **62**, 99–121.

FLOCK, H. R., 1964, Some conditions sufficient for accurate monocular perceptions of moving surface slant.   *Journal of Experimental Psychology*, **67**, 560–572.

FLOCK, H. R., 1965, Optical texture and linear perspective as stimuli for slant perception. *Psychological Review*, **72**, 505–514.

FREEMAN, R. B., 1966, Effect of size on visual slant.   *Journal of Experimental Psychology*, **71**, 96–103.

FREEMAN, R. B., 1969, A perspective metric for visual slant and shape.   *Psychologische Forschung*, **32**, 296–323.

GIBSON, J. J., 1950, *The Perception of the Visual World*.   (Boston: HOUGHTON MIFFLIN.)

GRUBER, H. E., and CLARK, W. C., 1956, Perception of slanted surfaces.   *Perceptual and Motor Skills*, **6**, 97–106.

HOCHBERG, J. E., 1969, Perception of objects: color and shape.   In *Experimental Psychology* by R. S. WOODWORTH (New York: HOLT, RINEHART & WINSTRON).

KÖHLER, W., and EMERY, D. A., 1947, Figural after-effects in the third dimension of visual space. *American Journal of Psychology*, **60**, 159–201.

KÖHLER, W., and WALLACH, H., 1944, Figural after-effects: an investigation of visual processes. *Proceedings of the American Philosophical Society*, **88**, 269–357.

OSGOOD, C. E., and HEYER, A. W., 1952, A new interpretation of figural after-effects.   *Psychological Review*, **59**, 98–118.

STEVENS, S. S., 1958, Problems and methods of psychophysics.   *Psychological Bulletin*, **55**, 177–196.

STEVENS, S. S., and GALANTER, E. H., 1957, Ratio scales and category scales for a dozen perceptual continua.   *Journal of Experimental Psychology*, **54**, 377–411.

The Influence of Identity of Objects on Whiteness Constancy

By M. Fatouros

University of Thessaloniki, Greece

and J. Glick

Yale University, New Haven, Connecticut, U.S.A.

An experiment is reported investigating whether judgment concerning the relative whiteness of objects is influenced by their degree of similarity, or as regards shape.

1. The Problem

It is well known that the whiteness of objects—that is their position on the continuum from white through grey to black—is recognized with remarkable accuracy over a wide range of illuminations, provided the objects are seen in a context of other objects or a background. It is a question of both theoretical interest and practical importance, how far this *whiteness constancy* depends on the identity of the objects seen in different illuminations, and how far it depends upon some more subtle abstraction of relationships between the reflectances of the objects concerned and of their backgrounds or other objects in the same field of illumination. Something of the latter nature must go on, but is it the whole answer to the question? Is it, perhaps, made easier if the objects concerned are identical? The purpose of the experiment reported here was to investigate whether judgment concerning the relative whiteness of objects is influenced by their degree of similarity, either type of figure (circle as opposed to triangle) or as regards shape (equilateral as opposed to right-angled triangle).

2. Apparatus, Subjects and Procedure

The apparatus was similar to one devised by Kozaki (1963). A box 45 in. long was divided lengthwise into two compartments, each 13 in. square. The subject sat in a dimly lit room in such a position that he could see into each compartment with one eye. The far ends of the compartments were covered with Colour Aid paper, grey No. 1. The left-hand compartment was illuminated by a 500 watt bulb through a neutral gelatine filter of density 1·0, and the right-hand by a similar bulb and filter of density 1·5. Otherwise the compartments were painted black. The ends could be hidden from, or revealed to, the subject by means of a shutter.

The objects to be judged consisted of circles or triangles of grey paper, each with a surface area of 2 sq. in. That on the left (the standard object) was always of No. 4 grey Colour Aid paper. That on the right (the comparison object) was, in different trials, Nos. 3A, 3, 4A, 4, 5A, 5 and 6A grey Colour Aid paper.

A pilot testing of 19 college students preceded the experiment in order to decide on the illumination of the two fields and the shape and brightness values of the stimuli. Three age groups were used for the experiment proper: 32 male undergraduate college students were tested within a period of one month. Thirty-two boys, 7 years old, and 32 boys, 11 years old, were tested within a period of two weeks.   The school population was drawn from a public school at East Haven, Connecticut, U.S.A.   The children were predominantly of Italian origin.

The instructions were as follows: ' Through the window in front of you, you are going to see circles and triangles (or triangles of different shapes). You will see them in pairs, and each time you will have to say whether the one on your right is lighter, darker or the same as the one on your left.'   Children were shown examples outside the apparatus beforehand, and were allowed to raise their left or right arm instead of making a verbal response.

Half the subjects in each age group were given a series of trials in which either two circles or one circle and one triangle were shown in random order— that is, conditions A and B in Table 1.   The side on which the circle appeared in condition A was also randomized, as was the order of the different greys of the comparison object.   There were thus $2 \times 2 \times 7$ combinations.   Subjects had 2 trials with each making a total of 56.   Arrangements for the other half of the subjects in each age group were similar except that they performed under conditions C and D in Table 1.

Table 1.   *Accuracy of matching grey patches of the same or different shapes shown in different illuminations.   The figures shown are mean coefficients of uncertainty.   In each age group, 16 subjects performed in conditions A and B, and 16 others in conditions C and D. Each subject made 56 judgments*

	Age group (years old)		
	7	11	18 to 20
Condition A: both objects circles or both equilateral triangles	6·38	5·31	4·25
Condition B: one object a circle, the other an equilateral triangle	6·25	6·66	5·00
Mean of A and B	6·31	5·98	4·63
Condition C: one object an equilateral and the other a right-angled triangle	6·25	5·13	5·19
Condition D: both objects equilateral or right-angled triangles	6·59	5·31	4·56
Mean of C and D	6·42	5·21	4·88
Mean of B and C, i.e. conditions in which objects were different	6·25	5·90	5·10
Mean of A and D, i.e. conditions in which objects were identical	6·49	5·31	4·41

3.   Results

The results shown in Table 1 are expressed in terms of mean intervals of uncertainty, measured in steps on the 7-point scale of grey used for the comparison objects.   The interval of uncertainty is the distance in steps between the point at which 50 per cent of the subject's judgments were that the comparison object was lighter than the standard, and the point at which 50 per cent of his judgments were that it was darker.   In other words it is twice the conventional measure of the difference limen.

Comparison of the last two rows of Table 1 shows that judgments by the two older groups were more precise under conditions in which the objects were identical (A and D) than when they were different (B and C) ($F = 11·06$, $p < 0·01$).   There seems to be no clear-cut difference between condition B in which circles and triangles were compared, and condition C in which different shapes of triangles were compared. Therefore, while comparisons seem to be better between identical objects, the types of difference between non-identical objects used in this experiment do not seem to have been important.

These differences do not show with the youngest age group. Their judgments were in any case very poor, possibly because, as several previous studies have shown, perceptual constancy has not fully developed at this age (cf. Burzlaff 1931; Bruner *et al.* 1966).

This research was carried out in 1966 at the Yale University Department of Developmental Psychology and was supported by Grant No. MH 11541. J. Glick is now at The Institute of Child Development, University of Minnesota, Minneapolis, Minn. 55755.

L'expérience relatée dans cet article avait pour but de déterminer, si le jugement concernant la leucie relative des objets était influencée par leur degré de similarité ou par leur forme.

Es wird ein Experiment beschrieben, das untersuchte, ob die Beurteilung der Weiße von Objekten durch den Grad der Ähnlichkeit ihrer Form beeinflusst wird. Identische Objekte wurden etwas sicherer beurteilt.

References

BRUNER, J. S., OLVER, ROSE, and GREENFIELD, PATRICIA M., 1966, *Studies in Cognitive Growth* (New York: WILEY).

BURZLAFF, W., 1931, Methodologische Beitrage zum Problem der Farbenkoustanz. *Z. Psychol.*, **119**, 177–235.

KOZAKI, AIKO, 1963, A further study in the relationship between brightness constancy and contrast. *Japanese Psychological Research*, **5**, 129–136.

Perception of Facial Expressions in Three Different Cultures

By D. M. Cüceloglu*

University of Illinois, U.S.A.

Sixty abstract facial expressions generated by the use of four eyebrow types, three eye types and five mouth types were rated on 40 emotion-name scales. These scales were constructed for each of three national groups, American, Japanese and Turkish, within their respective languages. By factor analysis three cross-cultural bi-polar dimensions which accounted for 72·4 per cent of the total variance were found and labelled Pleasantness, Irritation, and Non-Receptivity. Analysis of the components of the faces representing the two poles of each dimension revealed considerable similarity between the three language groups, but also some differences.

1. Introduction

One can distinguish three components which have usually been explicitly or implicitly involved in the study of facial expressions. These are the stimulus situation (S) eliciting a certain emotional experience, the emotional experience (E) resulting from the stimulus situation, and the facial expression (F) resulting from the emotional experience. Most studies of the interpretation of facial expressions have been mainly concerned with the relationship of this third component to the first and second, and the results of such studies have led some students in the field to question whether it is really possible to interpret facial expressions when they are isolated from the stimulus situation. One of the proponents of this view (Turhan 1966) puts it thus: ' When the subject is asked to interpret a facial expression he, in fact, is asked to do the impossible; as we all know from mathematics when there are three unknowns of an equation, say S, E and F, we need to know at least two of the unknowns to be able to find out the third one. Therefore, the argument follows, the interpretations of facial expressions, when presented without the context, are bound to be inconsistent and unreliable.'

We feel that this view overlooks the nature of the relations between S, E and F. Let us assume that S is mapped into E by a mapping function ϕ_1, and E is mapped into F by a second mapping function ϕ_2. If the two mapping functions and one of the components are known, then we can find the other two components. Investigation of these mapping functions at the present state of psychology seems to be impossible, since we do not have any direct way of observing E. However, when we look at the problem in terms of a communication model, we need to consider a third mapping function ϕ_3, between F and the interpretation of it by the observer, and the investigation of this function is feasible. The purpose of this study was to investigate the nature of ϕ_3, the ' facial code ', in three cultures. In other words we were interested in comparing the perception of facial expressions and the coding procedures underlying it in three different countries.

* Presently at Hocettepe University, Ankara, Turkey.

2. Method and Material

Sixty facial expressions were generated by combining four eyebrow types, three eye types and five mouth types as shown in Figure 1. These schematic faces were photographed on 4 × 3 in. cards and were randomized. Sixty male college students, 20 each in the United States, Japan and Turkey, were asked to name the emotion represented by each of the facial expressions. The consistency with which emotions were attributed to particular faces was analysed by means of a conditional entropy measure, and the 40 most consistently used names for each language were selected for the next stage of the study.

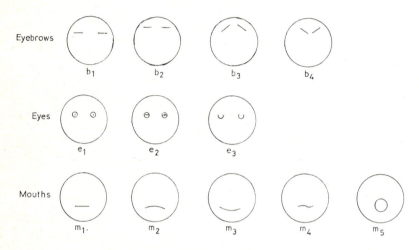

Figure 1.   Eyebrow, eye, and mouth types used to generate a matrix of facial expressions.

In the next stage, subjects rated each of the 60 faces in terms of each of the 40 emotion-names, marking a scale to indicate whether the expression on the face was *very* similar, *quite* similar or *a little* similar to that of the emotion concerned, or on the other hand *a little* different, *quite* different or *very* different from it. Judgments were scored $+3$, $+2$, $+1$, -1, -2 and -3 respectively. If there was more than one mark on a scale, or if it was not marked at all, a score of 0 was given.

The mean score for the subjects of each of the three language groups was worked out for each of the scales—i.e. $60 \times 40 \times 3$ mean scores in all. Correlations across the 60 faces were then worked out between the scores for each emotion-name in each language and every other emotion-name in all three languages, to make a matrix of 120×120 coefficients. This matrix was then subjected to a principal components factor-analysis. The translations of emotion labels may not have quite the same connotation in other languages, yet if the factors are represented by emotion-names from each language with roughly equal loadings they must be representing the same psychological entities. If so, the dimensions extracted by the factor-analysis can be claimed to be cross-cultural factors and the faces to have roughly the same affective meaning in different cultures. To the extent that this is not true, correlations are lower and the possibility of obtaining cross-cultural factors reduced.

3. Results

The analysis yielded six factors which together accounted for 81·9 per cent of the total variance, but only the first three seemed to be primary and truly cross-cultural in character. These accounted for 32·3, 29·8 and 10·3 per cent, respectively of the total variance. The main loadings on these three factors are indicated in Table 1. From these loadings Factor I seemed clearly identifiable as one of *Pleasantness* and Factor II as concerned with *Irritation*. Factor III seemed to group at its negative pole those emotional states which are ' open ' to the outside world, to stimulation, and thus receptive, and at its positive pole those emotional states which are ' closed ' to the outside world and thus non-receptive. If this is true a name such as *Non-Receptivity* would be proper for this dimension.

Table 1. Emotion-names selected as representative of three main factors describing facial postures generated from the components in Figure 1

PLEASANTNESS	Factors				Factors		
Positive Pole	I	II	III	*Negative Pole*	I	II	III
American				American			
happiness	0·92	−0·15	−0·13	depression	−0·91	−0·09	−0·12
amusement	0·85	−0·01	−0·15	disappointment	−0·90	0·14	−0·16
pride	0·81	−0·01	0·06	dejection	−0·89	−0·01	−0·06
Japanese				Japanese			
happy feeling	0·86	−0·25	0 15	disinterest	−0·82	−0·29	0·01
happiness	0·84	−0·36	0·17	being sorry	−0·79	0·04	−0·03
contentment	0·78	−0·40	0·25	anxiety	−0·78	−0·19	−0·38
Turkish				Turkish			
joy	0·86	−0·14	−0·25	bitterness	−0·88	−0·08	0·13
laughing	0·78	−0·11	−0·30	annoyance	−0·88	−0·12	0·15
contentment	0·60	−0·36	−0·12	worry	−0·87	−0·27	0·19
IRRITATION							
Positive Pole				*Negative Pole*			
American				American			
scolding	−0·38	0·83	0·27	sleepiness	−0·29	−0·80	0·37
anger	−0·36	0·82	0·35	drowsiness	−0·35	−0·77	0·33
growling	−0·37	0·79	0·34	unconcern	−0·06	−0·75	0·42
Japanese				Japanese			
short-temper	−0·23	0·88	0·28	inertness	−0·26	−0·83	−0·24
anger	−0·24	0·88	0·30	irksome	−0·37	−0·78	0·02
I will never be defeated	−0·11	0·88	0·32	sleepiness	−0·22	−0·77	0·11
Turkish				Turkish			
fury	−0·29	0·88	−0·01	innocence	−0·07	−0·90	0·11
anger	−0·35	0·83	0·07	shyness	−0·06	−0·83	0·22
irritated	−0·34	0·82	0·01	sleepy	−0·81	−0·32	0·27
NON-RECEPTIVITY							
Positive Pole				*Negative Pole*			
American				American			
asleep	−0·14	−0·71	0·53	bewilderment	−0·48	−0·02	−0·73
indifference	−0·39	−0·36	0·41	questioning	−0·39	0·24	−0·62
unemotional	0·13	−0·65	0·30	surprise	0·59	0·13	−0·63
Japanese				Japanese			
thought	−0·10	−0·01	0·57	help!	−0·52	−0·24	−0·65
thinking	−0·12	0·00	0·52	surprise	0·05	0·51	−0·49
perseverance	−0·48	−0·51	0·42	I am sorry	−0·51	−0·26	−0·40
Turkish				Turkish			
sleepiness	−0·24	−0·69	0·53	surprise	0·04	0·32	−0·82
unconcern	0·06	−0·23	0·47	bewilderment	−0·04	0·17	−0·81
offended	−0·66	−0·13	0·47	curiosity	0·20	0·19	−0·66

D. M. Cüceloglu

The emotion-names in Table 1 provide a set for each language which has maximum comparability with those of other language groups. They were chosen according to two criteria: (*a*) their loadings on the factor they represent should be as high as possible and (*b*) they should be *pure* as possible in the sense that their loadings on other factors should be low. It can be seen that in all three languages, the emotion-names representing the Pleasantness and Irritation dimensions achieve this aim well in that all were highly loaded and reasonably pure. On the third dimension they were relatively low in their loadings and were not pure in several cases—for example, *asleep*, *unemotional* and *surprise* in the American group, *perseverance* and *help* in the Japanese, and *sleepiness* and *offended* in the Turkish. They were, however, the most highly loaded and the purest available.

The mean score of each face on the scales for each of these sets of three emotion-names was then worked out. The four highest positively and negatively rated faces for the three factors are shown in Figures 2, 3 and 4 respectively.

The positive poles of the dimensions, i.e. Pleasantness, Irritation and Non-Receptivity, are defined by very nearly the same faces in all language groups, but this is not true for the negative poles, i.e. Unpleasantness, Non-Irritation and Receptivity.

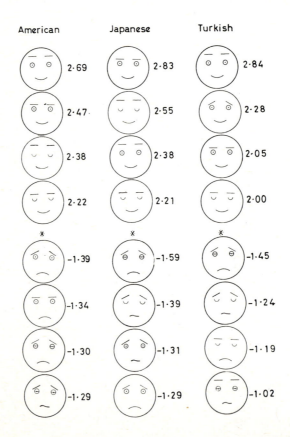

Figure 2.   The four faces rated most positively and the four rated most negatively for Pleasantness by each language group.   Mean scores are given beside the faces.

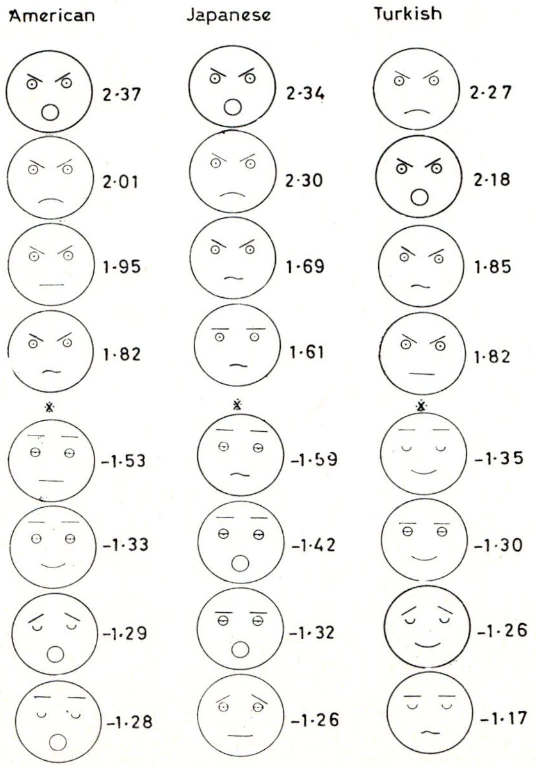

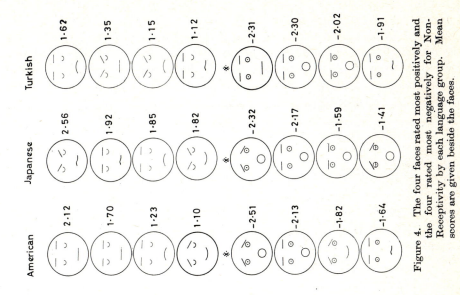

Figure 4. The four faces rated most positively and the four rated most negatively for Non-Receptivity by each language group. Mean scores are given beside the faces.

Figure 3. The four faces rated most positively and the four rated most negatively for Irritation by each language group. Mean scores are given beside the faces.

D. M. Cüceloglu

3.1. *Analysis of Facial Components Distinguishing Factor-Poles*

In Table 2 frequency distributions of facial features are given for the faces shown in Figures 2, 3 and 4. To obtain distinctive features which define a facial posture signifying a given emotional state two simultaneous criteria were employed: (*a*) the frequency of occurrence of the feature was more than half (i.e. 3 or 4); and at the same time (*b*) the frequency of the occurrence of the feature was less than half on the opposite pole of the dimension. Those features which conform to these criteria are underlined in the table, and features which indicate apparent cross-cultural *differences* are marked with an asterisk.

Table 2. Frequency distribution of facial features for the facial postures in Figures 2, 3 and 4

	Eyebrows								Eyes						Mouths									
	b_1		b_2		b_3		b_4		e_1		e_2		e_3		m_1		m_2		m_3		m_4		m_5	
Pole of factor	+	−	+	−	+	−	+	−	+	−	+	−	+	−	+	−	+	−	+	−	+	−	+	−
Pleasantness																								
American	2	1	2	0	0	3	0	0	2	2	0	2	2	0	0	0	0	3	4	0	0	1	0	0
Japanese	2	0	2	0	0	4	0	0	2	2	0	1	2	1	0	0	0	2	4	0	0	2	0	0
Turkish	2	1	1	1	1	2	0	0	3	0*	0	2	1	2	0	0	0	2	4	0	0	2	0	0
Irritation																								
American	0	0	0	3*	0	1	4	0	4	0	0	2	0	2	1	1	1	0	0	1	1	0	1	2
Japanese	1	1	0	2	0	1	3	0	4	0	0	4*	0	0	0	1	1	0	0	0	2	1	1	2
Turkish	0	2	0	1	0	1	4	0	4	0	0	1	0	3*	1	0	1	0	0	3*	1	1	1	0
Non-Receptivity																								
American	1	0	2	2	1	2	0	0	0	4	0	0	4	0	2	1	1	0	1	0	0	1	0	2
Japanese	1	1	1	1	0	2	2	0	0	3	0	1	4	0	0	0	1	0	1	0	2	0	0	4*
Turkish	0	1	2	3	0	0	2	0	0	4	0	0	4	0	1	1	2	0	0	0	1	1	0	2

The positive pole of the Pleasantness dimension is defined by the presence of m_3 (upturned) in all three groups, and for the American and Japanese groups by the absence of b_3 (downturned). In the Turkish group it is also defined by the presence of e_1 (open), but eyebrow types are not distinctive for the Americans and Japanese. The negative pole of the same dimension is defined by the absence of m_3 (upturned) in all three groups. Feature b_3 (downturned) is also definitive for the American and Japanese groups, but eyebrow types are not distinctive for the Turkish group.

In the definition of Irritated emotional states the three groups agree on the presence of b_4 (upturned) and e_1 (open). Mouth types are not significant for the Americans and Japanese, but are for the Turkish. The negative pole is defined by the absence of those features which are employed in the definition of the positive pole, i.e. b_4 (upturned) and e_1 (open), and for the Turkish group the presence of m_3 (downturned).

Non-Receptive emotional states are defined by the presence of the feature e_3 (closed) in the three communities, and for the Japanese by the absence of m_5 (open). Receptive states are signified by e_1 (open) in the three cultures, and also by m_5 for the Japanese.

4. Discussion

The first factor, Pleasantness, in the present study is in full agreement with the findings of Schlosberg (1941, 1952, 1954), Engen and Levy (1956), Abelson and Sermat (1962), Frijda and Philipszòon (1963), Harrison (1964) and Osgood (1966 a). However, the second dimension which we have termed Irritation seems to have been referred to under various names: Schlosberg called his second dimension Attention–Rejection, Osgood, Activation, while Harrison proposed two unipolar dimensions, Anger and Boredom, which seem to express the two poles of Irritation dimension. The third dimension, which we called Non-Receptivity, has been named Sleep–Tension by Schlosberg (1954), Intensity–Control by Frijda and Philipszoon, and Control by Osgood.

The dimensions found in this study are also comparable with those obtained through cross-cultural research carried out by the Center for Comparative Psycholinguistics at the University of Illinois, in some twenty countries on the generality of affective meaning systems. It was found that three primary factors identified as the Evaluative, Potency and Activity dimensions are shared by all the language groups under investigation. Our Pleasantness dimension seems to correspond to Evaluation, where pleasant expressions connote ' good ', and unpleasant expression ' bad ', affective tones, although it would be going too far to say that there is one-to-one correspondence between the two dimensions, or to claim that every unpleasant emotion is inherently ' bad '—for example, *worry* can be very ' good ' under certain conditions. The point is that there seems to be a parallelism between the way people perceive words and the way they perceive facial expressions. The Irritation dimension corresponds fairly well to the Potency dimension: angry, furious expressions indicate Potent, and quiet, non-irritated, smooth expressions indicate Non-Potent affects. Receptive expressions seem to resemble Active affects, and non-Receptive ones Passive.

The three dimensions found in our study accounted for a much higher amount of the total variance than was the case for similar dimensions found in other studies which used photographs of live human faces—for instance, Osgood's (*op. cit.*) study in which three dimensions accounted for only 46 per cent of the total variance. The use of live facial postures presumably introduces several extraneous factors such as the capacity of the actor, race of the person, his physiognomic structure, and the status and intelligence read into the face by the observer, all of which would tend to reduce the variance accounted for by factors concerned with emotions.

It may, of course, be objected that in any real emotion facial expression changes and evolves continuously over a period of time, whereas we, and many others, have used only static facial postures. It seems fair to assume, however, that in the developing series of postures in a real emotion there is *a modal posture* which, when taken by itself, best represents the emotion concerned. If so, when a study of facial expression employs static postures, it should not be assumed that *any* facial posture in the developing series of a particular emotion can adequately represent it; rather it seems likely that the modal posture should be employed. Conversely, it can perhaps be assumed that the static posture identified as expressing the emotion is the modal posture.

Whether this is so or not, the results of the present study indicate clearly that some static facial features are regarded as distinctive in the expression of a given emotion and some are not. Some of these distinctive features are shared across cultures reflecting what seem to be universals in facial communication, others seem to be peculiar to particular racial or cultural groups. In other words there seems to be a facial code employed in the communication of affective meaning which is to a great extent, although not wholly, common to different cultures.

Soixante expressions faciales schématisées, réalisées au moyen de quatre type de sourcils, trois types d'yeux et cinq types de bouches, ont été classées selon des échelles spécifiant 40 modes d'expressions émotionnelles. Ces échelles ont été construites pour trois groupes nationaux différents, Américains, Japonais et Turcs, en respectant leurs particularités linguistiques. L'analyse factorielle a permis de mettre en évidence trois dimensions interculturelles bipolaires absorbant 72,4 p. 100 de la variance totale et pouvant être interprétées comme " agrément ", " irritation " et " non-réceptivité ". L'analyse de la composition des schémas d'expression correspondant aux deux pôles de chaque dimension fait apparaître une grande similitude, mais également quelques différences entre les trois groupes linguistiques.

Sechzig abstrakte Gesichtsausdrücke wurden durch Kombination von vier Augenbrauentypen, drei Augentypen und fünf Mundtypen erzeugt und nach einer Skala von vierzig Bezeichnungen für Gefühlszustände bewertet. Diese Skala wurde für jede der drei nationalen Gruppen, die Amerikanische, Japanische und Türkische zusammengestellt. Durch Faktorenanalyse wurden drei interkulturelle bipolare Dimensionen gefunden, die für 72·4% der gesamten Varianz massgebend waren. Sie wurden " Wohlgefühl ", " Verdrießlichkeit " und " Unzugänglichkeit " benannt. Die Analyse der Gesichtskomponenten, welche beide Pole jeder Dimension erfasste, ergab eine beträchtliche Ähnlichkeit zwischen den drei Sprachgruppen, aber auch einige Unterschiede.

References

ABELSON, R. P., and SERMAT, V., 1962, Multidimensional scaling of facial expressions. *Journal of Experimental Psychology*, **63**, 546–554.

ENGEN, T., and LEVY, N., 1956, Constant-sum judgments of facial expression. *Journal of Experimental Psychology*, **51**, 6, 396.

FRIJDA, N. H., and PHILIPSZOON, E., 1963, Dimensions of recognition of expression. *Journal of Abnormal and Social Psychology*, **66**, 45–51.

HARRISON, R., 1964, Pictic analysis: Toward a vocabulary and syntax for the pictorial code; with research on facial communication. *Doctoral Dissertation, Michigan State University, Department of Communication.*

OSGOOD, C. E., 1962, Studies on the generality of affective meaning systems. *American Psychologist*, **17**, 10–28.

OSGOOD, C. E., 1966, Dimensionality of the semantic space for communication via facial expressions. *Scandinavian Journal of Psychology*, **7**, 1–30.

OSGOOD, C. E., SUCI, G. J., and TANNENBAUM, P. H., 1957, *The Measurement of Meaning* (Urbana: UNIVERSITY OF ILLINOIS PRESS).

OSGOOD, C. E., ARCHER, W. K., and MIRON, M. S., 1963, The cross-cultural generality of meaning systems. *Center for Comparative Psycholinguistics, Institute of Communications Research, University of Illinois.*

SCHLOSBERG, H., 1941, A scale for the judgment of facial expressions. *Journal of Experimental Psychology*, **29**, 497–510.

SCHLOSBERG, H., 1952, The description of facial expressions in terms of two dimensions. *Journal of Experimental Psychology*, **44**, 229–237.

SCHLOSBERG, H., 1954, Three dimensions of emotion. *Psychological Review*, **61**, 81–88.

TURHAN, M., 1966, Reconsiderations of theories and experiments on the interpretation of facial expressions. *Istanbul Studies in Experimental Psychology*, **5**, 12–37.

Some Aspects of the Selective Process in the Functional Visual Field

By A. F. SANDERS

Institute for Perception RVO–TNO, Soesterberg, Netherlands

A review is given of a group of experiments on performance as a function of display angle, aiming at a description of the perceptual strategies used with signals at various angular separations.

The first experiments were carried out using a simple four-choice discrimination task. The results show a non-linear decrease of performance as a function of display angle, which proved to be related to the necessity of making eye and head movements when shifting from one signal source to the other. It is suggested that the non-linearity is due to changes of strategy and a preliminary theory about selective processes is formulated and tested in a number of tasks.

1. Introduction

It is obvious that, if many possible sources of signals have to be inspected, larger eye movements are needed when wider display angles are involved, and that once a given angle is exceeded, eye movements must be complemented by head–eye movements. At the same time, even eye movements may not be necessary when the display angle is small and the task is simple. Much less can be said about the effects of display angle on *performance*, apart from a gradual increase of time required for the eye to move, when larger shifts are needed (White *et al.* 1962). There are, however, suggestions that changes occur in the strategy for handling information, which are connected with the degree of eye and head activity. Corbin *et al.* (1958), for example, found in some visual detection experiments that performance was better with peripheral viewing than when eye movements were made, and he concluded that, in some circumstances, ' the best search is no search at all '. In reaction time studies by the same authors, a large increase of variance appeared at angles between 40° and 80°, suggesting a change of strategy, which might well be related to the introduction of head movements.

These suggestions require systematic investigation of selective activity as a function of display angle, aiming at a description of the perceptual strategies involved. It seems likely that no simple relations will appear which are applicable to all tasks. The investigation seems basic, however, for the theory both of visual search and of perceptual coding. The present paper reviews the results of a project so far unpublished (Sanders 1964), and some important additions from subsequent research (Sanders 1967 a, b).

2. Performance as a Function of Display Angle in a Four-Choice Task

2.1. *An Introductory Experiment*

Two signals were simultaneously presented on a screen in a semi-dark room at equal distances from the subject's meridian and slightly above eye level. The visual field was otherwise empty. A signal consisted of a column of either four or five dots in one set of conditions, and either two or three in another set. Only one response was given based on the particular signal combination (e.g. 4–4, 4–5, 5–4, 5–5), each combination corresponding to one of four reaction keys. A new pair of signals arrived automatically 0·5 sec after a response, so that the task was serial and self-paced. The total number of responses made during a five-minute working period served as a score of performance. The main variables were (1) complexity of the signals, i.e. 4, 5 or 2, 3 dots, and the visual angle between the two columns of dots, i.e. 19°, 34°, 52°, 72°, 81° or 94°. The experiment used an analysis of covariance design. The corrected mean performance scores, shown in Figure 1, indicated *a non-linear decline of performance as a function of display angle*. There appear to be two significant drops, (1) at an angle between 20° and 40° depending on discriminability, and (2) at 80°–90°. It is obviously plausible to connect these two drops with the onset of eye and head movements respectively. Several experiments were carried out to test this suggestion.

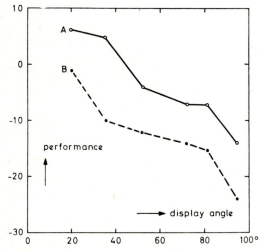

Figure 1.   Performance (corrected scores) as a function of display angle and discriminability
(A: 2, 3 dots; B: 4, 5 dots).

2.2. *Instructed Peripheral Viewing and Eye Movements*

In one of these tests, two well trained subjects were instructed to make observations under two conditions. In one they had to keep the position of the left signal (S_{L}) fixated and to observe the right signal (S_{R}) peripherally. In the other, they were instructed to make eye movements, even when they felt it to be unnecessary. Head movements were always prohibited. Medians of blocks of 20 reactions are shown in Figure 2. The main conclusion concerns the strict coincidence between the areas where the drops were found and those where peripheral viewing and eye movements are no longer sufficient to obtain optimal performance—i.e. at about 30° and 85° respectively.

2.3. *Direct Measurement of Eye and Head Movements*

The results of 2.2 encouraged tests in which eye and head movements were recorded during performance. The data of Figure 3 show the average results of two groups of subjects, who were tested with three different visual angles in a Latin square order. Each test consisted of three minutes' continuous serial performance and the visual angles were chosen in the area, where Drop 2 is expected.   In order to measure head movements the subject's head was connected to a string, which operated a variable potentiometer.   Each move-ment of the head altered the electrical resistance and these changes were recorded to an accuracy of 0·5° on a graphical writer.

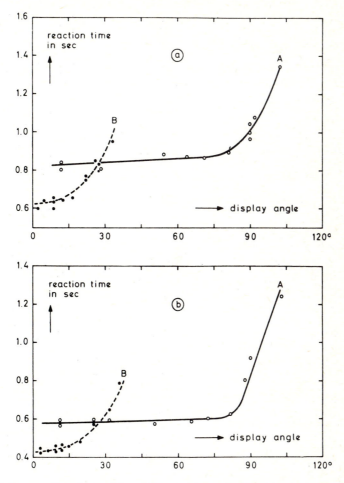

Figure 2.   Median reaction times with peripheral vision only (B) and with eye movements (A) as a function of display angle: *a* and *b* are the results of two different observers.

The data are clear in that Drop 2 appears once more in the expected area, and is accompanied by an increase of head activity.   Head movements were, however, also made at display angles between 60° and 80°, so that Drop 2 is not related to the mere *occurrence* of head movements: taking the results of 2.2 and 2.3 together it may rather be related to the *necessity* of making head movements.   Evidence regarding this possibility can be obtained only if the interplay between shifts of eye and head is studied.   Recordings of eye move-ments were therefore made, using the technique of electro-oculography (e.g. Shackel 1958).   Records of both eye and head movements were made for various display angles on different tracks of the same multichannel graphical writer.   An example is given in Figure 4.

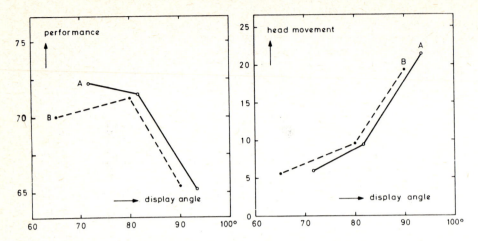

Figure 3.   Head movements (degrees) and performance (numbers of responses) as a function of display angle.   A and B indicate different groups of subjects.

It can be seen that eye and head start moving almost simultaneously.   The eye arrives at the right-hand signal (S_R) first, while the slower turning of the head still continues.   When the eye arrives at S_R the head begins to decelerate, while the eye keeps S_R fixated and thus has to make a compensatory movement. It is striking that secondary movements of the eye are almost absent when no head movements are made—S_R is found in one saccadic jump.   These phenomena were very consistent both within and between subjects.

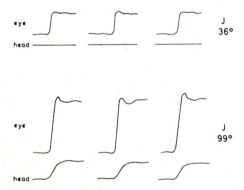

Figure 4.   Some examples of records of eye movements and of eye and head movements.

The relation between the amplitude of the movements and the size of the display angle is shown in Figure 5.   The eye movement covers the whole display angle up to about 80°, after which head activity also occurs.   Below 80°, the slight head movements which occurred seemed to match small secondary eye movements, perhaps made to prevent extreme positions of the eye. This supports the earlier suggestion that Drop 2 is related to *necessary* head movements and not to head movements *per se*.   The same seems to be true for Drop 1: when subjects are free to make eye movements, the eye is moved even when it is not necessary to do so to secure optimal performance.

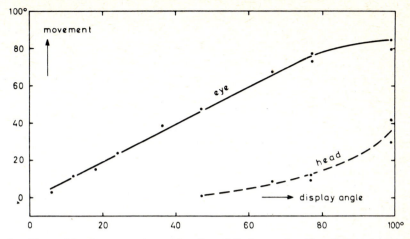

Figure 5. Eye and head movements as a function of display angle. Results from two groups of 6 subjects.

The data of Figures 4 and 5 are derived from a new experiment in which blocks of 20 separate trials were given at each display angle. The order of testing was again in a Latin square arrangement. Simultaneous recording of eye and head movements allowed a subdivision of reaction time into three parts: (1) inspection time of S_L (T_L), (2) movement time of the eye until fixation of S_R (m) and (3) inspection of S_R followed by a choice reaction (T_R). The average data for two groups of subjects and a summary of the statistical analyses are given in Table 1. The total times show, for each group, that the largest increases occur around 30° and between 77° and 90°, and thus confirm the earlier findings.

Table 1. Inspection- movement- and decision time as a function of display angle

	Display angle	Total time	T_L	m	T_R	$T_L + T_R$
Group 1	12°	0·86	0·44	0·04	0·38	0·82
	24°	0·92	0·42	0·06	0·44	0·86
	47°	1·05	0·43	0·11	0·51	0·94
	77°	1·15	0·43	0·18	0·54	0·97
	99°	1·29	0·47	0·22	0·60	1·07
Group 2	6°	0·70	0·37	0·01	0·32	0·69
	18°	0·76	0·37	0·05	0·34	0·71
	36°	0·85	0·37	0·09	0·39	0·76
	66°	0·95	0·36	0·17	0·42	0·78
	77°	0·99	0·36	0·20	0·43	0·79
	99°	1·14	0·41	0·24	0·49	0·90

Summary of the significant differences between display angles

Group 1

T_L: $F = 1·43$ $p < 70·05$

T_R: $F = 10·87$ $p < 0·001$ $M_1 - M_2 = 0·06$

$T_L + T_R$: $F = 32·82$ $p < 0·001$ $M_1 - M_2 = 0·08$

Group 2

T_L: $F = 1·20$ $p > 0·05$

T_R: $F = 18·95$ $p < 0·001$ $M_1 - M_2 = 0·05$

$T_L + T_R$: $F = 34·79$ $p < 0·001$ $M_1 - M_2 = 0·06$

These large increases, corresponding to the two drops of performance in previous experiments, do not occur in m, which shows a linear relation with visual angle, irrespective of the use of head movements. The drops appear largely in T_R, although T_L may play some part in Drop 2. The results thus make it clear that the drops are not due to the start of eye and head activity introducing an extra movement time to shift from S_L to S_R. The drops seem rather to result from changes of strategy, and more specifically, they seem related to the sequence of processing S_L and S_R. The fact that the drops are largely reflected in T_R suggests that, as the process of viewing becomes more complex, discrimination of S_R and final decision take more time.

Summarizing the results so far the following conclusions can be drawn.

1. The relation between performance and display angle in the present visual task cannot be described by a linear function. There appear to be two drops in performance at visual angles of about 20°–30° and 80°–90° respectively, the exact angles depending to some extent on the complexity of the signals.

2. The visual angles at which the drops are found coincide with (1) the marginal angle where the task can still be performed efficiently using peripheral vision without eye movements, and (2) the marginal angle where optimal performance is obtained using both peripheral viewing and eye movements but without invoking head movements.

3. Thus three levels of the functional visual field can be distinguished: the *stationary field*, where peripheral viewing is sufficient; the *eye field*, where the supplementary use of eye movements is required; and the *head field* where head movements are also necessary.

4. The drops cannot be explained in terms of a sudden increase of movement time at the transition from one level to another, but should rather be attributed to changes from a less to a more complex perceptual process.

Before passing to the next topic it should be noted that the experiment was repeated with small experimental variations, and that each time the results supported the same conclusions. In one study binocular and monocular vision were compared, the latter showing a shift of the head movements curve to a smaller display angle together with a similar shift of the drop in performance (Sanders, 1964 a, p. 55–59).

3. Grouping of Signals in the Functional Visual Field

3.1. *Grouping*

The correspondence between the drops and the necessity of eye and head movements may be related to the possibility of grouping signals in different areas of the functional visual field.

The concept of grouping has been used to account for results in several studies which appear to be analogous to the present one, namely those on the ' psychological refractory period '. In both cases two signals are presented, the main difference being a succession in time instead of a separation in space. In work on the psychological refractory period emphasis has been laid on findings which suggest that signals are treated successively and that information is processed along a single channel (for reviews see Bertelson 1966, Welford

1967). Now the results in experiments on the psychological refractory period appear to depend greatly on instruction. When subjects are asked to process the first signal (S_1) and to neglect the second one (S_2) completely until the first reaction is completed, the evidence indeed points to a quite strict single-channel mechanism, in the sense that the reaction time to S_1 is comparable to that which occurs when it is presented alone, and the reaction time to S_2 is lengthened to an extent varying with the size of the inter-signal interval. However, when subjects are instructed ' to collect all perceptual data before emitting any response ', reaction time to S_1 is lengthened while reaction time to S_2 is less so (Sanders 1964 b). Moreover when relationships between signals and responses are highly compatible and the inter-signal interval is short, the total processing time is considerably shorter with the ' grouping ' instruction than with the ' successive handling ' instruction (Sanders 1967 c). There appear to be at least three theories that might explain the greater efficiency that results from grouping. The first is a perceptual theory, emphasizing the possible effects of perceptual organization when signals are treated together. The idea of perceptual sampling over a short period of time (Broadbent 1958) suggests that signals which are taken in a sample are treated as one decision unit. Bertelson (*op. cit.*) has recently underlined the importance of the decision unit for the psychological refractory period, urging that ' no really predictive model of intermittency can be built as long as the size of the units to which it applies and the conditions under which they are grouped have not been stated ' (p. 157).

A second theory, related to the previous one, emphasizes the importance of overlearned sequences in recoding a group of signals into a single unit (Craik 1948, Miller 1956). This seems of less importance in psychological refractory period studies and also for the present investigation, since any correlation between S_1 and S_2 (or S_L and S_R) has always been carefully avoided.

Finally, a response feedback theory can be formulated which ascribes the relative efficiency of grouping to less monitoring of response. According to this theory, the main difference between grouping and successive handling would consist of successive perceptual intakes followed by simultaneous or almost simultaneous responses (grouping) versus strict alternation of intake and response. In the latter case monitoring of the response to S_1 before the processing of S_2 begins may lengthen the total processing time. If so, the decision units in successive handling and grouping would not differ—at least not in the usual type of task used in experiments on the psychological refractory period. The theory does not exclude the possibility that effects of perceptual organization and learned sequences may also occur.

Some evidence in favour of the last theory comes from a recent study in which four signals were successively presented, requiring selective responses. It was found that the efficiency of grouping was a function of the number of overt responses to be made. Instructions for grouping and for successive handling did not lead to different results when one, and sometimes when two, overt responses were required, but did so when more than two had to be made (Sanders and Keuss 1969). Grouping was unaffected by whether signals were positioned in one or two dimensions (Sanders 1967 c). In short, the relative efficiency of grouping seemed to depend on features of the responses rather than of the signals.

It is of course essential that both signals can be coded in rapid succession. When the interval between them is longer than the time needed to discriminate S_1, time is wasted waiting for the arrival of S_2: with successive handling, this time could have been used to carry out the first response.

3.2. *Grouping and the Functional Visual Field*

To bridge the gap between the preceding argument and the findings regarding the psychological refractory period an experiment was caried out in which two signals (columns of 4 or 5 dots) were simultaneously presented and where subjects were instructed either to handle S_L and S_R in strict succession or to group. Three separate groups of 8 subjects were practised with both instructions but tested at different display angles of 6°, 66° and 99°, corresponding to the stationary, eye and head fields respectively. The results of Table 2 show significantly shorter combined reaction times with grouping in the stationary field and in the eye field ($p < 0.01$). The tendency in this direction in the head field was not significant ($p < 0.1$). Thus grouping appears to be the more efficient

Table 2.   Mean reaction time to left signal (Rt_L) and sums of mean reaction times to left and right signals ($Rt_L + Rt_R$) with different instructions and display angles

	Display angle					
	6°		66°		99°	
Condition	Rt_L	$(Rt_L + Rt_R)$	Rt_L	$(Rt_L + Rt_R)$	Rt_L	$(Rt_L + Rt_R)$
Grouping	0·65	0·72	0·79	0·85	0·90	0·99
Successive treatment	0·46	0·87	0·44	0·97	0·43	1·06

strategy for the stationary and eye fields but much less so for the head field. It looks as if in the latter case S_R cannot be handled immediately after S_L, while this is possible within the limits of the eye field. Does a combined eye-head movement interrupt the processing, while this is not the case when only eye activity is involved? If so, an inability to deal immediately with S_R would not be the main explanation of Drop 1, but it could serve to explain Drop 2.

A further analysis of the data of Table 1 can be made in terms of the present argument. Subjects should have no difficulty in processing S_R immediately after S_L while keeping S_L fixated in the stationary field, where eye movements are not necessary (Figure 2) and where grouping is highly efficient (Table 2). This implies that T_L represents not only the time to discriminate S_L, but also includes at least a part of the time required to observe S_R peripherally. This is supported by the shortness of T_R, despite the fact that T_R includes both the processing of S_R and the motor response. If, now, in the eye and head fields, T_L represents discrimination of S_L only, it should be shorter than in the stationary field. This is not the case however: T_L remains at about the same value in the eye field and tends even to increase in the head field. The question arises of how the extra time is spent. One possibility might be that time is needed to preprogramme the movement of eye (and head), perhaps on the basis of peripherally obtained information about the location of S_R. As has been noted in section 2.3, saccadic eye movements hit their targets very precisely, so that programming before the movement begins is probable. Secondly, and especially in the eye field, subjects may not only obtain information about the location of S_R but also about its content. If so, the principal function of the fixation of S_R may be merely to confirm an expectation, which can be accomplished more quickly than a 'new' observation, and T_R is shortened accordingly (e.g. Senders *et al.* 1954, Senders 1955). In the head field, however, it may be that no information about the number of dots in S_R comes through, so that processing of the two signals is completely interrupted by the movement. This description can explain the results of both the last two experiments described. In the stationary field there would be immediate successive processing of S_L and S_R, perhaps facilitated by the perceptual structure, which may enable the subject to compare line lengths instead of counting dots. In the eye field, there is also immediate successive processing of S_L and S_R, but the information about S_R is not sufficiently clear and requires verification, which takes extra time. Finally, in the head field the observations of S_L and S_R would be separated by the movement of eye and head. As a result T_R is longer, and there may be some increase of T_L owing to time being required to prepare the movement.

An important aspect of this description is the assumption that subjects can acquire some evidence about S_R while inspecting S_L, as long as the display angle is within the borders of the eye field, but not after transition to the head field. In fact this is open to direct experimental test by presenting a pair of signals and having S_R disappear during fixation of S_L or during the eye movement to S_R. Subjects were required to report on both S_L and S_R. A summary of the results of four subjects is given in Table 3, in terms of the probability that the judgments they gave about S_R were better than chance. It appears that subjects can indeed judge S_R better than chance within the eye field but not in the head field.

Table 3. Probability that S_R will be judged better than chance, in relation to time of disappearance and visual angle. The moments at which S_R disappeared were divided into four classes: I, S_R disappeared at least 0·08 sec before the eye movement started; II, the same but from 0·00–0·08 sec; III, S_R disappeared during the eye movement; IV, S_R disappeared 0·00–0·08 sec after the eye had reached it.
— = not significant; + = $p < 0.05$; ++ = $p < 0.02$; +++ = $p < 0.01$. 0 = too few measurements to decide

		Visual angle 66°				81°			
	Subjects	J.M.	Th.E.	A.F.S.	B.S.	J.M.	Th.E.	A.F.S.	B.S.
Time of disappearance of S_R	I	0	+++	+++	0	0	0	+	−
	II	+	+++	++	+++	−	+++	+++	−
	III	+++	+++	+++	+++	+++	+++	+++	+
	IV	+++	+++	+++	+++	+++	+++	+++	+++

		88°			94°		99°
	Subjects	J.M.	Th.E.	B.S.	J.M.	A.F.S.	A.F.S.
Time of disappearance of S_R	I	−	−	−	−	−	−
	II	−	−	−	−	−	−
	III	+++	−	−	−	++	−
	IV	+++	+++	+++	+++	+++	+++

In this experiment also, confidence judgments on a five-point scale were asked after each judgment of S_R. It is consistent with the theory that confidence proved to be very low in the head field. A similar experiment at much smaller display angles showed high confidence ratings in the stationary field, falling rapidly when the display angle reached the eye field, which again fits the theory.

3.3. *Perception during Eye Movements*

So far, the data have been treated with the implicit assumption that no perception of S_R is possible during eye movements. In Table 1, $T_L + T_{lt}$ was considered as a processing time and m as an 'empty period' in between. There is some evidence that the perceptual threshold during saccadic eye movements is very considerably increased (Latour 1967), but does this mean that *no* perception occurs in the present context? To answer this question, an experiment was carried out in which S_R was presented only during the eye movement (for 0·1 sec), and judgments were compared with those in a situation where S_R was presented for the same period, while subjects fixated S_L. All subjects had a highly significant proportion of correct judgments in the latter condition, while nobody did better than chance in the former. So the assumption that information cannot be acquired during the eye movement seems justified. This does not mean, however, that information obtained during fixation of S_L cannot be further processed during the eye movement. There is considerable evidence that visual signals presented simultaneously are for a time processed in parallel—for a brief period a 'visual image' persists, in which specific visual characteristics will appear to be present and by means of which the material is retained for a short period of time after the signals have disappeared (Sperling 1960, 1967, Mackworth 1963). Some evidence exists that information from the periphery of the visual field is represented in this visual image, although less well at larger angles, as would be expected from the poorer acuity of the peripheral retinal system (Sanders 1967 b). Hence it might well be possible that information about S_R, obtained during T_L, is further processed during the eye movement. This might be especially true in the stationary field, perhaps enabling full use to be made of m in that area. It would be much less so in the eye field, since a checking fixation of S_R is always required, and can be considered to be absent in the head field. Hence, the relative possibilities of processing information during the movement may be an important factor in the different strategies of observation. It enhances a grouping strategy—i.e. immediate successive processing of S_L and S_R—in the stationary and eye fields, and leaves a real 'empty period' during m in the head field, which appears from Table 2 to make grouping more difficult to achieve.

4.   The Selective Process in More Complex Tasks

So far the whole account has been based on a very simple task, which of course cannot be considered as representative of selective activity in the normally highly structured functional visual field. It is essential, therefore, to see how far the results are an artefact of the task and to what extent they have wider implications. In the first place, some results of a visual search task will be summarized.

4.1. *Selective Strategies in a Visual Search Task*

A schematic drawing of the task is given in Figure 6. Six columns of dots were projected in a horizontal row. Each column contained four dots, except one which contained five. The task was to determine which this was and then to press the corresponding one of a row of six keys. A new signal appeared 0·1 sec after each response, so that the task was serial but unpaced. Each run lasted for 8 minutes. The location of the five-item column was randomly varied. Signals, responses and reaction times were separately recorded on a printer. Nine subjects practised with, and were subsequently tested with, each of three display angles—68°, 81° and 94° in a Latin square arrangement. The experiment was mainly planned to study the transition between eye and head fields, so that head movements were measured in all experimental runs. The main difficulty, in comparison with the earlier task, is that no constant visual angle is covered during a run. Hence, although the total display angle may exceed the eye field, many successive signals (for instance, a shift to an adjacent one) can still be in the eye field, or may even be in the stationary field.

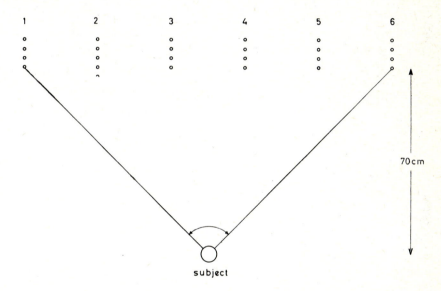

Figure 6. Schematic diagram of the visual search task.

The extreme case is when successive signals are the same: on the basis of the literature on repetitions of signals, a relatively short reaction time would be expected (e.g. Bertelson 1961) irrespective of the total angle subtended by the display. The visual angles covered by all possible pairs of successive signals were accordingly calculated and are listed in Table 4, for each of the

Table 4. Visual angle (in degrees) between successive signals

Signal II	Signal I 1	2	3	4	5	6	1	2	3	4	5	6	1	2	3	4	5	6
1	0	12	26	42	56	68	0	14	30	50	67	81	0	14	35	59	80	94
2		0	14	30	44	56		0	17	37	54	67		0	21	45	66	80
3			0	16	30	42			0	20	37	50			0	24	45	59
4				0	14	26				0	17	30				0	21	35
5					0	12					0	13					0	14
6						0						0						0

Total display angle: 68°   Total display angle: 81°   Total display angle: 94°

total display angles, 68°, 81° and 94°.   This made it possible to plot for every total display angle a function relating reaction time to the visual angle subtended by pairs of successive signals, assuming that the eye remains at the place where the last five-dot column appeared until the next signal arrives. In constructing these functions, equal or almost equal visual angles were combined in order to obtain sufficiently large samples of reaction times per subject.

The results are set out in Figure 7.   First they show ample evidence for the repetition effects in the difference between 0° and 12°–17°.   Secondly, the three curves coincide till about 35°.   There they diverge, in the sense that the 68° curve continues to have a linear course, while with the 81° and 94° an increase in reaction time occurs, followed by a linear trend, running parallel with that found for the 68°.   The flattening of the functions at the largest display angle may reflect an anchoring effect.   Head movements were almost absent at 68°, and quite large at the other display angles.   The 68° display can thus be regarded as within the eye field while the others exceed it.

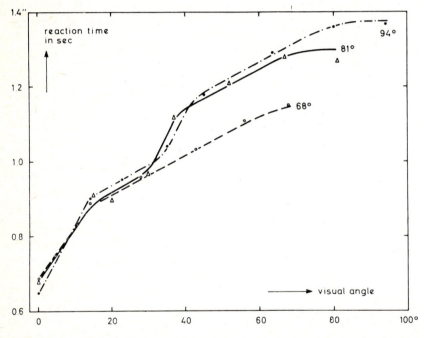

Figure 7.   Mean reaction times as a function of visual angle to be covered in successive signals.
The total display angles are indicated at the right of the curves.

When the five-dot column is observed peripherally but within the eye field, there is likely to be an eye movement to it from the previous position and an increase of reaction time.   This will be largely due to the movement time and will thus be linear with length of movement, which is in turn linear with visual angle.   As would be expected on this view, if a tentative movement time, derived from Table 1, is subtracted from the values for the 68° curve in Figure 7, the greater part of the slope does indeed disappear.   The remainder may be due to a longer time required to detect the signal peripherally, and the decreasing amount of information gathered during T_L as the visual angle becomes larger.

The most striking feature of Figure 7 concerns the increase of reaction time in the head field. The fact that reaction times for the 94° and 81° fields are markedly higher than for the 68° field at visual angles larger than 35° means that the efficiency of covering a specific angular area depends on the size of the total display angle involved. For example, an angular shift of 60° takes a smaller reaction time when the total display angle is in the eye field than when it is in the head field. It seems that, when a number of signal sources are involved, only the adjacent signals are observed in peripheral vision, except when the preceding signal was at the extreme end of the display, in which case two signals can be observed (compare Table 4 and Figure 7). Signals further away than this seem to involve a shift of fixation to another part of the field.

In conclusion, it can be said that the results of this experiment nicely fit the outline of the selective processes in the functional visual field, as connected with the occurrence of eye and head movements. They suggest that the theory is applicable more generally than to the particular experimental task used in the previous sections.

4.2. *Display Angle and Performance in a Memorizing Task*

It was suggested in a previous section that grouping is likely to be facilitated when a series of signals forms an overlearned sequence or has some inner structure which produces sequential redundancy. If, however, the angular separation of the signals is such that the total display angle exceeds the eye field, grouping will become impossible and the benefits of sequential redundancy should disappear.

To test this deduction, a memory span task was used, since it is common knowledge that the size of the memory span depends greatly on sequential redundancy. A number of visual signals ($+$ or $-$) were simultaneously presented. Three variables were introduced: number of signals (6 or 8); display angle (9°, 32°, 52°, 71° or 90°); and degree of sequential redundancy—either all items were random or the second half of the series was identical with the first. A factorial design with 20 experimental conditions was used, and a separate group of 5 subjects was assigned to each condition. Each subject had two practice trials followed by four experimental trials. Each signal, which was correctly reproduced as to item and order was counted as a correct response. Thus with a series of 6 items, subjects could obtain a maximum of 24 correct responses, and with 8 items, 32. Items were presented for 1 sec. Head movements were measured.

The results summarized in Figure 8 have the following main features.

(a) Except in the case of 8 random items, errors increased as a function of display angle, reaching a maximum of 30–40% at 90°. More errors than this are unlikely since 50% correct responses could be obtained on the basis of pure guessing, and subjects would be able to observe and recall one or two items even in very unfavourable circumstances. The main increase of errors is at the larger display angles: for example, in the case of 6 items the differences between 9° and 71° are not statistically significant.

(b) In the case of 8 random items, the percentage of errors appears to be independent of display angle. This is probably the result of overloading. A similar finding was obtained by Klemmer (1963), who presented randomly selected linear dot patterns and varied the display angle. It appears that a beneficial effect of redundancy is found only when the system is overloaded—i.e. with 8 items but not with 6.

(c) At the 90° display angle the effect of redundancy has also disappeared for 8 items. Apparently the redundancy was not recognized at that wide angle—which was in fact predicted by the theory. Subjects seem to be unable to obtain a general impression of the display at such a large angle. The necessity to make head movements at angles larger than 70° makes it reasonable to relate this to the transition from eye to head fields.

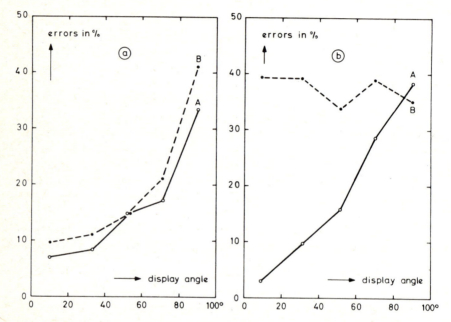

Figure 8.   Percentages of errors as a function of display angle in a memorizing task.   (a) six items; (b) eight items.   A: symmetrical sequences; B: random sequences.

A limitation of the procedure of this experiment is, of course, the presentation time, which probably did not allow more than one observation and the corresponding verificatory shift of the eye. In fact, head movements proved to be suppressed at 90°, implying that subjects had not had sufficient time to shift. The question therefore remains of whether redundancy would have a beneficial effect if presentation time was long enough to allow head movements to be carried out fully, but not so long as to allow rehearsal or a second inspection of the items. Pilot experiments showed that a presentation time of 2 sec satisfied these criteria. With this presentation time, 12 new subjects observing 8 items spread over 90° made 22·3% errors in the redundant case and 19·8% errors in the random case. The difference is small and suggests that redundancy is not easily recognized when two successive observations are needed to view the display. If this is found to be true generally, it would appear that the eye field limits the area within which perceived material can be recoded into a single unit.

5. Discussion

Several other studies have reported a sudden decline of performance as a function of display angle. The work of Corbin *et al.* (*op. cit.*) was discussed before. Adams and Boulter (1962) found a relatively large increase of the average reaction time in a vigilance task, when the display exceeded a critical display angle. Morrow and Salik (1962) reported a sharp decline in the efficiency of evaluating data in rear mirrors of cars when the angle with the driver's position exceeded 45°. Baker (1967) found that the speed of detecting radar signals was less with a moving than with a stationary search line.

Additional evidence about the effect of transition from eye to head fields has been obtained by the present author with a multi-source vigilance task (Sanders 1964 a, pp. 122–133) and with some position and size estimation tasks (pp. 150–156). Altogether, there seems to be fair evidence that the findings in paragraphs 2 and 3 are of general importance. While this was so for the transition from eye to head fields, it was not so for the stationary field. It may be that with a more complex display it becomes impossible to obtain information about items which are not centrally fixated, however small the display angle may be. For example, Mackworth (1965) reported some data about search for small details on complex pictures and on discrimination of letters in a page of printed text. In such tasks a cumbersome visual search goes on, without any evidence of data obtained from peripheral vision, although the display is certainly within the eye field. What can be peripherally viewed are rough structures, like open spaces, the side of the page and objects in the surroundings. The details in printed text or pictures are poorly represented on the visual image, due to a number of factors. One concerns the mutual inhibition of peripherally presented signals (Woodworth and Schlosberg 1954, Sanders 1967 b), which is demonstrated in Figure 9.

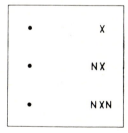

Figure 9. Demonstration of the mutual inhibition effect. When the dot on the left is fixated the letter on the right, seen in peripheral vision, is less well recognized the more it is surrounded by other items.

It should be further noted that the size of the eye field is not constant, but differs greatly as a function of the task. In the work under review the transition from eye field to head field ranged from 75° to 105°, depending on the complexity of the task. It is also clear that the effects of the transition are not always the same. In some tasks there is a change of reaction time at the transition point. In the search task reported here the total display angle had an effect on shifts which in itself did not exceed the eye field. In the memorizing task there seems to have been a breakdown of perceptual organization when the eye field was exceeded.

In conclusion it can be said that the experiments described in this paper concern the macrostructure of the functional visual field. Stationary field, eye field and head field are relevant in connection with this macrostructure. The important question for future research appears to be: where do microstructure and macrostructure meet and how do they interact?

Dans cet article on passe en revue quelques expériences destinées à évaluer la performance en fonction de l'écart angulaire du dispositif de présentation. Leur objectif était de décrire les stratégies perceptives qui s'élaborent lorsque les signaux sont presentés selon diverses séparations angulaires. Les premières expériences ont été réalisé au moyen d'une simple tâche de discrimination à quatre choix. Les résultats montrent que la performance décroît de manière non linéaire en fonction de l'angle du dispositif, ce qui est imputable aux mouvements oculaires et aux mouvements de la tête qui interviennent lors du balayage visuel des diverses sources de signaux. La non-linéarité semble dûe aux changements dans la stratégie, ce qui permit d'ébaucher une théorie des processus de sélection que l'on vérifie dans un certain nombre de tâches.

Es wird zusammenfassend über eine Gruppe von Experimenten über Leistung als Funktion des Darbietungswinkels berichtet, unternommen, um die Wahrnehmungsstrategie bei Signalen, die durch verschiedene Sehwinkel getrennt sind, zu beschreiben. Die ersten Experimente benutzten eine einfache Aufgabe mit vier Wahlmöglichkeiten. Die Resultate zeigen eine nicht-lineare Abnahme der Leistung als Funktion des Sehwinkels, der zwischen verschiedenen Signalen liegt. Das ist durch eine entsprechende Zunahme der Augen- und Kopfbewegungen bedingt. Die fehlende Linearität der Beziehung wird durch veränderte Strategie erklärt. Eine vorläufige Theorie des Wahlprozesses wird formuliert und an einer Reihe von Aufgaben getestet.

References

ADAMS, J. A., and BOULTER, L. R., 1962, An evaluation of the activationist hypothesis of human vigilance. *Journal of Experimental Psychology*, **64**, 495–504.

BAKER, C. H., 1967, Target detection performance with a stationary radar sweepline. In *Attention and Performance* (Edited by A. F. SANDERS). *Acta Psychologica*, **27**, 361–367.

BERTELSON, P., 1961, Sequential redundancy and speed in a serial two choice responding task. *Quarterly Journal of Experimental Psychology*, **13**, 90–102.

BERTELSON, P., 1966, Central intermittency twenty years later. *Quarterly Journal of Experimental Psychology*, **18**, 153–163.

BROADBENT, D. E., 1958, *Perception and Communication* (London: PERGAMON PRESS).

CORBIN, H., CARTER, J., REESE, E. P., and VOLKMANN, J., 1958, Experiments on visual search 1956–1957. *Psychological Research Unit, Mount Holyoke.*

CRAIK, K. J. W., 1948, Theory of the human operator in control systems. II: Man as an element in control systems. *British Journal of Psychology*, **38**, 142–148.

KLEMMER, E. T., 1963, Perception of linear dot patterns. *Journal of Experimental Psychology*, **65**, 468–474.

LATOUR, P. L., 1966, *Cortical Control of Eye Movements* (Assen: V. GORCUM).

MACKWORTH, J. F., 1963, The duration of the visual image. *Canadian Journal of Psychology*, **17**, 62–81.

MACKWORTH, N. H., 1965, Visual noise causes tunnel vision. *Psychonomic Science*, **3**, 67–68.

MILLER, G. A., 1956, The magical number seven plus or minus two: Some limits on our capacity for processing information. *Psychological Review*, **63**, 81–97.

MORROW, I. R. V., and SALIK, G., 1962, Vision in rear view mirrors. *Optician*, **8**, 314–344.

SANDERS, A. F., 1964 a, *The Selective Process in the Functional Visual Field* (Assen: V. GORCUM).

SANDERS, A. F., 1964 b, Selective strategies in the assimilation of successively presented signals. *Quarterly Journal of Experimental Psychology*, **16**, 368–372.

SANDERS, A. F., 1967 a, Informatie verwerking in het funktioneel gezichtsveld. *Nederlands Tÿdschrift voor Psychologie*, **22**, 137–149.

SANDERS, A. F., 1967 b, Centraal aflezen en wederzijdse inhibitie van signalen in het funktioneel gezichtsveld. *Nederlands Tÿdschrift voor Psychologie*, **22**, 251–262.

SANDERS, A. F., 1967 c, The effects of compatibility on grouping successively presented signals. *Acta Psychologica*, **26**, 373–382.

SANDERS, A. F., and KEUSS, P. J. G., 1969, Grouping and refractoriness in multiple selective responses. In *Attention and Performance II.* (Edited by W. KOSTER). *Acta Psychologica*, **30**, 177–195.

SENDERS, J. W., WEBB, J. B., and BAKER, C. A., 1955, The peripheral viewing of dials.   *Journal of Applied Psychology*, **39**, 433–436.

SENDERS, V. L., 1954, The effect of absolute and conditional probabilities distributions of instrument settings on scale reading.   *WADC Techn. Rep.* No. 54–253.

SHACKEL, B., 1958, A rubber section cup surface electrode with high electrical stability.   *Journal of Applied Physiology*, **13**, 153–158.

SPERLING, G., 1960, The information available in brief visual presentations.   *Psychological Monographs*, **74**, No. 11.

SPERLING, G., 1967, Successive approximations to a model for short term memory.   In *Attention and Performance* (Edited by A. F. SANDERS).   *Acta Psychologica*, **27**, 285–293.

WELFORD, A. T., 1967, Single channel operation in the brain.   In *Attention and Performance* (Edited by A. F. SANDERS).   *Acta Psychologica*, **27**, 5–23.

WHITE, C. T., EASON, R. G., and BARTLETT, N. R., 1962, Latency and duration of eye movements in the horizontal plane.   *Journal of the Optical Society of America*, **52**, 210–213.

WOODWORTH, R. S., and SCHLOSBERG, H., 1954, *Experimental Psychology* (London: METHUEN & Co.).

Visually-Guided Behaviour and Behaviourally-Guided Vision

By W. M. SMITH

Dartmouth College, Hanover, New Hampshire, U.S.A.

Temporal integration in perceptually-guided behaviour, and the effects of disturbing the normal temporal and spatial relationships between perceptual display and responding action, are outlined. The characteristics of the cybernetic, feedback model of behaviour they point to are discussed, and evidence is cited which shows that the effects are often highly specific to particular tasks and are affected by difficulties of the task which derive from factors other than temporal and spatial disturbances. A plea is made for a reappraisal of accepted ideas on sensory-motor performance, to incorporate the implications of sensory feedback resulting from action more thoroughly than has been done in the past.

1. Temporal Integration in Perceptually-Guided Behaviour

We look, see, and then we do
And in so doing we see anew.

This couplet (with apologies to the reader) identifies one of the most puzzling areas of concern in the study of psychology. On the one hand, it seems so obvious that behaviour is guided by what we see: we say—as in the title—visually-guided behaviour. Yet much research done during the past few years seems to be saying the reverse; namely, that vision is guided by behaviour (e.g. Kohler 1964, Held *et al.* 1966, Smith and Smith 1962, 1966). The point has been made repeatedly that movement-produced stimulation, that is, sensory effects of behaviour, modify, modulate and mould the perceived characteristics of the visual environment. Can behaviour be both visually guiding and guided? Do we see and then do and in so doing see anew and differently?

With these questions in mind let us turn to certain problems and experiments concerned with spatial and temporal factors bearing on the relationship between vision and overt behaviour. For purposes of context in the following discussion, let me first cite and elaborate upon some important general points.

For many years, indeed decades, psychologists have been disproportionately interested in problems of *spatial* integration and organization—at the expense, I think, of basic questions of *temporal* integration and organization. From the standpoint of experimental and procedural convenience this emphasis is not hard to understand, but from a conceptual or theoretical point of view the imbalance of emphasis is not defensible. Any attempt to interrelate perception and motion, vision and action, or what have you, cannot continue for long to avoid problems concerning temporal integration and organization.

Data on eye-movements obtained by the author and presented in Figure 1 illustrate this point. Here we see the subtle and complicated play of temporal integration and organization when the eye tracks a moving target. In this instance the target movement was horizontal, left to right over an angular distance of approximately 20 degrees. Each eye-movement record was analysed in such a way that the absolute time required for the pursuit component(s) was ascertained as well as the absolute time taken by the saccadic component or components. As the figure shows, the total time spent in pursuit motion was a direct function of the velocity of the target, whereas the amount of time taken for saccadic movement was the same at all velocities. Each eye-movement record, of course, could consist of more than one pursuit or saccadic component. At the higher target velocities the magnitudes of the saccadic movements were greater, but so were their velocities. When the times taken by the two components of eye-motion approach equality we find the general upper limit for seeing moving targets, i.e. at about 75° per sec. The important thing about these findings is the surprising degree of temporal precision and regularity found in the changing organization of the two components of eye motion. One can only speculate about the basis of such temporal organization, but we may note that in this particular case it is found only if the observer knows, at least roughly, how far the target will move on a given trial. When the extent of movement is unpredictable from trial to trial, the temporal integration and relationships shown in the figure are not found.

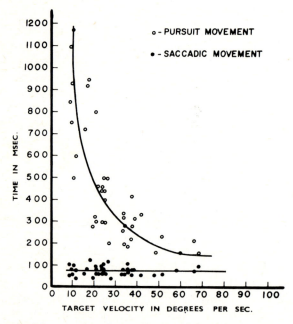

Figure 1.   Time required for pursuit and saccadic components of eye-movement as a function of target velocity.

A second point worth noting is that we still suffer from a long-established tradition in psychology of emphasis on the phenomenal aspects of perception—perception *is* phenomenological. Such an emphasis forced many earlier psychologists to miss or ignore the sensory and perceptual consequences of behaviour related to a particular phenomenal event. In contemplating the sheer beauty of a sunset it is perhaps easy to ignore the behaviour of the viewer. On the other hand, and in contrast, later and more modern psychologists—mostly American—with their intense interest in behaviour have tended to ignore the phenomenal aspects of perception, and thus the consequences of perception related to behaviour. It is true that we easily conclude that perception guides action—we see and thus do—but how many of us have really tried to comprehend or explain what great complexity that easy conclusion embodies? What is the secret of the 'final common path' or, as Miller *et al.* (1960, p. 11) put it, what fills the 'theoretical vacuum between cognition and action'? The point, of course, is that we explain little, if anything, when we state that perception guides action. There is as much a theoretical vacuum between perception and action as there is between cognition and action—indeed, it is the same vacuum.

Another important point which should be kept to the fore in a list of guidelines for the study of visually-guided behaviour is suggested by the adjective 'visually-guided'. It is that we must continually remind ourselves that the complex of action we loosely call perceptual-motor is *multi-sensory* or *multi-perceptual* in nature. The sensory information—exteroceptive, proprioceptive and probably always interoceptive—related to some expression of action is inevitably multi-sensory in nature. Thus, the problem of perceptual-motor behaviour (not, in fact, a very good term) is really the problem of how simultaneous multi-sensory information controls a kinetic system whose output is part of that multi-sensory information. When, for example, we make a placing motion of a hand in relation to an object, the visual information about the object and the hand and arm is not the only relevant information used. There is, in addition, sensory information derived from the movement itself plus important postural information of a sensory nature. Were it not awkward in expression we might say sensory–motor-sensory or even sensory–sensory–motor-sensory–sensory. Indeed, the organization and integration of multi-sensory information in relation to a specific expression of action might *be* the cognitive component of perceptual-motor behaviour. In other words, it is only when the temporal and spatial aspects of different sources of sensory information relative to some movement are properly integrated, that we finally know the movement in question has been achieved and a subsequent movement can begin.

Study of the temporal patterning of events in perceptual-motor behaviour is therefore crucial, particularly in relation to the multi-sensory nature of such behaviour. Within single sensory systems the study of temporal patterning is, of course, an old and established tradition, dating from very early investigations of apparent movement (the phi-phenomenon) to modern studies of brightness enhancement, short-term memory, and figural after-effects, among others. In recent years, however, increasing emphasis upon the temporal aspects of perception and motion has come from a growing interest in the concept of feedback. This emphasis has in turn required investigators to look more closely at problems of temporal integration in which multi-sensory information is involved. We see this emphasis best illustrated in studies of delayed sensory feedback, to which we now turn.

2. Studies of Delayed Feedback in Visually-Guided Behaviour

With the post-war development of cybernetics, it was inevitable that some psychologists should turn to detailed studies of sensory feedback and its importance in the control of behaviour. Indeed, studies made during World

War II had emphasized the significance of feedback in various tracking tasks, and pointed up the importance of delay in feedback—most tracking systems had inherent time-lags which affected performance.

The study of sensory feedback and its experimental delay has been possible for only a relatively few years.   In the early 1950s, starting with the work by Lee (1950 a, b), the use of magnetic tape recorders made possible the delay of auditory feedback in speech and certain other forms of behaviour, such as tapping.   Since that time, extensive research has been carried out on delayed auditory feedback in the control and expression of speech.   It is not possible to discuss this important work in detail here, but it is worth noting that the experimental control and manipulation of this form of sensory feedback have opened up significant research problems which are basically concerned with the temporal organization and control of behaviour.

The development of video-tape recording made it possible to delay visual feedback of the motion of the hands when performing a task, in a manner analogous to the delay of auditory feedback in speech: the movements are recorded on video-tape and played back after a brief interval.   The first observations on delayed vision were obtained by myself and two colleagues almost ten years ago (Smith *et al.* 1960).   The technical problem, unfortunately, has yet to be solved in a satisfactory manner, but in the last decade several interesting studies of delayed pictorial and non-pictorial visual feedback have been made (Bergeijk and David 1959, Kalmus *et al.* 1960, K. Smith 1962, Smith and Smith 1962, 1966, Sheridan and Ferrell 1963, 1965, W. Smith 1964, Held *et al.* 1966).

We learn from these studies the important fact that delaying visual information in the continuous execution of some task is extremely disorganizing, usually more so than the effects of spatially distorted information.   If the delay is long enough, a strategy of look, wait, and then move can be employed, but at delays less than one second this strategy does not serve well.   Indeed, from the observation obtained in the first study of its kind (Smith *et al. op. cit.*), it was clear that in a task like maze-tracing, with a delay of about half a second performance was next to impossible.   These studies also tell us, at least tentatively, that the effects of delay are a function of the difficulty of the task, of task complexity, and the level of initial skill.

The importance of these studies lies not so much in what we have already learned from them, but in the questions they raise.   Why should delayed visual feedback disorganize behaviour in an extreme fashion?   Why should more difficult and more complex tasks be more severely affected by delay? Perhaps future studies will enable us to learn precisely how much visual guidance is involved in a variety of tasks.   At this time we have no effective way of knowing the degree to which visual guidance is involved in a particular task at different stages of learning and performance.   In learning a visual-motor task, there is no reason to assume that the degree or amount of visual guidance is linearly, or in any other particular way, related to the various stages of skill.   The technique of delayed visual feedback provides a way for investigating such questions by assessing the decrements of performance produced by various amounts of delay at different levels of proficiency.   We like to think that some visual-motor tasks learned to a very high degree of proficiency essentially ' run themselves off ' unaided by vision once they have been initiated—we can do something so well that we can perform it ' blind '. Such an assumption could be put to precise test.

We may further ask whether *learning* is impaired under conditions of delayed visual feedback. I suspect that at very short delays such as 50 to 300 msecs only limited learning, if any, is possible. I say this because of the suspicion that delays of this magnitude prevent basic integrative mechanisms from operating, which in turn would negate the normal effects of reinforcement. Or, put another way, the temporal organization of sensory events in regard to motor output is a high-speed process, and if prevented, the normal effects of reinforcement, knowledge of results, etc., will be prevented.

Another promising idea with respect to future studies of delayed visual feedback concerns its experimental use in assessing the effects of drugs. In discussions with colleagues in the medical field, I have frequently been told that disorders of the motor system are often so subtle that standard neurological tests do not provide a sound basis for assessment. The extremely disorganizing effects of delayed visual feedback may prove to be an effective way of amplifying such subtle effects of perceptual-motor dysfunction and thus of providing valuable diagnostic information. Similar possibilities apply to other impairments of behaviour such as those due to brain damage, stress, etc.

Visual delay of on-going behaviour is a form of temporal disarrangement and, as such, is related to certain problems of spatial disarrangement. It has been found, for example, that if an observer wears prisms which distort the visual scene, his actions are at first inaccurate because they are not adjusted to take account of the distortion. After practice, however, a new co-ordination is achieved and accuracy is restored. Held *et al.* (*op. cit.*) found that the achievement of the new co-ordination was prevented if, in addition to the visual distortion, visual feedback was delayed by 0·3 to 3·3 sec. The importance of this study, it seems to me, taken in conjunction with other studies of delayed visual feedback, is that the temporal disturbance of normal feedback relationships in visual-motor behaviour not only affects motor organization but may also affect perceived dimensions such as spatial locations. Further studies along the same line are, however, needed in order to be sure that this is so. Specifically, we need to know the answer to the question: does delay of visual information in visually guided tasks not only disturb *motor* organization but also make things *appear* differently?

3. Spatially-Altered Feedback in Visually-Guided Behaviour

I now turn to a discussion of some problems concerning spatial factors in visually-guided behaviour. Specifically I shall concentrate upon the question of motor organization in relation to the two major spatial co-ordinates of space —right–left and up–down or, more conveniently, to normal, reversed, inverted–reversed and inverted dimensions of perceived space.

Recent years have seen something like an explosion of research dealing with such problems as adaptation to visual disarrangement and displacement. The theoretical questions and empirical issues behind this research are not entirely new: for example, the work of Stratton (1897) on the effects of wearing lenses which invert the retinal image is classical. In considering the research of recent years of such adaptation, I cannot help but be impressed by the very grave difficulty investigators have had in conceptualizing the perceptual problem in the same or similar terms to the behavioural one. Many agree that the two are inextricably related, yet by the end of a report, conclusions read as if the author has been talking only about one or the other. Consider for a moment the process of adaptation shown in the studies by Kohler (1964), Held (1966), Harris (1965), Rock (1966) and others in which subjects come, after practice, to locate objects accurately with their hands while viewing them through inverting or distorting spectacles. If we call this adaptation, what is it that we have adapted to? Harris discussed this point well and at length (1965). Is it the visual system which has adapted? Is it the motor system, or the proprioceptive system? Is the adaptation perhaps even cognitive? In any case, what has adapted to what? Maybe several systems are involved.

If we turn to consider studies of response to extreme visual disorientation such as Stratton started with inverting lenses, our question becomes even further complicated. Can the human observer adapt to optical inversion of his visual field? Is adaptation here the right concept? Is it the same question as adapting to a limited lateral angular displacement of the visual field? Maybe we adapt to slight visual displacements and *learn to adjust* to visual inversion or reversal. I would argue that this distinction may be a valid one and that we should assume tentatively that fundamental processes underlying the two are different.

In the first place, I would stress that disturbing the normal directional properties of the visual field necessarily has a profound effect on, and relation to, the postural base of all behaviour, and in addition, to the intrinsic and unlearned dimensions of body symmetry and bilateral movements of the limbs of the body. To relate the bilateral and co-ordinate dimensions of limb, hand and body (including head) movement to, say, optically inverted vision, is to require the learning not of new movement patterns, nor of new visual directions, but of new relationships between the two. Moreover, it is not evident that all such relationships can be established through learning. Smith and Smith (1962) emphasize the idea that the spatial organization of visually-guided behaviour is based on (1) the geometric properties of the visual stimulation and its orientation, together with (2) the spatial and temporal patterning of feedback stimulation arising from the postural and bilateral movement systems of the body. For example, it is instructive to consider the results of an experiment by Smith and Greene (1963) which showed a critical period at about 12 years of age when youngsters were first able to write upside down while viewing an inverted television image, in such a way as to make the writing appear normal—so-called compensatory writing. Such results clearly support the conception that something more basic than just *learning* underlies the human capability of organizing overt behaviour to conform to changed co-ordinates of visual space—something more that develops in the early teens.

Such development seems to be of an intrinsic organization of human motion in terms of a postural up–down dimension and bilateral right–left symmetry. The importance of these has been shown time and again in our studies of the effects of reversed, inverted, and reversed–inverted vision. We have found repeatedly that these different changes in visual direction differ in difficulty and can often behave as if they were relatively independent of one another. For example, in an experiment using televised displays, it was found with tasks such as maze-tracing that performance under inverted vision was the most difficult, with inverted–reversed next, followed by reversal alone (Smith and Smith 1962).   This order of difficulty has been found in other studies subsequently and appears to be a predictable one.

The independence of which I spoke above can be found in a study by Smith and Wargo (1963).   In this experiment a group of subjects (the control group) practiced a star-tracing task with inverted visual feedback for half an hour per day on each of 20 days.   A second group of subjects (the experimental group) practiced for 15 minutes each day with normal feedback and for 15 minutes with inverted feedback.   A third (normal) group traced with normal upright feedback throughout.   The time required to complete the maze decreased with practice each day for all groups.   Understandably the normal group did better than the others.   The surprising finding was the superiority of the experimental group, which was consistently better than the control group throughout the 20-day period.   The obvious question, of course, is why the subjects who alternated each day between normal and inverted conditions of feedback were superior to those who consistently practiced under conditions of inverted feedback.   Clearly, the expected interference between the two conditions of practice did not occur.   Apparently performance with normal vision did not impair subsequent performance with inverted vision—the two performances seemed to be independent.

Further evidence in support of the position that visually-guided behaviour is primarily organized around the up–down and left–right dimensions can be seen from the effects of angular displacement of visual feedback.   Most studies of these, other than those carried out in the Wisconsin and Dartmouth laboratories, have not adequately emphasized the particular significance of the problem of angular displacement because they have dealt only with very small magnitudes of displacement.   Here I have in mind the numerous studies of adaptation made during recent years (see Rock *op. cit.*).   We find in our studies that adjustment to angular displacement is highly specific to the various meridians of the visual field, and differs with difficulty of task.   In studies of this kind, we have defined the normal breakdown angle of displacement for certain kinds of visually-guided behaviour.   The value of the angle varies with the precision of the movements required, being smaller (10–15°) for very precise tasks and larger (30–40°) for tasks requiring only general movements of the limbs and minimal accuracy.   This finding again illustrates that the effects of displaced visual feedback do not depend only on learning to deal with the reorientation implied, but also on other aspects of movement reflected in the difficulty of the task.

We obviously have much to learn about how the major co-ordinates of visual space are related to the corresponding co-ordinates of human motion.   That the relationship between the two is not simply dependent upon how ' normal ' the visual environment appears can be illustrated by studies of inverted vision with direct and compensatory motion.   The former motion is illustrated by the subject who is required to write inverted letters or words and sees them as such.   Compensatory motions in the same task are, as we have already noted, writing in an inverted fashion to make the written material appear as normal. When these forms of writing are compared (Smith and Smith 1962) it is usually found that, after extensive practice, differences between the two are not reliable, notwithstanding the fact that subjects who practice under the

compensatory conditions see their writing as ' normal ' throughout an experiment.   Similarly, results from a recent pilot experiment by the author, shown
in Table 1, indicate that subjects who practiced compensatory inverted writing
for half an hour a day on each of 19 days showed little or no effects when they
were required to continue to write inverted letters with normal upright vision.
Their performance was, however, degraded more if they switched from writing
single letters to three- and five-letter words, that is, to groups of letters they
had not practiced during the 19 days.   Still more errors occurred with numbers,
which had not been written at all during the previous 19 practice sessions.
In other words, even though one may learn to write inverted letters without
error under direct or compensatory inverted vision, it does not enable one to
write unpracticed material in an inverted manner without considerable error.
Direct inverted vision during practice appears to be less disturbing than
compensatory, but under both conditions the error rates for numbers were
relatively high.   Such results suggest that the organization of visual-motor
behaviour is not a simple function of either how the environment appears
(normal, inverted, etc.) or what motions specifically have been practiced, but
is a function of the interaction of both in relation to specific requirements of
the task existing at the moment.   Such a conclusion is in harmony with the
earlier discussion in this paper of the relative independence of effects under
extreme changes in visual direction.   It also supports the thesis (Smith and
Smith 1962) that adaptation to various conditions of visual displacement
posesses a high degree of specificity, and produces complicated and unpredictable transfer effects, particularly in relation to such things as visual direction,
the nature of feedback, and the form of motion required by the task or tasks
in question.

Table 1.   Percentage error for inverted writing on two days of testing after 19 days of practice
with either compensatory or direct inverted writing

Practice conditions	Compensatory				Direct			
Subject	1		2		3		4	
Test day	1	2	1	2	1	2	1	2
Test material								
Individual letters	0	0	20	4	0	0	0	0
3-letter words	4	7	60	4	0	0	0	0
5-letter words	0	3	47	3	0	0	0	3
Numbers	40	20	70	62	20	12	24	4

4.   Conclusion

Taking into consideration what we know (though it may be little) about
the role of delayed sensory feedback in relation to behaviour, and also what
we know (it may be more) about spatially altered feedback in relation to
behaviour, it seems compelling to me to conclude one thing, if nothing else:
namely, that we must accept conceptually what the whole concept of feedback
implies.   The implication is that our traditional cause-and-effect model as
applied to perception and motor behaviour must be set aside.   When we
incorporate the concept of feedback into our thinking, we are using a cybernetic
model in which not only does perception lead to behaviour, but behaviour
inevitably alters sensory feedback, both afferent and re-afferent; and the

resulting multi-sensory information in its turn alters behaviour in some measure. Perception guides behaviour; behaviour guides perception. Cause and effect? Each is both.

It seems, therefore, that the chief task before us is not to concentrate upon new and different variations of the kinds of experiments many of us have done to study temporally and spatially displaced feedback, but rather to turn our major effort toward trying to conceptualize this whole problem area in a new way—in a manner which conforms more to a cybernetic model. Few of us, if any, are yet really able to think effectively in these terms about so-called perception and motor behaviour. I know I am not.

Cet article donne un aperçu des mécanismes de l'intégration temporelle dans les comportements guidés par la perception et souligne les conséquences de la perturbation des relations spatio-temporelles entre le dispositif de présentation et la réponse. La discussion porte sur les caractéristiques du modèle cybernétique à rétroaction auquel on se réfère. On montre que les effets sont souvent très dépendants des tâches spécifiques et sont parfois modulés par des difficultés de la tâche ayant leur origine dans des facteurs autres que les perturbations spatio-temporelles. Il est fortement suggéré de réévaluer les idées reçues concernant les performances sensori-motrices afin d'y incorporer plus que par le passé, les effets de la rétroaction sensorielle d'origine motrice.

Die zeitliche Integration eines wahrnehmungsgelenkten Verhaltens und die Wirkungen einer Störung der normalen zeitleichen und räumlichen Beziehung zwischen Darbietung und Antwortsreaktion werden umrissen. Die Charakteristik des kybernetischen Rückkoppelungs-Modells des Verhaltens wird diskutiert. Beweise werden angeführt, die zeigen, dass diese Wirkungen oft sehr spezifisch für bestimmte Aufgaben sind und dass sie durch Schwierigkeiten der Aufgaben be-einflusst werden, die von anderen Faktoren herrühren als zeitlichen oder räumlichen Störungen. Eine Wierderaufwertung der sens-motorischen Leistung wird empfohlen, um die Auswirkungen der sensorischen Rück—koppelunggründlicher einzubauen als es in der Vergangenheit geschehen ist.

References

BERGEIJK, W. A. VAN, and DAVID, E. E., JR., 1959, Delayed handwriting. *Perceptual and Motor Skills*, **9**, 347–357.

FERRELL, W., 1965, Remote manipulation with transmission delay. *IEEE Transactions of human Factors in Electronics*, HFE–6, 24–32.

HARRIS, C. S., 1965, Perceptual adaptation to inverted, reversed, and displaced vision. *Psychological Review*, **72**, 419–444.

HELD, R., EFSTATHION, A., and GREENE, M., 1966, Adaptation to displaced and delayed visual feedback from the hand. *Journal of Experimental Psychology*, **72**, 887–891.

KALMUS, H., FRY, D. B., and DENES, P., 1960, Effects of delayed visual control on writing, drawing, and tracing. *Language and Speech*, **3**, 96–108.

KOHLER, I., 1964, The formation and transformation of the perceptual world. (Trans. by H. FISS.) *Psychological Issues*, **3**, 1–173.

LEE, B. S., 1950 a, Some effects of side-tone delay. *Journal of the Acoustical Society of America*, **22**, 639–640.

LEE, B. S., 1950 b, Effects of delayed speech feedback. *Journal of the Acoustical Society of America*, **22**, 824–826.

MILLER, G. A., GALANTER, E., and PRIBRAM, K. H., 1960, *Plans and the Structure of Behavior* (New York: HOLT).

ROCK, I., 1966, *The Nature of Perceptual Adaptation* (New York: BASIC BOOKS).

SHERIDAN, T. B., and FERRELL, W. R., 1963, Remote manipulative control with transmission delay. *IEEE Transactions of human Factors in Electronics*, HFE–4, 25–29.

SMITH, K. U., 1962, *Delayed Sensory Feedback and Behavior* (Philadelphia: SAUNDERS).

SMITH, K. U., and GREENE, P., 1963, A critical period in maturation of performance with space-displaced vision. *Perceptual and Motor Skills*, **17**, 627–639.

SMITH, K. U., and SMITH, W. M., 1962, *Perception and Motion* (Philadephia: SAUNDERS).

SMITH, K. U., and SMITH, M. F., 1966, *Cybernetic Principles of Learning and Educational Design* (New York: HOLT).

SMITH, K. U., and WARGO, L., 1963, Sensory-feedback analysis of specialization of movements in learning. *Perceptual and Motor Skills*, **16**, 749–756.

SMITH, W. M., 1964, Control of eye-fixation by auditory feedback. *Psychonomic Science*, **1**, 233–234.

SMITH, W. M., McCRARY, J. W., and SMITH, K. U., 1960, Delayed visual feedback and behavior. *Science*, **132**, 1013–1014.

STRATTON, G. M., 1897, Vision without inversion of the retinal image. *Psychological Review*, **4**, 341–360 and 463–481.

A Theory of Pattern Perception Based on Human Physiology

By M. Kabrisky and O. Tallman
Wright-Patterson Air Force Base, Ohio

C. M. Day
U.S. Air Force Institute of Technology

and C. M. Radoy
U.S. Air Force Cambridge Research and Development Center, Lexington,
Massachusetts, U.S.A.

The gross connectivity patterns of information pathways in the primate and human visual systems, when examined by an information processing engineer, bear a curious resemblance to the two-dimensional-pattern optical computers which he builds himself in an attempt to achieve pattern recognition. The portions of the visual system inferior to the primary visual cortex are essentially a topologically accurate homeo-morphic mapping of the retinal image, at least in the vicinity of the fovea. Analysis of the topological aspects of the visual scene and hence 'Pattern Recognition' must therefore take place in the primary visual cortex and successive cortical areas.

We have previously reported how intra- and inter-cortical connectivity could support a combined memory and computation scheme capable of performing pattern recognition by a variation of two-dimensional cross correlation. This paper is a report of an extension of the previous model enabling it to perform pattern recognition by computing the two-dimensional Fourier transform of input images in a manner isomorphic to computation of the Fraunhofer diffraction pattern in optical computers. It is shown that the use of the Fourier transform of an unknown pattern in a subsequent correlation scheme results in a pattern recognition system which is not easily faulted by the small local mutilations of input patterns which badly compromise straight correlation pattern recognition schemes.

1. Introduction

Let us consider a hypothetical experiment. If a person is seated before a projection screen and monochromatic photographic slides of typical objects and scenes are projected, he will find it an easy task to 'identify' virtually all of them. If we were to imagine his responses to a randomly chosen sequence of pictures they might go as follows: 'Capital letter A; Harold Wilson; Telephone, probably not an English one; Poodle; Looks like an etching by Dürer; Aerial photo of an airport; Don't know, perhaps the mouth parts of an insect'; and so on. This 'identification game', although probably requiring the utilization of all of the human eye–brain system, is in fact, a simplified sub-task of that system in that it excludes colour, temporal aspects, binocular depth perception, optical illusions, and behaviour of the system at other than normal bright illumination. Preliminary experiments in our laboratory show that many or all significant portions of complex scenes may be 'identified' after viewing times as short as 2 msec (the time available to us with our present mechanical shutter and projector system). These preliminary tests seem to show that complexity does not affect identification nearly as much as does familiarity and that, provided the projected image contains elements of the viewer's repertoire of stored visual memories of the very general sort enumerated above, the identification game is a simple one—and, we think, probably a very fundamental one. We do not know at all how the eye–brain system accomplishes this simplified task, but the task would seem so fundamental that an explanation of how an existing biological system can do it might be the first step in a description of the function of the entire human visual system and, perhaps, give us an insight into the ways in which the visual system is coupled to other major information handling systems in the brain. With such information we might even be tempted to consider the construction of an equivalent simulacrum.

The subject playing the identification game classifies each new projected picture into his own personal categories which, for the most part, are similar to those possessed by persons of similar background. After classification, he can make statements about the pictures which are personally relevant; in other words, the subject, as a result of the stimulus, has produced a list of related items. The production of such a list is what we shall define as ' pattern recognition '. The lists, categories or statements produced following the visual stimuli are not neat, precisely defined elements, and, in fact, are adjustable to suit the particular task at hand; for instance, separating a series of World War II aircraft into categories marked: American, British, German, none of the above, don't know; and then for a second task, going back and classifying the same photos according to whether the aircraft have liquid- or air-cooled or jet engines.

An information processing engineer is embarrassed by such a performance because of the comparatively trivial capabilities that his own machines have with respect to this game. If he looks to the biological machine to provide a clue as to how to build an identification game machine he finds a paradoxical situation.

(1) Very little is known about the integrative internal operation of the entire human (or primate) visual system—especially when considered in the light of the identification game.

(2) There is an enormous amount of data concerning small sections of the system (such as anatomical minutiae, neurone physiology and electrical activity, photo-receptor chemistry, etc.) which at present cannot be incorporated in any model of the complete system.

An, as yet, unknown portion of the existing data is certainly irrelevant to the identification game. For instance, does the EEG have anything to do with it? For that matter, are neurones themselves important or is it only the pattern of their interconnection which need concern us? After all, *in retrospect*, it is obvious that feathers have nothing to do with flying any more than vacuum tubes have anything to do with digital computation.

The problem of the selection of pertinent aspects of known data about the human visual system in an attempt to hypothesize a useful model of one aspect of its function is a tricky and dangerous business. At worst, the model builder may fasten his attention on what will eventually turn out to be irrelevancies;

at best he will succeed in outraging some of his friends and co-workers when they discover that his prejudices and penchants are different from theirs.   He may also be wasting his time completely because, for all we know, some key set of facts or some essential theoretical discipline not yet dreamed of may be required before the job can be done.

With such forebodings lurking in the background, our group has focused its attention on what we think are the essential information-handling processes occurring in the human visual system when performing the identification game. In doing this, we think that it is important to try and locate where in the system specific sub-tasks of the identification game are being carried out; the idea being that perhaps some specific structure, together with what is known of its function, may provide clues to the identification of what the sub-tasks actually are in the game—at least as employed by the biological system.

2.   Infra-Cortical Data Transmission Systems

The first step in the identification game computation is, in relation to the entire task, a trivial one: the formation of an optical image of the viewed scene on the retina.   Optical diffraction theory predicts an ultimate visual acuity (depending, however, upon the definition of the width of the Airy disc pertinent to a retinal signal detection system) of less than 1 minute of arc, perhaps as little as 30 seconds.   Certain subjective foveal acuity tasks (which, of course, also require the operation of the *entire* visual system) do achieve this level of acuity and thus seem to verify the theoretical optical computations.   It is very important to note that the assumption must then be made that the foveal retinal receptor system is capable of transmitting with an acuity as good as that of the optics and that this acuity is maintained in the foveal portion of the system through to subjective analysis centres in the brain.   Otherwise it is impossible to account for the ultimate subjective awareness of the acuity of the optical input to the system.

The simplest sort of system which is capable of transmitting foveal optical images with no loss of acuity is a point-by-point transfer of the optical image. with ' points ' having the approximate dimensions of the optical Airy disc, As we might expect then, the cones occur in the fovea at this density: that is their centres are about 14 sec. of arc apart.   However, data from the retina are actually reported to the central nervous system in terms of the behaviour of receptive fields which are organized in the retina (Kuffler 1953, Wiesel and Hubel 1966).   These are about 2 degrees in overall diameter and have a smaller concentric centre area.   The information reported from the retina to the brain describes what is happening in the small central area compared to the larger surrounding annulus.   Such arrangement could easily form the basis of an automatic sensitivity control mechanism in a system reporting, essentially, local intensity of illumination on the retina in terms of Dirac delta functions in two spatial dimensions.   Such two-dimensional intensity functions are certainly sufficiently elemental decompositions of the components of two-dimensional scenes to provide a universal pattern transmission system; that is, one capable of transmitting every possible pattern.   The human system is evidently a universal pattern-handling system to within the limits of its optical acuity; there do not exist two different patterns, in the sense of the identification game, which cannot be distinguished by the system.

The receptive field system is intrinsically capable of computing the two-dimensional derivative of images, thereby enabling edge enhancement and the formation of Mach bands to occur and, apparently, providing the basis of colour vision where the receptive field centre and its surround are sensitive to different colours (Wiesel and Hubel *op. cit.*).

It is the size of the field centre, of course, which controls the ultimate possible acuity of the overall system—assuming that the field centres are sufficiently numerous to cover the entire retinal area. Note that the receptive fields would then overlap extensively. Considering the subjective acuity of the entire visual system, one would expect that, in the fovea, the field centres are about the size of cones and that they occur, spatially, at the same rate as the cones. Histological evidence (Dowling and Boycott 1966) confirms this as does physiological experimentation in infra-human primates (Wiesel and Hubel *op. cit.*). Outside the fovea the size of the receptive field centres increases and their spatial rate of occurrence decreases; the subjectively experienced result of this is well known: acuity and capability of form perception fall substantially and increasingly as the image moves from the fovea to the far periphery of the retina.

The two-dimensional optical image, now coded spatially in the form of two-dimensional delta functions, is transmitted from the retina to the lateral geniculate bodies in the thalamus and thence to the primary visual cortex. It is most unlikely that significant information processing with respect to the identification game is performed in the human (or primate) lateral geniculate body (Wiesel and Hubel *op. cit.*, Kabrisky 1966, 1967). Since the same is obviously true for the retina, attention then turns to the cortical centres of the brain. The principal, and certainly most striking, feature of the retina–thalamus–cortex transmission channel, at least in primates and man, is that it maps the retina homeomorphically (Polyak 1957) on to the functionally flat, thin cortex (Bok 1959). As a result of this homeomorphic transfer the information implicit in the *shapes* of objects, which is precisely the information required to play the identification game, is preserved until it can be processed by cortical structures. The care with which these shape and form data are preserved, and the fact that the form data are maintained in fairly well isolated channels which individually do not have access to most of the other points required to represent any significant entity in a retinal scene, strongly suggest that it is in the cortex that the crux of the identification game is played.

3. The Cortex and Computations it could Support

Although structurally a large sheet, the cortex is organized *functionally* to operate in small, integral and independent units. A rough analogy would be the flat, sheet-like structure of a honey comb wherein the functional units, the individual cells, are separate and distinct. Their arrangement in a large flat sheet is an artefact consequent on mechanical expediency and the necessity of having access to each of the distinct and different functional units.

The basic connectivity within the cortex was first described by Cajal in 1898 (see Lorente de No 1949) based purely on histological studies. The flow of data, as shown by the general orientation of axonal direction, is perpendicular to the plane of the sheet of cortex: input data are received through axons which are effectively perpendicular to the sheet, roughly like hair growing on the scalp, and the output corresponding to a particular input departs from the cortex at the same point at which the data went in. There is virtually no transmission of data across the sheet—at least so far as concerns the identification game. Functional verification of the fact that the cortex operates as a collection of distinct cell-like units has been communicated by Mountcastle (1957) and by Hubel and Wiesel (1962). Hubel and Wiesel gave dimensions of these units in the cat as 0·5 mm in diameter and extending completely through all six layers of the cortex. Based on considerations of information theory, Kabrisky (1961, 1966) predicted that these cortical elements, which he termed 'basic computing elements', should have dimensions of about 0·05 mm in the human striate cortex (area 17). Since this region of the cortex is about 1·5 mm thick they would be roughly in the form of thin cylindrical cells about thirty times longer than their diameter.

What sort of calculation and memory functions could be obtained in such an element is now the subject of some interesting observations and speculations. Hubel and Wiesel have made some functional evaluation of the units they have found in live, anaesthetized animals; unfortunately their experimental procedure is a little crude in the sense that the variety of visual stimuli to the animal was limited, and the behaviour of the functional units being examined was evaluated by simply listening to the amplified clicks picked up from single neurone micro-electrodes. A more elegant experiment on the effects of stimulation has been done by Ervin (1964); the stimuli were generated by a computer and presented as two-dimensional patterns on the face of a cathode-ray tube placed in the animal's line of sight. The patterns generated depended upon the behaviour of the data picked up by a micro-electrode in the visual cortex, thus completing an information processing feedback system which included the animal. The behaviour of individual neurones were analysed in great detail, on-line, by the computer and showed many dimensions of cortical behaviour that could not possibly be discerned by listening to clicks. For instance, the idea that a cortical computing element might be handling, say, only straight-line elements having a specific angular orientation in the visual scene, as suggested by the results of Hubel and Wiesel, seems to be erroneous in the light of Ervin's experiments. These showed, among other facets of behaviour, that individual cortical elements may respond, for example, to all angular orientations of a line, but with different temporal patterns according to orientation.

Important as it may be to deduce the nature of the computation that can be performed by the sharply localized units in the cortex, it is of equal importance to understand how arrays of these elements can be made to function together. It is only through the mutual interaction of large two-dimensional arrays of the elements that the cortex can analyse sensory data, at least as regards the identification game.

Since visual sensory data are mapped homeomorphically on to the primary sensory cortex, and since at this stage of their processing the localized nature of the cortical computation denies them any sort of computation extending over a significant portion of any interesting visual pattern, one seeks to know where the data are relayed following their reception in area 17. It can only be after this first cortico–cortical relay that significant areas of an input pattern can be made to interact. Unfortunately, little is known about systems and methods of data transmission between various portions of the cortical sheet. Such information is very difficult to elucidate and finding it is not a popular contemporary research interest. This is regrettable since a full understanding of cortical brain function is not likely to be achieved until the scheme of cortico–cortical interconnection is understood. What little is known of the scheme suggests that data from local cortical areas are broadcast widely to succeeding cortical areas by means of multitudinous axonal pathways originating from the discrete localized computing regions. McCulloch, for instance, described this phenomenon in terms of the strychnine neuronography experiments he was using to deduce cortico–cortical and thalamo–cortical connectivity patterns, as follows: 'When Dusser de Barenne and Kabrisky strychninized a pinhead spot on the area striata, strychnine spikes appeared at many points in the secondary visual areas as if the output from each spot in the area striata were scattered at random in the secondary visual area ' (see Dusser de Barenne *et al.* 1951). Such a statement seems to summarize basically what is known about the destination of data following its neat mapping on primary sensory cortex and it is necessary to try and deduce what sort of computation—in at least the sense of the identification game—can be performed by a device which broadcasts data widely and, seemingly, randomly to successive cortical sheets. A one-dimensional representation of this cortico–cortical connection scheme is shown in Figure 1.

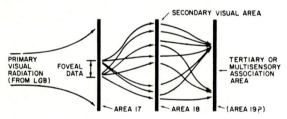

Figure 1. Cortico–cortical connection scheme transmitting visual data incoming from the lateral geniculate body (LGB).

Curiously enough, optical systems (which can easily be set up to perform interesting computations with two-dimensional patterns) fit McCulloch's description. For instance, the scheme of light-ray paths in a slide projector fits the diagram above; and the projector, if excited with a coherent light source, generates as an inadvertent concomitant of its projection of the slide, the two-dimensional Fourier transform of the slide image in an optical plane corresponding to the secondary visual area in the above diagram.

While two-dimensional optical computers are usually constructed with lenses (which are continuous two-dimensional refracting systems) and designed to operate in homogeneous propagation media such as air or water, such computational systems can be approximated by discrete pathway systems—mimicking the above diagram—using a fibre optical system. They can also be simulated and extensively investigated in digital computing machines using the same sort of discrete approximations to a spatially continuous system (Radoy 1967). Thus many of the interesting computational techniques possible in optical systems can be realized in equivalents employing discrete fibres.

As mentioned above, one of the interesting computations that an optical system can perform is to produce the two-dimensional Fourier transform of any two-dimensional photo transparency. It produces this transform because of the interference and reinforcement of various portions of sinusoidal electro-magnetic (light) fields propagating along pathways of different lengths within the system of lenses. The differences in path lengths—and hence time of propagation in a homogeneous medium—depend upon the refractive properties of, and the mutual physical relation among, the lenses in the system. In an optical homologue using fibres, or in a digital computation simulation, it is necessary to control propagation times in the individual pathways to mimic the cancellation and reinforcement that occurs intrinsically in the spatially continuous optical system. For a neurone homologue of such a system it would probably be necessary to maintain *consistent relative* propagation times in axonal pathways and provide sufficient overall synchronization of activity to allow the possibility of excitory post-synaptic potential and inhibitory post-synaptic potential interaction in individual neurones to provide the equivalent of reinforcement and interference found in the optical system. Whether or not these timing requirements are met in the cortico–cortical information propagation system has never been investigated to the authors' knowledge; to do so would require careful analysis of large amounts of data recorded from many closely spaced electrodes (probably between 0·5 to 0·05 mm separation) in several areas of related cortex, say in areas 17, 18 and 19. The fact that the mechanical arrangement of the cortico–cortical pathways is suggestive of such an interesting computation would probably make such an experiment worth while. It has suggested to us a digital computer investigation of the pattern recognition capabilities of such a system. This will now be described.

4. Pattern Recognition by Fourier Transformation

It is easy to show (Kabrisky 1961, 1966, 1967) that the pathway scheme shown in Figure 1 can support a two-dimensional pattern recognition scheme based on cross-correlation computations—including a learning and memory mechanism requiring no 'teacher'. However, it is easy to defeat a pattern recognition device based solely on cross-correlation, with patterns only slightly mutilated (by human standards) with respect to some previously 'learned' pattern. For instance, two H patterns such as the solid and dotted ones shown below will, in general, not be placed in the same list by a cross-correlator:

If, however, the low frequency components of the Fourier transforms of such H patterns are compared, it will be found that they do not differ substantially; thus the hope is raised that the small-local-mutilation problem, as a part of the general pattern recognition problem, might be solved by a universal, 'simple-minded' algorithm scheme—and one which might be feasible for neurone based computation. One might speculate that the lists required by the identification game might be produced by comparing easily and algorithmically derived transformations of input sensory patterns.

In this paper two-dimensional patterns will be characterized in the following manner. A given pattern will be entirely contained on a rectangular (or square) grid of finite dimensions. The extent of this grid will be designated by the co-ordinates $|x| < X$ and $|y| < Y$, where X and Y are chosen for mathematical convenience to be equal to one-half plus some integer. The pattern will be completely described by a real valued function, $f(x, y)$, which is defined only at the co-ordinate points at which x and y are both integers. These mathematical restraints correspond to the characterizing of a given pattern solely by the values of its intensity at a finite set of evenly spaced points. This type of pattern characterization is compatible with the human visual system as pointed out previously.

It can be shown (Radoy *op. cit.*) that for the type of function or pattern characterization described above the following transform pair exists.

$$F\left(j\frac{\pi}{X}, k\frac{\pi}{Y}\right) = \sum_{n=-(X-\frac{1}{2})}^{X-\frac{1}{2}} \sum_{m=-(Y-\frac{1}{2})}^{Y-\frac{1}{2}} f(n, m) \exp\left[i\left(nj\frac{\pi}{X} + mk\frac{\pi}{Y}\right)\right] \quad (1)$$

$$n, m = \text{integers}$$

$$f(n, m) = \frac{1}{4XY} \sum_{j=-(X-\frac{1}{2})}^{X-\frac{1}{2}} \sum_{k=-(Y-\frac{1}{2})}^{Y-\frac{1}{2}} F\left(j\frac{\pi}{X}, k\frac{\pi}{Y}\right) \exp\left[-i\left(nj\frac{\pi}{X} + mk\frac{\pi}{Y}\right)\right]. \quad (2)$$

$$j, k = \text{integers}$$

In this notation, $f(n, m)$ is the value of the function at the co-ordinate points at which x and y are integers. $F(j\pi/X, k\pi/Y)$ is the value of the pattern transformation at specific points in what is commonly called the spatial frequency plane.

Since this transform pair exists and since $f(x, y)$ is defined only at the points $f(n, m)$, it is clear from Equation (2) that $f(x, y)$, or the pattern characterization, is completely and uniquely described by the finite set of values $F(j\pi/X, k\pi/Y)$. Also, since the summation indices j and k cover the same range of integers as do the indices n and m respectively, for an N by M grid of values of $f(x, y)$, there exists a unique and invertible N by M grid of values of $F(j\pi/X, k\pi/Y)$.

For ease of notation, in the following discussion, the pattern characterization will be referred to as $f(x, y)$ and its transform will be denoted by $F(A, B)$. One should keep in mind, however, that these functions are defined only at specific points in their respective planes.

Equation (1) may also be written

$$F(A, B) = \sum \sum f(x, y) \left[\cos (Ax + By) + i \sin (Ax + By)\right]. \quad (3)$$

And, since $f(x, y)$ is real valued,

$$\text{Re}[F(A, B)] = \sum \sum f(x, y) \cos (Ax + By) \quad (4)$$

$$\text{Im}[F(A, B)] = \sum \sum f(x, y) \sin (Ax + By). \quad (5)$$

Re and Im refer to the 'real' and 'imaginary' components of Equation 3. In general $\exp(i\theta) = \cos \theta + i \sin \theta$, $\text{Re}[\exp(i\theta)] = \cos \theta$ and $\text{Im}[\exp(i\theta)] = \sin \theta$.

Since the cosine is an even valued and the sine is an odd valued function, one has the following relationships.

$$\text{Re}\,[F(A, B)] \quad = \quad \text{Re}\,[F(-A, -B)] \quad (6)$$

$$\text{Re}\,[F(A, -B)] = \quad \text{Re}\,[F(-A, B)] \quad (7)$$

$$\text{Im}\,[F(A, B)] \quad = -\text{Im}\,[F(-A, -B)] \quad (8)$$

$$\text{Im}\,[F(A, -B)] = -\text{Im}\,[F(-A, B)]. \quad (9)$$

From Equation (6) through (9) it is clear that all values of $F(A, B)$ may be determined if only some of them are known. Consider the set

$$F(A, B) \qquad A, B > 0$$
$$F(A, -B) \qquad A, B > 0$$
$$F(0, B) \qquad B > 0$$
$$F(A, 0) \qquad A \geqslant 0.$$

All values of $F(A, B)$ may be calculated if the above set is known. Consequently, this set can also be used to determine mathematically all values of $f(x, y)$.

The variables, A and B, of the transform $F(A, B)$ are spatial frequency parameters. From a qualitative standpoint the values of $F(A, B)$, for large values of A and B, relate to the degree of 'sharpness' or the high spatial frequency content of the pattern, $f(x, y)$. Correspondingly, $F(0, 0)$ relates to the 'D.C. level' or the total intensity contained in $f(x, y)$. If one sets $F(A, B)$ equal to zero for large values of A and B (or, equivalently, does not store these values), and then computes $f(x, y)$ by Equation (2), the function obtained will be a somewhat blurred representation of the original pattern characterization. Such a process is analogous to the passing of a sharp, or fast rise-time electrical pulse through a low-pass filter. The filter output will be a pulse which is a less sharp replica of the input pulse.

It seems reasonable to postulate that, in most pattern recognition mechanisms, the storing of a blurred representation of a particular pattern would be adequate for the purposes of recognizing other equivalent or highly similar patterns. Indeed, it may be argued that the human recognition system does just this to a certain degree: one does not 'remember' all the detail or the 'sharpness' of a particular pattern. Rather, what is retained is a somewhat more vague or 'blurred' representation of it.

The above line of reasoning leads to the questions, 'How much of the high spatial frequency content is not essential for pattern recognition?' and 'How much saving in pattern storage space may be achieved by not storing this "inessential" high frequency content?'. Experiments have been conducted with simple patterns in an effort to determine how much of the transform need be retained in order to keep the blurred representation 'recognizable'.

One might postulate that a pattern recognition device could operate on the following principle. The device evaluates and stores part of the transforms of the patterns which it is to remember. When it is called upon to recognize some input pattern, it obtains the inverse transforms of the data which it has stored and, in some way, compares these inverses with the input. The input is recognized as being that pattern whose inverse compares most favourably to the input or to the inverse transform of the input.

5. Pattern Recognition Using an 11 by 11 Unit Format

In order to test this last suggestion, simple patterns were described on 11 by 11 grids of data points. The complete transform of each of these patterns was calculated (running time = 5 sec on an IBM 7094). Then, using various amounts of the transforms, inverse patterns were calculated. An 11 by 11 pattern grid results in a transform function $F(A, B)$ which is evaluated at the points

$$A = -\frac{5\pi}{5\cdot5}, \ -\frac{4\pi}{5\cdot5}, \cdots, \ -\frac{\pi}{5\cdot5}, \ 0, \ \frac{\pi}{5\cdot5}, \cdots, \ \frac{5\pi}{5\cdot5}$$

$$B = -\frac{5\pi}{5\cdot5}, \ -\frac{4\pi}{5\cdot5}, \cdots, \ -\frac{\pi}{5\cdot5}, \ 0, \ \frac{\pi}{5\cdot5}, \cdots, \ \frac{5\pi}{5\cdot5}.$$

Inverse patterns were constructed using the following sets of points of $F(A, B)$.

Set I:

$$A = -\frac{2\pi}{5\cdot5}, \ -\frac{\pi}{5\cdot5}, \ 0, \ \frac{\pi}{5\cdot5}, \ \frac{2\pi}{5\cdot5}$$

i.e. only the two lowest spatial frequency components.

$$B = -\frac{2\pi}{5\cdot5}, \ -\frac{\pi}{5\cdot5}, \ 0, \ \frac{\pi}{5\cdot5}, \ \frac{2\pi}{5\cdot5}$$

Set II:

$$A = -\frac{3\pi}{5\cdot5}, \cdots, \ \frac{3\pi}{5\cdot5}$$

Set I plus an additional frequency component.

$$B = -\frac{3\pi}{5\cdot5}, \cdots, \ \frac{3\pi}{5\cdot5}$$

Set III:

$$A = -\frac{4\pi}{5\cdot5}, \cdots, \ \frac{4\pi}{5\cdot5}$$

Set II plus an additional frequency component.

$$B = -\frac{4\pi}{5\cdot5}, \cdots, \ \frac{4\pi}{5\cdot5}$$

A typical result of this sort of procedure can be seen using a capital H as the test pattern. Figure 2 shows the 11 by 11 characterization of the letter ' H ' which was used. In this figure an ' X ' denotes a data point at which the intensity of the pattern was set, arbitrarily, to 50 units. All other data points on the individual 11 by 11 grid were of zero intensity.

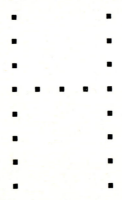

Figure 2.   Representation of H pattern.

The reconstructions of this pattern using Sets I, II and III of its transform are illustrated in Figures 3, 4 and 5 respectively. The contours of Figure 3 are not easily recognizable as being representative of the letter H. However, Figure 4 was identified by most observers as being an H and Figure 5 was clearly identifiable. On the basis of this one test it would appear that the

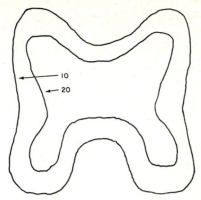

Figure 3.   Reconstruction of H pattern using only low spatial frequency components (Set I).

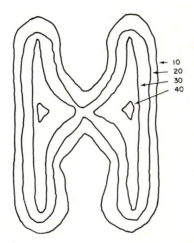

Figure 4.   Reconstruction of H pattern using Set II frequency components.

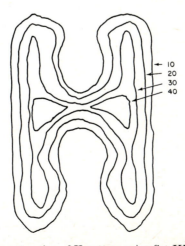

Figure 5.   Reconstruction of H pattern using Set III components.

retaining of Set II of the transform grid might be sufficient to enable a system to recognize 11 by 11 pattern representations of alphabetic characters.

An identification game-playing machine must be able to do more than answer the question, ' Is this an H ? '   In particular it would have to store or remember not just one pattern but many, and it would have to be able to identify which of those stored patterns a given input pattern was most similar to.   Figure 6

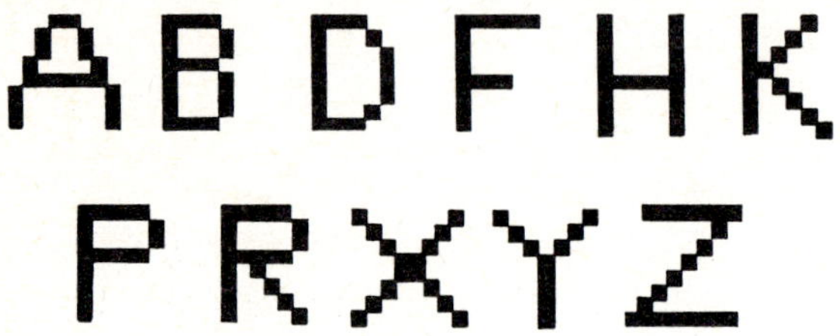

Figure 6.   11 × 11 master patterns.

contains the 11 by 11 master pattern characterizations stored by the system tested.   Each of these was stored solely as eight data points.   These were,
$\mathrm{Re}[F(0, \pi/5\cdot5)]$, $\mathrm{Re}[F(\pi/5\cdot5, \pi/5\cdot5)]$, $\mathrm{Re}[F(\pi/5\cdot5, 0)]$, $\mathrm{Re}[F(\pi/5\cdot5, -\pi/5\cdot5)]$
and
$\mathrm{Im}[F(0, \pi/5\cdot5)]$, $\mathrm{Im}[F(\pi/5\cdot5, \pi/5\cdot5)]$, $\mathrm{Im}[F(\pi/5\cdot5, 0)]$, $\mathrm{Im}[F(\pi/5\cdot5, -\pi/5\cdot5)]$.
Each test pattern was also characterized by these eight data points.   Figure 7 illustrates the test patterns used.   The absolute magnitude of the difference between each test pattern data point and a corresponding master pattern data point was calculated, and these differences were totalled over all eight points. The system chose the master pattern for which this total was the smallest. Table 1 contains the results of these tests.   Listed in this table are the first and second ' choices ' of the system and the corresponding difference levels computed for each test pattern.

Table 1.   11 by 11 pattern test results

Pattern number	First choice	Second choice
1	A: 346	H: 777
2	A: 453	H: 858
3	A: 508	R: 715
4	R: 650	A: 675
5	A: 928	R:1027
6	D: 689	Z: 961
7	F: 816	P: 849
8	H: 710	D: 870
9	B: 398	R: 514
10	R: 568	P: 711
11	P: 345	R: 816
12	B:1095	Y:1167
13	Y: 277	B: 692

Exact evaluation of the results contained in Table 1 is not possible, since it is not always clear to a human observer which of the master patterns the system should have chosen.   However, since the authors made up most of the test patterns used, and since they were made with specific master patterns in mind, it is at least possible to use that basis in evaluating the system's performance.   In the author's opinion, the system made an erroneous decision only in the case of test pattern 12.   Whether or not the reader agrees exactly with this evaluation, it is clear that the system, tested this way, works fairly well.

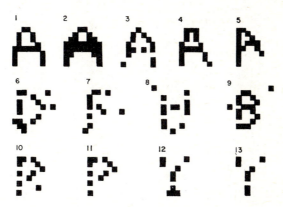

Figure 7.   11 × 11 test pattern set.   Test numbers are given beside the patterns.

Another important point is that the 'shape sensitivity' of the system appears to be quite high.   This is illustrated most graphically by a comparison of the results of test patterns 10 and 11.   These two patterns differ at only one point.   However, this slight difference is enough to enable the system to switch from an unambiguous identification of an 'R' to an unambiguous identification of a 'P'.   A discussion of the results of tests 12 and 13 is contained in Section 6.

5.1. *21 by 21 Pattern Test Results*

The degree of success achieved with 11 by 11 alphabetic pattern representations suggested the consideration of larger pattern arrays.   If one transforms 21 by 21 pattern characterizations, the lowest spatial frequency terms, $F(A, B)$, obtained involve A or B or both, being equal to $\pi/10\cdot5$.   This is a comparatively low frequency term; it would seem that very little of a pattern's shape could affect such a term and also that it would be unlikely that a 21 by 21 pattern could be adequately represented solely by terms of this order. Additionally, a 21 by 21 pattern is potentially more complex than is an 11 by 11 pattern, and it might be argued that, in general, one could not effectively describe a 21 by 21 pattern with, perhaps, only eight data points even though this might be adequate for the simpler 11 by 11 patterns.   Still, though, in light of the 11 by 11 results, one might hope to operate a recognition scheme with rather limited sets of stored data especially compared to the, say, $(21)^2$ storage elements that would be required if such a pattern were to be stored completely.

Figure 8 illustrates the master pattern set used in the 21 by 21 unit tests. Each of these ten patterns was characterized solely by the following spatial frequency values.

$$F(0, \pi/10\cdot5),\ \ F(\pi/10\cdot5\ \pi/10\cdot5),\ \ F(\pi/10\cdot5.\ 0),\ \ F(\pi/10\cdot5, -\pi/10\cdot5).$$

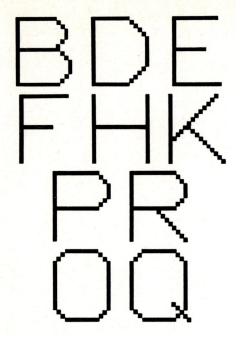

Figure 8.   21 × 21 master patterns.

The five patterns illustrated in Figure 9 were used as test patterns.   The system was set to choose patterns in the same way that the 11 by 11 grid system operated.

The results of these tests are shown in Table 2.   They indicate that, at least for the pattern tested, the system can indeed operate with only these lowest spatial frequencies.   The ability of the method to identify correctly both

Table 2.   21 by 21 pattern test results

Pattern number	First choice	Second choice
1	O: 403	Q: 531
2	Q: 396	O: 488
3	F: 810	E:1353
4	F: 651	E: 909
5	E: 647	F: 894

Patterns 1 and 2 in Figure 9 is particularly striking.   Patterns 3 and 5 were also properly identified.   The result of test 4 is, however, not as good.   Whether the test figure was closer to an 'F' or to an 'E' was subject to debate.   However, it was clear to a human observer, *SKILLED WITH THIS ALPHABET*, that Pattern 4 was not a *better* 'F' than Pattern 3, despite the fact that the system evaluated it as being so, as can be seen by comparing tests 3 and 4.

It would thus appear that this method of pattern recognition is quite successful, though not infallible.

6. Analysis of Recognition by Low Spatial Frequencies

In the preceding section systems were discussed which identified a pattern characterization, $f(n, m)$, by the value of terms of the form,

$$F(A, B) = \sum_n \sum_m f(n, m) \exp [i(nA + mB)].$$

The choice of the values of A and B used in that section had been dictated by the mathematical considerations contained in Section 4, i.e. A and B must be of the form $j\pi/X$ and $k\pi/Y$ respectively, where X and Y related to the grid size. These particular values of A and B are of importance if one wishes to be able to reconstruct $f(n, m)$ from $F(A, B)$. For an identification game machine, however, the choice of A and B need not necessarily be of the form used in Section 5. Consequently, one might wonder if there might not be some other values of A or B or both which would be more suitable for the types of systems discussed in that section.

Consider the following simple one-dimensional situation.

$$f_1(x) = \begin{matrix} 1 & x = x_0 \\ 0 & \text{elsewhere} \end{matrix}$$

$$f_2(x) = \begin{matrix} 1 & x = x_0 + d \\ 0 & \text{elsewhere.} \end{matrix}$$

We intend to ' code ' $f_1(x)$ and $f_2(x)$ in the forms

$$F_1(A) = \sum f_1(x) \exp (iAx)$$
$$F_2(A) = \sum f_2(x) \exp (iAx).$$

Intuitively, we want the difference between $F_1(A)$ and $F_2(A)$ to be the greatest when d is greatest. In fact, it seems that we should require $F_1(A) - F_2(A)$ to be a monotonically increasing function of d. For this example,

$$|F_1(A) - F_2(A)| = |\exp (iAx_0) - \exp [iA(x_0 + d)]|$$
$$= |1 - \exp (iAd)|$$

where d represents a shift between two otherwise identical functions $f_1(x)$ and $f_2(x)$. The quantity $[1 - \exp (iAd)]$ is a maximum when Ad is equal to π. If the maximum attainable value of d is equal to N, one should choose A equal to π/N. (Notice also that the computation of the difference between $F_1(A)$ and $F_2(A)$ is based on the phasors themselves rather than on the components of these phasors. The use of the difference in the components of the phasors does not yield a result which is solely a function of d.) Thus, for a one-dimensional grid which is $N + 1$ units long, one has A equal to π/N, whereas to develop a Fourier Series representation of patterns described on such a grid, the lowest, non-zero, spatial frequency computed would be equal to $\pi/(N + 1)/2$.

The above reasoning does not extend easily to two dimensions. But, using it as a rough guide, it would appear that, for 21 by 21 patterns, possibly better pattern identification could be achieved by using A or B or both equal to $\pi/20$, rather than $\pi/10\cdot5$. In order to test this possibility, a system was simulated which computed

$$|F_1(\pi/20, 0) - F_2(\pi/20, 0)| + |F_1(0, \pi/20) - F_2(0, \pi/20)|$$
$$+ |F_1(\pi/20, \pi/20) - F_2(\pi/20, \pi/20)| + |F_1(\pi/20, -\pi/20) - F_2(\pi/20, -\pi/20)|$$

as a means of comparing 21 by 21 pattern characterizations. The same five test

patterns illustrated in Figure 9 were compared against the master patterns of
Figure 8. The results of these tests are compared in Table 3 with the results
which were obtained for these same patterns in Section 5.

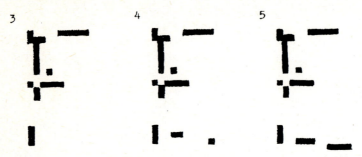

Figure 9. 21×21 test patterns.

To state flatly that one of these methods was superior to the other would
be unwarranted. These results clearly demonstrate, however, that there is
nothing special about using A or B or both equal to $\pi/10\cdot5$ when working with
a 21 by 21 pattern grid. Indeed, one might find it advantageous to characterize a pattern by several terms (not necessarily four) of the form $F(A, B)$,
where A and B each take on many different values. Work in this direction
is continuing.

Table 3.   Comparison of 21 by 21 pattern test results

Pattern number	$(\pi/10\cdot5)$ test		$(\pi/20)$ test	
	First choice	Second choice	First choice	Second choice
1	O: 403	Q: 531	O: 161	Q: 313
2	Q: 396	O: 488	Q: 186	O: 208
3	F: 810	E: 1353	F: 317	P: 779
4	F: 651	E: 909	F: 393	P: 679
5	E: 647	F: 894	E: 276	K: 611

Using systems of this sort, the representation of a pattern for a particular
value of A and B is a phasor. If two different patterns have the same, or
nearly the same, phasors for all values of A and B considered, the patterns
will be rated as similar by the system. Consider the following three patterns.

1	2	3
X	X	X
X	X	X
X	X	X
X	X	X
$x=0$	$x=0$ $x=d_1$	$x=0$ $x=d_2$

A pattern recognition system should note some similarity between 1 and 2
and should interpret 3 as being somewhat different from the other two. If A
is equal to π/d_2, one has the following relationships.

$$F_1(A, 0) = 4$$

$$F_3(A, 0) = 0.$$

$$F_2(A, 0) \approx F_1(A, 0)$$

If

$$A = \pi/d_1 \text{ and } d_2 = 6d_1,$$
$$F_1(A, 0) = F_3(A, 0) = 4, \quad F_2(A, 0) = 0.$$

The above is a simple illustration of the fact that A and B should be chosen small enough so that $|(nA + mB)| < \pi/2$. This restriction helps to keep highly dissimilar spatial effects from having similar terms of the form

$$\exp[i(nA + mB)].$$

Also, it ensures that terms due to similar shape or structure will be nearly equal.

The above precaution alone will not serve to make the system infallible. It is still possible for the net phasors of two patterns to be nearly equal though the individual terms in each sum,

$$\sum \sum \exp[i(nA + mB)]$$

are dissimilar. Thus, two unfortunate situations may arise. Two different master patterns may have essentially the same net phasors or a distortion of one master pattern may have net phasors which are close to those of another master pattern.

This latter situation is the type which occurred when testing Pattern 12 of the 11 by 11 pattern set. This pattern and the patterns ' Y ' and ' B ' are illustrated again in Figure 10. In this figure, the grid origin, $x = y = 0$, is noted with $a +$. From this figure, one can see that Pattern 12 and pattern ' B ' are both fairly symmetric about the origin, while pattern ' Y ' is very ' top-heavy '. This similarity between Pattern 12 and pattern ' B ' was enough to make all of their net phasors nearly equal, and it resulted in the ' confusing ' of the system. Pattern 13 not only ' looks ' like a ' Y ', but it is also ' top-heavy '. As a result, 13 was correctly identified.

```
                                  12                   13

XXXX         X       X       X       X       X       X
X    X       X    X          X               X
X    X       X  X                 X                      X
XXXX         X                    X               X
X +  X       +                    +               +
X    X       X
X    X       X                    X               X
XXXX         X                  XXX               X
```

Figure 10. 11×11 test patterns.

The results may be summarized in the following broad generalities. The spatial frequencies used in this method of pattern identification should be comparatively low. In such a case, small spatial distortions will not confuse the system. If the frequencies are chosen to be ' too ' low, significant but small structural differences (like the difference between an ' O ' and a ' Q ') will not be detectable. The more master patterns which a system must store, the more chance there is that two of these patterns will have highly similar phasors. Such a situation would cause considerable difficulty for the system. Large spatial distortions or considerable ' noise ' can cause erroneous decisions to be made. Decisions made by the system are not necessarily of the type which the human visual system would or could make—no one thinks that Pattern 12 looks like a ' B '. Much more work, both theoretical and experimental, will probably have to be done before the above generalities can be made more specific or quantitative.

7. Conclusion

Several aspects of the Fourier Series Transformation which might have a bearing on methods of pattern recognition have been investigated. The conclusions which can be drawn from this investigation are:

1. An N by M pattern characterization has a unique and invertible N by M Fourier Series Transform.

2. Only one-half of the transform is required in order to describe a real-valued pattern uniquely.

3. This transform may be obtained by a digital computer, by optical diffraction, by a finite fibre optic net, and possibly by the human neural network.

4. A recognizable reconstruction of most patterns can be made by inverting only the lower frequency portion of the transform.

5. By simply correlating the lowest spatial frequencies of transforms, a start can be made in playing the ' identification game '.

Le réseau des connexions et des voies cheminant l'information dans le système visuel des Primates et de l'Homme présente, aux yeux de l'ingénieur informaticien, une curieuse ressemblance avec un ordinateur optique à structure bi-dimensionnelle destiné à la reconnaissance des structures. Les portions du système visuel situées en avant du cortex visuel primaire se présentent essentielle-ment comme une reproduction homéomorphe topologiquement précise de l'image réitnienne, du moins dans la proximité de la fovéa. L'analyse des aspects topologiques de l'image visuelle et, par conséquent, la " reconnaissance des structures " doit donc avoir lieu dans le cortex visuel primaire et dans les aires corticales plus profondes. Nous avons montré, dans un travail antérieur, comment les modes de connexions intra- et intercorticales pouvaient donner lieu à un schème de fonctionnement combinant des opérations mnésiques et arithmétiques et capable de reconnaître des structures par une variation dans la corrélation croisée bi-dimensionnelle. Cet article présente un développement du modèle précédent et permet de réaliser une reconnaissance de structures par le calcul de la transformée bi-dimensionnelle de Fourier des images d'entrée, d'une façon analogue au calcul des réseaux de diffraction de Fraunhofer au moyen d'ordinateurs optiques. On montre que l'utilisation de la transformée de Fourier d'une structure inconnue traitée par la suite au moyen d'un schème de corrélations, aboutit à un système de reconnaissance de structures qui n'est pas facilement perturbé par de petites mutilations locales des structures d'entrée qui cependant compromettent sérieusement les schèmes de reconnaissance des structures à corrélations linéaires.

Die groben Verbindungsmuster der Informationswege im visuellen System der Primaten und Menschen, geprüft von einem Informations—Verarbeitungs—Ingenieur, ähneln merkwürdiger-weise dem zweidimensionalen optischen Computer, den er selbst in der Absicht baut, das Erkennen von Mustern zu verwirklichen. Die Teile des visuellen Systems unterhalb der primären Hirnrinde besorgen in der Hauptsache eine topographisch genaue, homeomorphe Aufzeichnung des Netzhaut bildes, wenigstens in der Nachbarschaft der Fovea. Die Analyse der topologischen Aspekte der visuellen Szene und die " Muster-Erkennung " muss daher in der primären Hirnrinde und den anschliessenden Hirnpartien stattfinden.

Wir haben früher mitgeteilt, wie intra- und intercorticale Verbindungen ein kombiniertes Gedächtnis—und Berechnungssystem enthalten könnten, welches zur Muster—Erkennung durch Variation zwei-dimensionaler Kreuz-Korrelationen fähig ist. Diese Atbeit ist der Bericht über eine Ausdehnung des früheren Modells, die es ermöglicht, Muster zu erkennen durch Berechnung zwei-dimensionaler Fourier-Transformationen eingegangener Bilder in einer Weise, die der Berechnung von Fraunhofer Diffractionsmustern in optischen Computern isomorph ist. Es wird gezeigt, dass die Verwendung der Fourier-Transformation an einem unbekannten Muster in einem Korrelations-Folge-Schema zu einem Muster-Erkennungs-System führt, das nicht leicht durch die lokalen kleinen Verzerrungen des eingegebenen Musters verfälscht werden kann, welche in hässlicher Weise lineare Korrelations-Erkennungs-Schemata belasten.

References

Bok, S. T., 1959, *Histonomy of the Cerebral Cortex* (New York: Elsevier Publishing Company).

Dowling, J. E., and Boycott, B. B., 1966, Organization of the primate retina: electron micro-scopy. *Proceedings of the Royal Society*, Series B, **166,** 80–111.

DUSSER DE BARENNE, H. G., BAILEY, P., VON BONIN, G., and McCULLOCH, W. S., 1951, *The Isocortex of the Chimpanzee* (Urbana: UNIVERSITY OF ILLINOIS PRESS).

ERVIN, F. R., 1964, On-line computer techniques for analysis of the visual system. *Symposium on the Analysis of Central Nervous System and Cardiovascular Data using Computer Methods* (Washington, D.C.: NASA (SP–72)).

HUBEL, D. H., and WIESEL, T. N., 1962, Receptive fields, binocular interaction, and functional architecture in the cat's visual cortex. *Journal of Physiology*, **160**, 106–154.

KABRISKY, M., 1961, A spatially iterated memory organ patterned after the cerebral cortex. *Preprints of the Papers Presented at the 16th National Meeting of the Association for Computing Machinery.*

KABRISKY, M., 1966, *A Proposed Model for Visual Information Processing in the Human Brain* (Urbana and London: UNIVERSITY OF ILLINOIS PRESS).

KABRISKY, M., 1967, Visual information processing in the brain. *Models for the Perception of Speech and Visual Form* (Edited by WATHEN-DUNN) (Cambridge, Mass: MASSACHUSETTS INSTITUTE OF TECHNOLOGY PRESS).

KUFFLER, S. W., 1953, Discharge patterns and functional organization of mammalian retina. *Journal of Neurophysiology*, **16**, 37–68.

LORENTE DE NÓ, R., 1949, Cerebral cortex: architecture, intracortical connections, motor projections. One section in *Physiology of the Nervous System* (3rd edition by J. F. FULTON) (London: OXFORD UNIVERSITY PRESS).

MOUNTCASTLE, V. B., 1957, Modality and topographic properties of single neurons of cat's somatic sensory cortex. *Journal of Neurophysiology*, **20**, 408–434.

POLYAK, S., 1957, *The Vertebrate Visual System* (Chicago: UNIVERSITY OF CHICAGO PRESS).

RADOY, C. M., 1967, *Pattern Recognition by Fourier Series Transformation.* MSEE Thesis GE/EE/67A–11, United States Air Force Institute of Technology (U.S. Defence Documentation Center, Washington, D.C.).

WIESEL, T. N., and HUBEL, D. H., 1966, Spatial and chromatic interactions in the lateral geniculate body of the Rhesus monkey. *Journal of Neurophysiology*, **29**, 1115–1156.

The Perception of Symbols for Machine Displays

By R. S. EASTERBY

Applied Psychology Department, University of Aston in Birmingham, England

The role of pattern perception theory based on the Gestalt view of perception is discussed in relation to the practical design of symbols for machine displays. Experimental studies of discrimination and apprehension of meaning of symbols are reviewed, and some recommended perceptual principles important to symbol design are summarized.

1. Introduction: The Need for Symbolic Representation

The application of psychology to problems of equipment design requires the development of new skills to exploit current knowledge from ' pure ' research. One aspect which needs attention is the narrowing of the gap between the elucidation of some theoretical principles and their utilization in some practical design task; the ergonomist of course sees himself in this role, and it was while actively engaging in ergonomics work that the need to study the psychological aspects of symbol design became apparent.

Previously, the identification of display and control elements for machines had been achieved predominantly by written words and abbreviations, but in the last decade designers have resorted to highly structured and simplified symbols to convey information.   The use of symbols is not, of course, confined to machine displays, but mass technology systems, such as transportation systems, rely to an ever-increasing extent on symbolic information transmission.

With international boundaries being diffused by rapidly increasing trade, many machine systems involving human participation require language-free displays.   While the motivation for such displays may be blatantly commercial, the issues it raises are of theoretical and practical importance, and the need to pay particular attention to symbol displays has been the beneficial effect of much more detailed attention to display design as a whole.

An obvious question to pose is the relative efficacy of symbolic display representation and verbal identification using normal printed text.   Certainly, from an applied standpoint, this relative utility should have been evaluated, but to date there are few published studies available.   A study by Walker and Nicolay in 1965 compared European and American road signs (where the essential difference is symbolic versus verbal information display) and their experiments demonstrate superior recognition performance for the symbolic, European-style road signs.   In most applications it is tacitly assumed that symbols are a superior form of information display.   But it is possible that it is the technical and commercial advantages offered by symbolic displays (rather than their psychological advantages) which are the primary reasons for their widespread use in many machine systems.

It is, of course, paradoxical that man has used pictographic and iconic recording (which was followed by the development of alphabets and language) and now, with increasingly complex technology, he must revert to symbolic representation.   There may well be unexplored ideas in Egyptian hieroglyphics which we could use to define more adequately the principles of symbol design.

What is manifestly apparent is the need for procedures to facilitate in many different contexts this contemporary design activity; it is the purpose of this paper to propose such procedures and to elaborate some of the desirable visual characteristics of symbols for optimum perception.

2.   Structural Factors in Symbol Design

If we wish to establish a usable sign set, it must be based on some systematic rationale, otherwise the user may well interpret signs differently on successive occasions.   Sign sets are in fact a form of simple symbolic language with interacting concepts being identified by sets of interacting pictorial or abstract signs.   We may therefore exploit some of the formal properties of languages to guide us in the construction of a simple symbol language.   Thus we can consider pragmatic principles which specify the context in which we wish the signs to be interpreted; we can consider semantic principles which define the relationships between the signs and the things they stand for; and lastly we can specify the syntactic principles which define the relationships of the signs with one another.   These inherent pragmatic, semantic and syntactic structural properties of the sign system are important determinates of the perceptibility since they provide the desirable 'set' and contextual cues to the observer who is attempting to define the meaning of the symbols.   These structural notions have been fully explored in other papers (Easterby 1967, 1969).   Suffice to note here that there must be agreement on these pragmatic, semantic and syntactic principles before the visual geometric characteristics of the symbols are defined.   The important inference here is that it is of little use deciding on the visual qualities of the symbol until the context in which they are to be interpreted is agreed, together with adequate definition of the required symbolic referents and the interrelations between these individual concepts. With these propositions settled it is then appropriate to investigate the visual qualities of the symbols for optimum perceptibility.

3.   Experience, Stereotypes and Learning of Symbols

The notion of 'perceptual set' is an important theoretical aspect of symbol perception.   The observer's experience of using symbolic information, the stereotype symbol for a particular function together with learning and training are all factors likely to influence approaches to symbol design.

It is often assumed that observers should be able to guess the meaning of symbols at first exposure.   This concept has little operational relevance except to indicate the presence of transfer of training effects (positive or negative) from one context to another.   Speed and accuracy of recall after suitable training are far more reliable indices of symbol utility.

Laboratory studies have, however, emphasized the relative or absolute apprehension of meaning; e.g. Karsh and Mudd (1962) demonstrated that observers using only prior experience assigned meaning with equal facility, no matter whether the symbols were presented all together or serially in random order.   Their intention here was to develop a suitably sensitive measure of the utility of an individual symbol in defining a functional concept.   This measurement was in fact achieved, thus enabling unsatisfactory symbols to be identified and then redesigned after successive experimental trials.   But this form of study can only lead to a more rapid convergence to an optimum set of symbol shapes.   There also is scope for evaluation of the role of training of the user population so that the recognition and apprehension of meaning is 100 per cent accurate.

For small sets of symbols (less than 10) accurate recognition would appear to be easily achieved (Brainard *et al.* 1961).   For large sets of symbols, Mackie's (1967) report on the learning of road traffic signs indicates that exposure to symbols in the context of everyday use as the sole form of training gives a very slow rate of acquisition of meaning.   In these studies only 60 per cent accuracy was achieved after two years' operational use of new signs.   The obvious point here is that small sets (of about 7–9 symbols) impose no severe load on memory and perception—a not uncommon finding in other memory tasks (Miller 1956); but larger sets of symbols (usually up to 100 in most applications) are more difficult to remember.   Obviously structural aspects of the large sign sets can be an important factor in the perceiving and memorizing of the individual signs.

Thus simple laboratory studies can discriminate between individual symbols in terms of ease of assignation and ease of recall of meaning and they can determine whether a shape satisfactorily signifies a particular functional concept (Mudd and Karsh 1961).   But of course the shape and its graphic interpretation, in terms of line outline thickness, contrasting figures, etc., may interact at the operational level.   Hopefully, though, we can have some separation of these two significant decisions about a design of symbol.

We can evaluate the shape for a given concept based on the definition, by experiment if necessary, of the response stereotype for a particular function. There would appear to be no absolutes in allocating a symbolic realization of a particular concept.   An intuitive design approach guesses at a good symbol while an experimental approach, which we advocate here, attempts to define a symbol stereotype and then, further, to validate this stereotype by experiment. To achieve the optimum form of that particular shape we may then proceed to manipulate this shape using perceptual notions from the theory of pattern perception and discrimination.   Thus it is to these figural factors in symbol perception that we must now devote some attention.

4.   Detail Definition of Symbol Forms

Two separate, but related, issues are important in symbol design—discriminability and meaning.   The observer must be able to distinguish the elements of the set from one another and then define the concepts for which the individual symbols stand.

4.1. *Symbol Discriminability*

Discrimination studies of different basic abstract forms (circles, ellipses, stars, crosses) have shown that no single geometrical dimension universally qualifies optimum discrimination.   These discrimination studies are of course purely psychophysical—the discriminations were made without any reference to meaning.   Studies such as the one by Casperson (in 1950) have concluded that for six different figures, the best predictors of discriminability are:

      triangles and ellipses—area
      rectangles and diamonds—maximum dimension
      stars and crosses—perimeter.

Between these different classes of symbol there are important relative differences in their discriminability both as regards search time and accuracy (Williams and Falzon 1963 a and b). These data refer to symbols which, within the context of the experiment, were not meaningful, but the results enable useful generalizations to be made about suitable shapes. Simple solid geometric shapes give good accuracy and low search time (confirming the discussions on contour generation in Section 4.2 below), but when solid figures require superimposed lines (e.g. slashes for negation) they then prove less satisfactory than outline forms. Thus simple outline shapes—circles, squares —may be subjected to superimposed horizontal and vertical lines without significant impairment of their discriminability.

These discrimination experiments are important for two reasons. Firstly they identify the limiting geometrical characteristics of a symbol design, unrelated to its meaning. Secondly, they define the best characteristics for abstract symbols which visually portray an abstract concept. We need these abstract elements, circles, triangles, as constituent parts of symbols, e.g. arrow-heads, enclosing circles, triangles and squares. These discrimination data enable accurate definition of these forms so that they are discriminable from one another. For the optimum definition of more meaningful shapes, we must take the evaluation process one stage further than the psychophysical, and define the best features for perception.

4.2. *Symbol Perceptibility*

The real difficulties arise when we try to define what we mean by a ' good ' symbol. Any attempt to formulate an aesthetic judgment is subject to wide individual differences and prejudices, and it is thus important to treat symbols as more than just an exercise in applied art. We could argue that as long as a symbol is visible, it will in fact be satisfactory; but it is possible to conceive a whole range of shapes which are all equally visible, but some of the symbols distinguish themselves by appearing more usable (more meaningful) than others. Consider, for example, the many different interpretations of the common arrow as a direction indicator. All these different shapes are quite legible, but many of them distort the arrow form to such an extent that we intuitively feel that some are much better than others, and in fact some studies have demonstrated this feature (Rutley and Christie 1966). In some early studies Mackworth also appreciated these aspects when considering shape coding of display material for aircraft operations control rooms (Bartlett and Mackworth 1950).

Thus, while it is important to appreciate that size, area, perimeter, brightness and contrast are significant, more important perceptual features may be vital in terms of performance, especially when the task situation is critical (e.g. Provins *et al.* 1957). Visibility and discriminability are necessary but not sufficient conditions for perceptibility; it is relatively easy to ensure that a sign can be seen, but there are other more subtle characteristics which may be varied to ensure that the meaning of a symbol is accurately and readily perceived. There is, for example, a basic meaning associated with a particular shape (e.g. an arrow) and the apprehension of this meaning may be facilitated or hindered depending on how the form is defined—in the case of an arrow, the size and relative proportions and shape of the shaft and the head, etc. The determinants of shape and form are the *figures* in the visual field, which in turn are characterized by their contour. The contour may be defined by a line outline or, as in the case of a solid figure, a contrast boundary. This delineation of one part of the visual field from the other, the 'figure/ground' phenomenon, was first recognized and investigated by the Gestalt psychologists, and much of the perceptual theory which would appear to be of any practical value in symbol design derives from their ideas and experiments. From these Gestalt principles comes the concept of 'figural goodness'. The perceptual processes, in attempting to decode the incoming visual stimuli, examine the different structural patterns for clarity and stability. The more this perceptual process is enhanced by the inherent clarity and stability in the visual sensation supplied by the form, then the more 'figural goodness' that form is said to possess. The percept, i.e. the meaning of the form, is based on the clearest and stablest pattern. Thus, if we wish to avoid confusion and ambiguity, we must have maximum 'figural goodness' which in turn implies high internal organization and stability of the visual form (Figure 1).

As Vernon (1952) reports.

> 'With any perception process there is a spontaneous tendency on the part of the observer to segregate the incoming sensory patterns into groups. The observer segregates the visual field into separate comprehensible parts; some of these parts are ignored while the remainder command detailed attention. Even the apparently formless visual fields do not manifest themselves in human perception as entirely amorphous, unorganised masses. We strive to comprehend the superficially formless by perceiving multiplicities of figure groupings in an effort after meaning.'

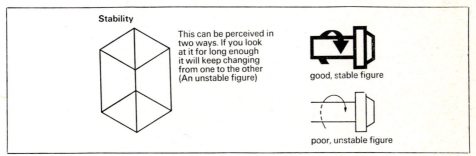

Figure 1.   Definition of figure/ground : stability.

4.3. *Detail Figural Features for Optimum Perception*

For a figure to be defined it must possess contour, and this contour can be generated either by a line or a contrast boundary. Now although a line actually has a finite area in physical terms, geometrically and psychologically this is not so; we perceive lines as lines—not as areas. Lines exhibit shape, and more important, if a line forms a closed or nearly closed figure, we no longer perceive *a line* on a homogeneous ground but perceive *a surface figure* bounded by that edge defined by the line. We could equally well define a surface figure by a contrast boundary, i.e. a solid shape with the outline generated by an abrupt change in contrast at the edges of the surface figure.

An important principle first defined experimentally by Gottschaldt (reported in Koffka 1935) is the psychological superiority of the contrast-bounded figure (silhouette) over the line form. It may be that the line-bounded form is potentially ambiguous since there is a surface figure defined by the ' inside ' of the line as well as the ' outside ', whereas the contrast-bounded figure only has an ' outside ' boundary. These differences between the perceptual qualities of line and contrast-bounded figures lead to a useful principle applicable to symbol design; we may exploit these differential psychological features to emphasize one part of a symbol figure at the expense of another. Thus with simple two-dimensional symbol images we can make one part (contrast bounded) appear to lie on top of another less important part (line bounded) (Figure 2).

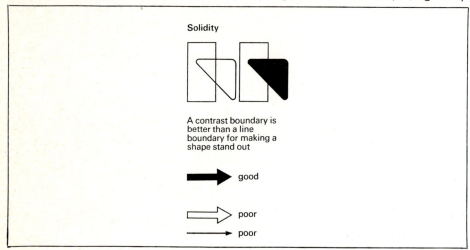

Figure 2.   Contour definition: line and contrast boundaries.

A discussion of contour involves two further issues—closure and continuity. Experimental evidence points to the superiority of closed figures. The tendency of human perceptual mechanisms is to choose figures so as to achieve high internal figural organization (Bartlett 1931, Vernon *op. cit.*). In many studies, summarized by these two, subjects asked to produce *unclosed* figures invariably drew the figures as *closed*.

Equally the continuity of the figure has a strong influence on its perceptibility. Gottschaldt's early experiments (see Koffka 1935) with figures of differing smoothness of outline ably demonstrate a principle applicable to symbol designs. Figures with a strong tendency to smooth continuous outline are figurally good. (This explains the unique qualities of the circle and its fundamental contribution to all symbol sets.   See Figures 3 and 4.)

The visual integration of a symbol has a significant influence on its perception. Symmetry, simplicity and unity of the visual form naturally facilitate its organization in the perceptual process (Figure 5). In addition, integration by use of similarly shaped visual elements in different symbols relates the members of the symbol set to one another and ensures that they are perceived as belonging together. The most important of these integrating elements in machine symbols is the arrow; by consistent application of the different forms of the arrow shape (directional, functional, relative motion, dimensional) the observer can be ' set ' to perceive particular meaning in the symbols containing those elements, by having previously encountered the arrow in other elements (Figure 6).

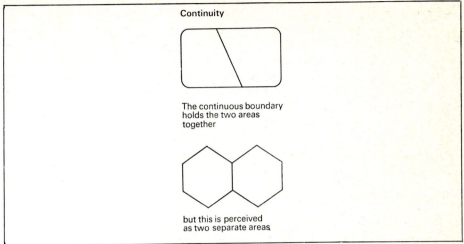

Figure 3.   Contour definition: the importance of continuity.

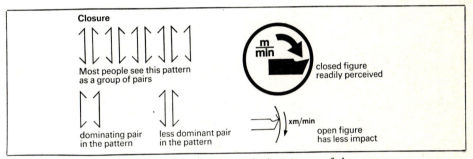

Figure 4.   Contour definition: the importance of closure.

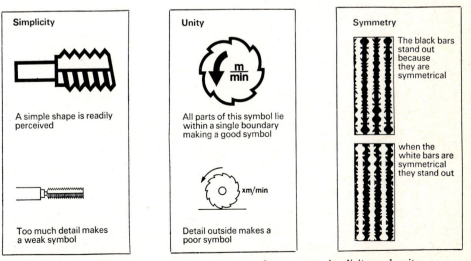

Figure 5.   Figure definition: the importance of symmetry, simplicity and unity.

5. Summary

All of the propositions explored above have some relevance to symbol design. Indeed the implications of some of these theoretical notions is quite general and decisive. The more we can match the characteristics of the visual image to the idealized process of discrimination and perception, the more rapidly and unambiguously will the symbol be perceived. From a practical point of view some basic principles of symbol design may now be formally stated.

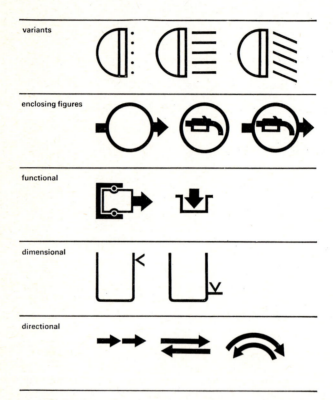

variants

enclosing figures

functional

dimensional

directional

Figure 6.   Symbol integration: using a common symbol component to integrate symbols.

Figure/ground.   Clear and stable figure to ground articulation is essential.

Figure boundary.   The figures should be bounded by a contrast boundary in preference to a line boundary. Where more than one graphic element is required for a symbol, the most important should have a solid contrast-bounded element. Rationalization of these principles leads to the following consistent allocation between solid and outline elements of the symbol

Symbol dynamic	:	Solid
Moving or active part	:	Outline
Stationary or inactive part	:	Solid

This allows a consistent approach to the design of complex symbols, since the stationary part (solid figure) will, by definition, never require the dynamic part (also a solid figure) to be superimposed. Problems of overlapping solid parts of a composite symbol should therefore not occur.

Geometrical forms. Where simple geometrical shapes are used it is preferable to have a solid rather than an outline figure.

For these solid contrast-bounded figures, optimum discriminability will be achievèd if the geometrical relationships are as follows.

triangles and ellipses	:	maximize area
rectangles and diamonds	:	maximize one dimension
stars and crosses	:	maximize perimeter

Closed figures. Line contour figures should always form a closed figure unless, of course, it is essential to the meaning of the symbol for the outline to be discontinuous. In this case the discontinuity should be unequivocal to avoid misleading interpretations due to the psychological phenomenon of closure.

Continuity of figures. The smoothest continuous outline for the figure should be used. Again as in closure, if a discontinuity is required to enhance the meaning it should be unambiguously defined.

Simplicity. The symbols should be as simple as possible. Fine detail makes no contribution to unambiguous and rapid interpretation of a symbol.

Symmetry. Symbols should be as symmetrical as possible, providing that assymetry adds no further meaning to the figure.

Unity. Symbols should be as unified as possible. This can be achieved by consistent use of the same size and proportions of individual elements when they repeat. Secondly, when solid and line outline figures occur together, more unity is achieved when solid figures are integrated by enclosing them, within the line outline figures.

Orientation. The prevailing outlines of the symbol should follow as far as possible the main spatial axes of the horizontal and the vertical.

Much of the work discussed here derives from an earlier report written for the Machine Tool Industry Research Association whilst the author was at the Ergonomics Laboratory at Cranfield. None of this work would have been possible without encouragement and support given by Mr. A. E. DeBarr, Research Director of MTIRA, and the author is most grateful for his interest and encouragement.

Continuing research based on this report is now in progress under Science Research Council Sponsorship. The collaboration in the preparation of the visual material by R. G. Taylor, of MTIRA, and Miss Gill Scott, of the Applied Psychology Department at the University of Aston in Birmingham, is gratefully acknowledged.

References

Bartlett, F. C., 1932, *Remembering* (London: Cambridge University Press).

Bartlett, F. C., and Mackworth, N. H., 1950, *Planned Seeing.* Air Ministry Publication No. 31398 (London: H.M.S.O.).

Brainard, R. W., Campbell, R. J., and Elkin, E. H., 1961, Design and interpretability of road signs. *Journal of Applied Psychology*, **45**, 130–136.

Casperson, R. C., 1950, The visual discrimination of geometric forms. *Journal of Experimental Psychology*, **40**, 668–681.

Christie, R., and Rutley, K., 1964, An evaluation of different designs of traffic filter arrow. *Road Research Laboratory Report* No. R.46.

Easterby, R. S., 1965, An evaluation of British Standard proposals for symbols on machine tool indicator plates. *M.T.I.R.A. Research Report No.* 10.

Easterby, R. S., 1967, Perceptual organization in static displays for man–machine systems. *Ergonomics*, **10**, 193–205.

Easterby, R. S., 1969, The grammar of symbols. *Print*, **13**, 6.

FROSCHAUG, 1963, Roadside traffic signs. *Design,* **178,** 37–50.

KARSH, R., and MUDD, S. A., 1962, Design of a picture language to identify vehicle controls: III. A comparative evaluation of selected picture symbol designs. *Human Engineering Laboratory Technical Memo,* 15–62.

KOFFKA, K., 1935, *Principles of Gestalt Psychology* (New York: HARCOURT BRACE).

MACKIE, A. M., 1967, Progress in learning the meanings of symbolic traffic signs. *Road Research Laboratory Report No. LF* 91.

MILLER, G. A., 1956, The magic number seven plus or minus two: some reflections on our capacity to process information. *Psychological Review,* **63,** 81–97.

MUDD, S. A., and KARSH, R., 1961, Design of a picture language to identify vehicle controls: I. General method; II. Investigation of population stereotypes. *Human Engineering Laboratory Technical Memo,* 22–61.

PROVINS, K. A., *et al.,* 1957, The representation of aircraft by pictorial signs. *Occupational Psychology,* **1,** 1–15.

RUTLEY, K. S., and CHRISTIE, A. W., 1966, Comparison of ten varieties of signal filter arrow. *Road Research Laboratory Report No. 33.*

VERNON, M. D., 1952, *A Further Study of Visual Perception* (London: CAMBRIDGE UNIVERSITY PRESS).

WALKER, R. E., NICOLAY, R. C., and STEARNS, C. R., 1965, Comparative accuracy of recognizing American and International road signs. *Journal of Applied Psychology,* **49,** 322–325.

WILLIAMS, J. R., and FALZON, R. P., 1963 a, Relationship of display system variables to symbol recognition and search time. *Journal of Engineering Psychology,* **2,** 197–111.

WILLIAMS, J. R., and FALZON, R. P., 1963 b, Comparisons of search time and accuracy among selected outlined geometric symbols with various overlays. *Journal of Engineering Psychology,* **2,** 112–118.

Subject Index

A

accommodation, 74, 75, 76, 78
acuity
    of peripheral retinal system, 110
    tasks, 131
adaptation
    to visual inversion, 123–4, 125
aerial perspective, 74
after effects
    visual, 16
age
    judgments by the young, 90
Airy disk, 131
Ames distorted rooms, 17
analogue
    synthetical, 34
analytical procedure
    for computer, 33, 34
animals
    communication with, 32
Applied Psychology Department,
    University of Aston, 157
arousal
    changes in, 54
    physiological measures of, 54
attention, 7, 18
auditory localisation, 6
Australian Research Grants Council,
    55

B

behaviour
    appropriate, 25, 27, 28
    choice, 37–38
    control of, 121, 122
    controlled by information, 25–35
    cortical, 133
    cybernetic feedback model, 119,
        126
    overt, 119, 124
    perceptual-motor, 121, 126
    related to perception, 119, 120
    sensory effects of, 119, 120
    visually-guided, 119–128
Berkeley, George, *New Theory of*
    Vision, 73
Bernouilli trials, 43
binocular
    convergence, 74
    depth perception, 129
    disparity, 73, 75
    parallax, 74, 78
    vision, 74, 80, 106
biological reflexes, 31
blindness, 29
blood pressure
    changes in, 55
brain
    cortical activity, 54, 132
    models, 29
        analogue, 32
        biological status of, 32
        digital, 32
        engineering status of, 32
        logical status of, 32
    perceptual, 32
    synthetical, 34
burlap, 83

160

C

Cambridge University Psychological Laboratory, 13, 55
car driving, 27, 28
    position for, 115
car mirrors, 115
causality, 67, 68
Center for Comparative Psycholinguistics, University of Illinois, 99
central nervous system, 25, 29, 33
changes of form, 67–72
Charles Babbage's Analytical Machine, 34
choice
    -reaction tasks, 7
    response, 8, 20
classification criteria, 8
coding
    of signals, 108
    perceptual, 101
    procedures, 93
cognition, 121, 124
colour
    as part of human eye–brain system, 129
    changed when seen through film, 59
    continuum, 89
    judgments of, 90
    Talbot's law of mixture, 61
    whiteness constancy, 89–91
colour aid paper, 89
communication model, 93
computation scheme, 129
computational techniques
    used in optical systems, 134
computer
    analytical, 32–33, 34
    digital, 32–33, 134, 135, 146
    perceptual mechanism compared with, 34
    programming, 5, 34
    simulation of accumulator process, 47, 49, 50, 51
    simulation to obtain predictions, 44

    synthetical, 34
    systems, 32–33
    two-dimensional optical, 129, 134
    two-dimensional patterns of, 133
computing device, 33
conditional entropy measure, 94
confidence judgments, 109
contour, 83
    closure, 154, 157
    continuity, 154, 155, 157
    of objects, 75
control panels
    design of, 20
convergence, 74, 75, 76, 78
corneal grafting, 29
Cranfield Ergonomics Laboratory, 157
critical task situation, 152
cross-culture bipolar dimensions, 93, 98
cultures
    cross-cultural differences, 93–100
    cross-cultural factors, 93–100
    different, 93–100
cue
    concept of, 74
    dimensions, 73
    geometrical analysis of, 75
    measurement of, 76
    psychophysical analysis of, 75
    spatial, 76
    theory, 73, 74
    thresholds, 76
    use of texture, 87

D

data
    accumulation models, 37, 39
    scale setting, 28
    semantic aspects of, 5
data processing
    perceptual, 33
decision, 5
    economy of, 5, 19
    process, 7
    rate, 26
    time, 105

170

transparency
  conditions for seeing, 60
  perceptual theory, 59–66
trials
  random order, 90
two-dimensional symbol images, 154
typing
  learning of, 26, 27

V

variables
  input, 34
Venner Digital Counter Type
  TSA 6634, 46
viewing process
  complexity of, 106
vigilance
  task, 115
vision, 5, 27, 28, 29
  behaviourally-guided, 119–128
  binocular, 74, 106
  inverted, performance under,
    124–125, 126
  monocular, 84, 106
  peripheral, 101, 102, 103, 106,
    110, 112, 115
  process of, 73
  related to behaviour, 119
  volunteers with normal or cor-
    rected, 47
visual
  acuity, 131
  after-effects, 16, 83–88
  angle, 75, 76, 103, 106, 111, 112,
    113
  cortex, 11, 129, 132
  cues, 74, 75, 80
  cues, measurement of, 73
  detection experiments, 115
  disorientation, 124, 126
  display, 16, 21
  distance, 30
  distance, scaling of, 75
  distortion, 126
  environment, perceived charac-
    teristics of, 119–125
  features, perspective con-
    vergence of lines, 28

feedback, 122
field, 76, 84, 101, 153
field, shape and form as figures
  in, 152
field, functional, 106, 108
field, information from periphery
  of, 110
field, optical inversion of, 124,
  125
form, internal organisation of,
  153, 154
form, simplicity of, 154, 155, 157
form, stability of, 153
form, symmetry of, 154, 155, 157
form, unity of, 154, 155, 157
frameworks, 18–19
guidance, 122
illusions, 15, 25, 28–29
image, 110, 115
information, 121
interpretation, 73
inversion, 123
memory, 130
perception, 68, 73, 84
reversals, 30
scene, distortions, 124–126
scientists, 73
search, 115
search task, 110, 111, 115
search theory, 101
shape, judgments of, 73, 76
signal, 110
size, 30
slant, judgments of, 73, 76, 78
space perception, 73–81
stimuli, 11, 67, 130, 153
system, 75, 76, 124
system, acuity of, 131
system, human, 129, 130, 131,
  132
system, primate, 129, 130

W

Weber fractions, 79
Weber's law, 79
Wheatstone bridge, 29–30
World War II
  studies made during, 121

Author Index

A

Abelson, R. P., 98, 100
Abrams, M., 20, 23
Adams, J. A., 115, 116
Anderson, Nancy, 22
Anderson, N. H., 19, 21
Archer, W. K., 100
Arrow, K. J., 57
Aseyev, V. G., 54, 56
Attneave, F., 9, 13, 18, 21
Audley, R. J., 39, 40, 53, 56

B

Bailey, P., 147
Bainbridge-Bell, L. H., 20, 21
Baker, C. A., 117
Baker, C. H., 115, 116
Baker, K. E., 81
Barnett, G. P., 57
Bartlett, F. C., 17, 18, 20, 21, 25, 35, 152, 154, 157
Bartlett, N. R., 117
Beishon, R. J., 19, 21
von Bekesy, G., 11, 21
Bekker, J. A. M., 38, 53, 58
Beller, H. K., 8, 23
van Bergeijk, W. A., 122, 127
Bergman, R., 83, 84, 87, 88
Berry, R. N., 76, 81
Bertelson, P., 106, 107, 111, 116
Bindra, D., 55, 56
Birdsall, T. G., 57
Birren, J. E., 38, 52, 56
Blodgett, H. C., 35
Bok, S. T., 132, 146
von Bonin, G., 147
Boring, E. G., 74, 81

Botwinick, J., 38, 52, 56, 57
Boulter, L. R., 115, 116
Bower, G. H., 39, 57
Boycott, B. B., 132, 146
Brainard, R. W., 151, 157
Brebner, J., 8, 21, 22
Bricker, P. D., 10, 22
Brindley, J. F., 57
Broadbent, D. E., 6, 7, 22, 54, 57, 107, 116
Bruner, J. S., 91
Brunswik, E., 70, 72
Buck, L., 54, 57
Buckner, D. N., 57
Burzlaff, W., 91
Bush, R. R., 57

C

Campbell, R. J., 157
Carmichael, L., 17, 22
Carr, H. A., 74, 81
Carter, J., 116
Cartwright, D., 38, 39, 54, 57
Carvellas, T., 8, 23
Casperson, R. C., 151, 157
Christie, A. W., 152, 158
Christie, R., 157
Clark, W. C., 87, 88
Clynes, M., 55, 57
Coghill, G. E., 25, 35
Coleman, P. D., 54, 57
Collins, J. F., 18, 22
Corbin, H., 101, 115, 116
Corcoran, D. W. J., 5, 11, 22
Corso, J. F., 51, 57
Crabbé, G., 67, 69, 72

174

O

Ogle, K. N., 74, 81
Olver, Rose, 91
Oostlander, A. M., 8, 23
Osgood, C. E., 83, 86, 88, 98, 99, 100
Oswald, I., 41, 54, 58

P

Pearson, E. S., 43, 58
Pearson, K., 44, 58
Philipszoon, E., 98, 99, 100
Pickett, R. M., 40, 51, 53, 58
Pike, A. R., 39, 40, 41, 53, 56, 58
Polyak, S., 132, 147
Posner, M. I., 9, 23
Poulton, E. C., 20, 23
Pribram, K. H., 127
Provins, K. A., 152, 158

Q

Quastler, M., 58

R

Rabe, A., 88
Radoy, C. M., 23, 129, 134, 147
Rappoport, M., 22
Reese, E. P., 116
Riggs, L. A., 81
Riley, Jenefer G. A., 7, 23
Robbin, J. S., 57
Robinson, J. O., 11, 16, 23
Rock, I., 124, 125, 127
Ross, Helen E., 29, 35
Rutley, K. S., 152, 157, 158

S

Salik, G., 115, 116
Sampaio, A. C., 69, 72
Sanders, A. F., 23, 57, 58, 101, 107, 110, 115, 116, 117
Schlosberg, H., 98, 99, 100, 115, 117
Schouten, J. F., 38, 53, 58
Sekuler, R. W., 20, 23, 55, 58

Senders, J. W., 109, 117
Senders, V. L., 109, 117
Sermat, V., 98, 100
Shackel, B., 103, 117
Shallice, T., 38, 46, 52, 58
Sheppard, P. M., 51, 57
Sheridan, T. B., 122, 127
Shipley, E. F., 58
Shopland, C., 30, 35
Simon, H. A., 13, 23
Smith, A. H., 88
Smith, E. E., 39, 58
Smith, K. U., 119, 122, 124, 125, 126, 127, 128
Smith, M. F., 119, 122, 124, 125, 126, 127
Smith, W. M., 119, 122, 124, 125, 126, 127, 128
Solomon, R. L., 81
Southall, J. P. C., 81
Spencer, J., 19, 23
Sperling, G., 110, 117
Stearns, C. R., 158
Stevens, S. S., 86, 88
Stone, M., 38, 39, 55, 58
Stratton, G. M., 123, 128
Stroud, J. M., 48, 58
Suci, G. J., 100
Suppes, P., 57
de Swart, H., 8, 23
Swets, J. A., 38, 58

T

Tallman, O., 23, 129
Tannenbaum, P. H., 100
Tanner, W. P., 57
Taub, Thelma, 22
Taylor, M. M., 38, 58
Thierman, T., 17, 23
Thinès, G., 67, 72
Thomas, L. F., 20, 23
Thouless, R. H., 16, 23
Titchener, E. B., 74, 81
Tognazzo, D. P., 70, 71, 72
Treisman, Anne M., 6, 7, 23
Tudor-Hart, B., 59, 66
Turhan, M., 93, 100